LIVING "ILLEGAL"

LIVING "ILLEGAL"

THE HUMAN FACE OF

UNAUTHORIZED IMMIGRATION

Marie Friedmann Marquardt,
Timothy J. Steigenga,
Philip J. Williams,
and Manuel A. Vásquez

THE NEW PRESS

NEW YORK
LONDON

Requests for permission to reproduce selections
from this book should be mailed to:
Permissions Department, The New Press, 38 Greene Street,
New York, NY 10013.

First published in the United States by The New Press, New York, 2011
This paperback edition published by The New Press, 2013
Distributed by Perseus Distribution

ISBN 978-1-59558-881-4 (pbk.)
ISBN 978-1-59558-901-9 (e-book)

LIBRARY OF CONGRESS CATALOGING-IN-PUBLICATION DATA

Living "illegal" : the human face of unauthorized immigration /
Marie Friedmann Marquardt ... [et al.].
p.   cm.
Includes bibliographical references and index.
ISBN 978-1-59558-651-3 (hc. : alk. paper)
1. Illegal aliens—United States.   2. United States—
Emigration and immigration—Social aspects.
I. Marquardt, Marie F. 1972–
JV6475.L58   2011
305.9'0691—dc22   2011007499

The New Press publishes books that promote and enrich public discussion and understanding of the issues vital to our democracy and to a more equitable world. These books are made possible by the enthusiasm of our readers; the support of a committed group of donors, large and small; the collaboration of our many partners in the independent media and the not-for-profit sector; booksellers, who often hand-sell New Press books; librarians; and above all by our authors.

www.thenewpress.com

Composition by dix!
This book was set in Walbaum

Printed in the United States of America

2   4   6   8   10   9   7   5   3   1

CONTENTS

FOREWORD

At DePaul University, where I am president, a bright student approached us two years ago in desperate need of help after finding herself in a terrible bind. The student—I will call her Julia—had been the salutatorian of her high school class and kept up the good work after coming to DePaul, earning a very high grade-point average and taking a variety of leadership positions in student organizations. Working when possible, Julia also volunteered to help the poor every week. She was the type of student we prize: a high achiever who is engaged in our community and contributes to society.

By many accounts, Julia's life was flourishing, except for one important aspect: she was an unauthorized immigrant. This meant she was unable to qualify for federal scholarship funds, federally backed loans, or DePaul's work-study program. Her educational funds were quickly depleting. Charity, along with the few private scholarships that DePaul was able to find for her, could not compensate for her shortfall of funds. Unable to pay her tuition, this young woman's life began to crumble, all because she was born on the wrong side of a border in a country she did not know—she had spent all but the first few months of her life in the United States.

A graduate student I'll call Ahmed first wrote me to beg that I help him become eligible to accept a job offer from a major U.S. firm. I was unable to do so, and, following his education at DePaul in finance and information technology, he returned to a Pakistan he never knew. Ahmed had gone to high school here. He has a Chicago accent and a brilliant mind, and wants nothing more than to work and build a life in this country. Numerous employers desperately wanted his combination of skills, but the United States' limit on employment-based green cards each year could not accommodate him or the many businesses who cannot find sufficient U.S. citizens to apply for these positions. Although Ahmed introduced himself to distant relatives to try to build a life in Pakistan, he has finally found a more welcome reception in Canada and will soon move there.

Because the legal issues surrounding immigration are complex, it is easy to lose sight of the human element in the debates over policy and border enforcement. Unauthorized immigrants celebrate birthdays, care for their families, start businesses, worry about money, and, yes, go to college, like anyone else. The authors of *Living "Illegal"* illustrate this dilemma—human and ordinary lives juxtaposed against the fear of discrimination and deportation. This very real depiction of living "illegal" in America is a side of the issue very few contemplate and is precisely why I selected the book for the DePaul President's Book Club.

Living "Illegal" lays bare the realities of unauthorized immigrants living in our midst and demonstrates what happens to people's lives when politics cloud smart social choices. The stories detailed in these pages are heartbreaking, but not surprising. Unauthorized immigrants come to the United States for the same reasons many of our own ancestors boarded boats to make the perilous trip from Europe, Cuba, or Asia. They are fleeing political oppression, seeking a steady paycheck to support their families, or searching for a better quality of life. They worry constantly about being deported over something as simple as not having a driver's license.

The conundrums described in *Living "Illegal"* show why
the issue of unauthorized immigration merits closer attention. Few people realize that common misconceptions about
the socioeconomic value of unauthorized immigrants are fed
by government policies. For instance, take the issue faced
by students such as Julia. The federal government makes
financial aid available to young people with the idea that
this aid is an affordable, short-term investment that eventually turns students into contributing taxpayers. Yet the
government withholds that assistance from unauthorized
immigrants, making it extremely difficult for them to attend college. Now consider the often-heard complaint that
unauthorized immigrants are long-term financial drains on
society and ask, "What is the government's better investment: short-term financial aid for college with a longer-term
yield of tax revenues or years of welfare, health care, or lower
to no tax revenues because most of these unauthorized immigrants will obtain only low-paying jobs without a college
education?"

DePaul's stance on immigration is rooted in the words
and actions of our namesake, St. Vincent de Paul, who, in
his day, shaped France's approach to the overwhelming postwar influx of the rural poor into urban Paris. We admit students regardless of their citizenship and thus have no way of
knowing exactly how many of our students are unauthorized
immigrants. Typically, we learn about these students when
they reach a breaking point in their lives, as with Julia and
Ahmed. Their college funding dries up, perhaps because a
parent has lost a job or their savings have been depleted.
Sometimes we are able to find other avenues to assist them
so they can continue their educations. Often we cannot. We
help them because they are human beings who have every right to pursue the same dreams our ancestors not only
dreamed but also realized.

Throughout history, society has confronted a fear of incorporating the stranger. The United States justified slavery and Jim Crow by claiming those of African descent were less than human. Women were portrayed as too simple-minded and emotionally unstable to vote. Hitler fanned fears that Jews were plotting the overthrow of German society. Today, entire classes of unauthorized immigrants have been demonized by unfair portrayals of immigrants' perceived negative effects on the United States' economy, crime rate, and social order. The benefits of their influence are rarely brought to light, let alone discussed. Rarely do we hear stories about the contributions unauthorized immigrants make to small businesses, industries, churches, or once-failing neighborhoods.

The authors of *Living "Illegal"* do us a great service by painstakingly collecting the stories of unauthorized immigrants, but so do the women and men who took the risk to share their experiences. How can anyone read about the lives, journeys, and obstacles detailed in this book and not see a shade of themselves, their ancestors, or their families? Who among us does not dream of a life that is safe, stable, and prosperous? By virtue of our humanity, we have more in common with unauthorized immigrants than some might care to admit. As we debate the shape of responsible and comprehensive immigration reform, our conversations must always find their touchstone here.

—Reverend Dennis H. Holtschneider, C.M.
November 2012

INTRODUCTION

"Waves of illegal aliens swarming across our border, joining violent gangs, forcing families to live in fear." As the narrator speaks, a crowd of dark figures passes through a hole in the soaring fence. Crouching low and holding flashlights, they grin as they move furtively beyond it. The fence gives way to a shadowy alley, where a group of young men dressed in the fashion of gang members advances menacingly. The television advertisement continues, and these images, intended to portray "illegal aliens," are juxtaposed with images that aim to portray American citizens. In one version of the television commercial, two working-class American men in hard hats express bafflement and annoyance. In another version, the two workers are replaced by a white family fretting together, as scowling young Latino men wearing bandanas and sporting tattooed chests fill the screen. While these dark images flash across the television, viewers are told that federal legislators who support immigration reform aim to "give tax breaks and social security benefits to illegal aliens" and support "a plan that gives illegals a pathway to amnesty and even special college tuition rates." A final image of young white schoolchildren gathering eagerly around their teacher emerges, as the narrator decries the Senate majority leader's decision to vote "against making English the national language." [1]

At the height of the 2010 midterm election campaigns, the American public was inundated with powerfully charged depictions of unauthorized immigrants and with strong claims about the devastating impact of unauthorized immigration on the life of the nation. But as this and other widely publicized campaign ads circulated throughout the United States, entering into the spotlight of national media attention and the consciousness of many Americans, other stories more quietly unfolded.

Until the morning of March 29, 2010, Jessica Colotl lived the rather uneventful life of a typical hardworking college student. Her parents brought her from Mexico in 1996 at the age of seven, and she studied hard, eventually earning a 3.8 grade point average and graduating with academic honors from Lakeside High School in DeKalb County, Georgia. According to Lila Parra, a close friend and sorority sister, when Colotl discovered that her parents had brought her into the United States without the proper documentation, she filed papers to regularize her and her younger sibling's status. Parra explained, "She took it upon herself to do that for herself and her younger sibling. She was like, 'I've been here forever, I consider America my country.' "[2]

Undeterred by the lack of resolution on her legal status, Colotl applied to and was accepted into Kennesaw State University (KSU), where she became a political science major, with the hope of eventually going to law school. To support her studies, Colotl worked with her mother, cleaning office buildings in Atlanta until late at night. Despite the long working hours, Jessica found the time to establish a Latina sorority that has been active in the local community.

Colotl's plans were derailed on that morning in March, when she was stopped by a campus police officer for a minor traffic infraction. Unable to produce a valid driver's license,

she was turned over to the Cobb County sheriff's department, which has a 287(g) agreement with Immigration and
Customs Enforcement (ICE). This arrangement allowed the
sheriff to check her immigration status. After authorities con-
firmed that Colotl was in the country without authorization,
they sent her to an ICE detention center in Etowah, a small
rural community in the northeastern corner of Alabama.

Upon learning about Colotl's situation, a myriad of local
organizations, including her own sorority and the president
of KSU, quickly mobilized to secure her release. After spending more than a month in the Etowah detention center, she
was released, and ICE deferred action on her case for a year
to enable her to finish her degree at KSU before being sent
back to Mexico, a country that she has not visited since her
parents brought her to the United States. But this was not
the end of Colotl's ordeal. Cobb County sheriff Neil Warren
obtained a new warrant for her arrest, adducing that she had
lied about her address during her first arrest. Under Georgia
law, making false statements to a law enforcement official
is a felony. Colotl, who turned herself in voluntarily to the
Cobb County jail, is awaiting a decision from the judge on
the felony charge. Reflecting on Jessica's case, Lila Parra expressed admiration for her sorority sister: "I've never seen
anybody fight so hard for their education. . . . [Jessica] pays
for it all on her own and pays out-of-state tuition. She doesn't
want to just get by—she wants to get that 4.0 GPA. . . . We
want other students to not get discouraged by situations like
this, and for them to move forward. . . . So many students,
they just want to be educated, because they realize their family is not."[3]

Jessica's situation is not unique. Recently, the *Los Angeles Times* reported the case of Cal State Fresno student body
president Pedro Ramirez, who was brought from Mexico by
his undocumented parents at the age of three. Under a law

that allows anyone who attended high school in California for three years to pay in-state tuition, Ramirez was able to attend college. However, he could not receive any financial aid from the federal government nor could he work legally, often having to resort to working with his father mowing lawns and with his mother cleaning houses. He also refused to accept a $9,000 stipend that comes with the office of student body president, volunteering to serve without pay. When an anonymous tip to the college newspaper revealed his undocumented status, Ramirez declared: "In a way, I'm relieved. . . . I don't want to be a liability or cost the school donations. I never really thought this was going to happen. But now that it's out there, I finally feel ready to say 'Yes, it's me. I'm one of the thousands.' "⁴

Although Jessica Colotl and Pedro Ramirez do not know each other and live on opposite sides of the country, when they were asked about their aspirations, their answers were remarkably similar. Summoning a version of the narrative that has inspired countless immigrants to come to America, from the heyday of Ellis Island to the present, each of them stated: "I'm just trying to live the American dream and finish my education."⁵

These stories lay bare the emotional intensity surrounding the issue of unauthorized immigration, as well as the enormous gulf between the potent images circulating in our media and the complex reality of life as an unauthorized immigrant in the United States today. On one side of the gulf, such potent imagery has helped doom attempts to pass comprehensive federal immigration reform in 2006 and 2007 and has since shut down all alternatives beyond the enforcement of a system that most politicians and scholars agree is broken. The arguments underlying these images is best summarized by the expression popular among groups opposing immigration reform: "What part of illegal don't you understand?" After all, a lawbreaker is a lawbreaker. There is nothing to discuss. To advocate anything but punishment—in this case deportation—simply amounts to aiding and abetting criminals, opening the way for others to commit the same offense with total impunity.

The simple contrast between "legal" and "illegal" is bolstered through the repeated use of four broadly articulated claims about unauthorized immigrants:

1. Unauthorized immigrants flood across the U.S.–Mexico border to take advantage of public benefits and social services, while contributing very little to U.S. society. Thus, the solution to the problem of unauthorized immigration is to seal U.S. borders. If they want to come to America, they should get in line and do it legally.

2. Unauthorized immigrants are a burden on the U.S. economy. They take jobs from U.S. citizens, exacerbating unemployment and depressing wages for working-class Americans. In addition, taxpayers pay heavily for the government services they use. For this reason, the solution to the problem of unauthorized immigration is to deny them any access to social services and public benefits.

3. Unauthorized immigrants are closely associated with criminality, violence, drugs, and gangs. They threaten the safety and stability of local communities. Therefore, the solution to the problem of unauthorized immigration lies in vigorous local and state enforcement. Any other approach represents amnesty for lawbreakers.

4. Unauthorized immigrants cannot be integrated into U.S. society because they bring values that are contrary to the values of this nation. Furthermore, these immigrants do not want to integrate. They choose instead

to retain their language and to have dual national allegiances facilitated by connections with their countries of origin. Therefore, unauthorized immigrants threaten the sovereignty and the future of the nation.

These broad claims obscure the complex human stories that lie behind the phenomenon of unauthorized immigration. Furthermore, as we will see throughout the course of this book, they generate a patchwork of policies that simply fail to solve the complex problems associated with unauthorized immigration.

From the other side of the enormous gulf, we recognize that there is a lot about illegality that we do not fully understand. The reality on the ground is much more complicated than the simple contrast between "legal" and "illegal" that characterizes mainstream media and political discourse. Jessica Colotl's and Pedro Ramirez's cases suggest that if we take a closer look into the lives of unauthorized immigrants, we might find that these immigrants share many of the core values that have shaped the history of the United States: hard work, individual initiative, willingness to take risks in the quest for self-improvement, dedication to families and communities. Colotl's and Ramirez's cases also point to the strong desire of unauthorized immigrants to integrate and contribute to their adopted society. As Colotl attempted to do without success, these immigrants would readily regularize their status if given the opportunity, paying fines, enlisting in the army, or doing community service to make up for having entered the country without proper authorization. Drawing from a helpful distinction that scholars of citizenship and immigration make, we may say that although Colotl and Ramirez are not citizens in the liberal sense, since they do not have legal membership in the U.S. polity, they certainly behave like citizens in the civic republican mode, for which engagement in the life and well-being of the community is key. The trouble lies in the fact that lack of formal citizenship limits the kinds of civic engagement these immigrants can have. This tension may have negative consequences not only for Colotl and Ramirez, who carry the stigma of illegality, but also for this nation's democracy, which fails to tap into the civic values and energy they bring.[6]

This book is an effort to go beyond the highly charged stereotypes that have become associated with the term illegal and to shed light on what it means to be unauthorized in America. From the outset, we recognize that unauthorized immigration is an issue that raises valid concerns and that has real costs for our society, as well as for immigrants and their communities of origin. In particular, communities in the United States that have witnessed the growing presence of unauthorized immigrants as part of their economic boom have legitimate concerns about the strain put on school systems, emergency units, hospitals, and other local services at a time when resources are scare. Furthermore, there are understandable reasons to worry about the presence of a large group of unskilled and vulnerable workers in the labor market. As we will see, many Americans are ambivalent about unauthorized immigration. For instance, they recognize the needs that lead many Latin Americans to come to the United States without legal status and admire the work and family-centered ethics of Latino immigrants. Yet they also worry that, because these immigrants are willing to work under any conditions and to be paid less than the minimum wage, the native born will be "underbid" and displaced by unauthorized Latino workers.

The people and communities raising these valid concerns should not be labeled and dismissed as racists or xenophobes. These concerns certainly call for rational, open-minded, and careful reflection on the causes, costs, and benefits of unauthorized immigration, as well as thoughtful debate and discussion of potential solutions. We might disagree in the end on these solutions, but such a debate should be informed by the realities on the ground, by moral considerations, and by a robust knowledge of the historical and contemporary forces that have led to unauthorized immigration. Americans must account for the ways in which actions by the U.S. government and even American lifestyles and patterns of consumption have contributed to this phenomenon. Instead, the valid concerns and struggles of local communities have been overshadowed and profoundly distorted by an increasingly shrill discourse surrounding immigration.

In this book, we hope to introduce a more full and complex portrait of contemporary unauthorized immigration, one that might contribute to robust debate and discussion of the issue and to thoughtful and deliberate attempts at devising solutions to the real problems that cause and are caused by this phenomenon. To avoid the negative and polarizing emotional baggage that has become attached to the word *illegal*, we will refrain from using it. Instead, we will use the term *unauthorized immigrant*, since it is factually correct. This term indicates that the immigrants who are the subjects of this book are out of status, having entered the country or remained in the country without following proper procedures. In other words, they might have crossed the border at a place other than a designated port of entry or they might have overstayed their tourist or work-based visas. Occasionally we will also use the term *undocumented immigrant*, which is far more common in everyday discourse but is not always accurate. Many unauthorized immigrants do have documents, such as passports from their home countries, driver's licenses from their state of residence in the United States (as in New Mexico, which allows the issuance of driver's licenses without proof of legal residence), or *matrículas consulares*, identification cards distributed by consulates. What they do not have is valid social security numbers, green cards, or U.S. passports, documents that mark their formal status as members of our polity. Debates about unauthorized immigration, however, are not merely about semantics. They are shaped by a widespread lack of knowledge of the root causes of this immigration and, most important, of the situation unauthorized immigrants face in their daily lives. Our task is to show the human face of unauthorized immigration from Latin America, not to romanticize unauthorized immigrants but to gain a better understanding of the historical complexities, political paradoxes, moral dilemmas, and sometimes tragic predicaments that are hidden behind the labels we attach to unauthorized immigration and which shape the lives of the almost twelve million people who are "living illegal" in the United States today.[7] We hope that by offering a rich portrait of the everyday lives of unauthorized Latin American immigrants, and by listening to their voices, we can help move the public conversation beyond the polarizing frames that equate unauthorized status with criminality, and a path to citizenship with amnesty for lawbreakers and free riders.

Moving beyond these frames is crucial to thinking about the kind of country the United States wants to be. Currently, many politicians use unauthorized immigration as a hot-button issue and link it with racial stereotypes and violent criminality. This indicates that they and their media consultants feel this strategy will resonate with the frustrations and fears of voters. Yet, the word *illegal* has become so emotionally charged that it dehumanizes not only unauthorized immigrants, who are objectified as nothing more than faceless criminals, but even those who use the term uncritically. The widespread use of the term *illegal* leaves no room to consider the moral and policy contradictions that are behind the need for people to leave their homes and risk their lives crossing the border without authorization or to overstay visas and live in a precarious status. When a congressman can say that "illegal" immigrant women "multiply like rats" and not have to apologize for such a derogatory remark, it is clear that the public discourse on the topic has reached its nadir.[8]

The media have tended to magnify the raw passions elicited by the term *illegal*, contributing to an overall climate of mistrust, hostility, and incivility, which, as we shall show, stymies constructive public debate, impeding the search for rational, pragmatic, and long-term repairs to the broken immigration system. Furthermore, the federal government has not been able to articulate a compelling narrative of why the United States needs comprehensive immigration reform that is in line with the values of the nation and its evolving place in the world. In the absence of immigration reform at the federal level, states and communities that are directly experiencing the contradictions of immigration are left to cope with the issue on their own, often with dwindling resources. In response, these states and localities have passed an incongruent patchwork of ordinances and laws. Many of these do not address the root causes of unauthorized migration but instead seek short-term solutions that at best merely deflect the problem and at worst threaten civil liberties and increase local tensions. These laws put an especially heavy burden on families, often separating unauthorized parents from their U.S.-born children. They also may lead to racial profiling, eroding the overall sense of community, interethnic trust, openness, and tolerance to pluralism that is at the heart of American civil society. Moreover, these laws have in effect criminalized unauthorized immigrants. What is often lost in our immigration debates is the simple fact that immigration law is administrative law, and illegal entry and presence are in violation of administrative procedures. The growing patchwork of state and local ordinances, in practice, turn unauthorized presence from civil infraction into felony. Equally troubling has been the rapid growth of a culture of enforcement that threatens to spin out of control. Recent figures published by the *Washington Post* reveal the magnitude of enforcement efforts: "The Immigration and Customs Enforcement agency expects to deport about 400,000 people this fiscal year, nearly 10 percent above the Bush administration's 2008 total and 25 percent more than were deported in 2007."[9] But simply quoting these statistics obscures several problematic shifts in immigration enforcement practices. Immigration enforcement increasingly is being placed in the hands of local law enforcement agencies, and immigrants increasingly are being detained in for-profit, privately run prisons. In Cobb County, Georgia, where we conducted some of our field work, the ACLU reports a situation of "policing run amok [as] . . . law enforcement and jail personnel routinely abuse their power under 287(g)." Of the 3,180 inmates the county jail processed for ICE detention in 2008, almost 69 percent were arrested for traffic violations, belying the avowed focus on removing criminals from local communities.[10] This trend will likely increase, since the Secure Communities Program, which also relies on local and state law enforcement agencies for implementation, is scheduled to be in all U.S. jurisdictions by 2013. The increasing criminalization and incarceration of unauthorized immigrants distracts local communities and the nation, drawing attention and efforts away from addressing the forces that propel unauthorized immigration.

In response to the problematic move to criminalize all unauthorized immigrants, we felt the urgent need to write a book that would draw from the facts—the reality—of America's contemporary immigrant experience. To paint a textured portrait of life as an unauthorized Latino immigrant, we draw from more than seven years of field research that we have conducted among the three immigrant groups—Brazilians, Guatemalans, and Mexicans—who represent a wide cross section of Latin American immigration to the United States today.[11] The portrait that emerges from this face-to-face encounter challenges the one-dimensional characterizations of unauthorized immigrants that set them up as the "unlawful other" that can be dismissed through enforcement and deportation. Instead, we present immigrants as people living in our midst, people Americans once welcomed into the most intimate spaces of our society, trusting children and elderly parents to them, relying on them to build and clean homes, and depending on them to produce, often at the cost of backbreaking labor and unsafe work conditions, the food that Americans eat, the tomatoes and meat that go into those burgers that are taken for granted as part of the American cornucopia. These immigrants are not simply workers; they are complex and fully human people, with families, dreams, and desires. Their children, more than two million of whom are unauthorized immigrants, have become deeply imbedded in the civic, cultural, and social life of the United States. Like all young people, they struggle and sometimes make mistakes. As they reach adulthood, though, the possibilities that their predecessors had—the very possibilities that built a nation of immigrants—are not available to this "second generation."

The cost of coming to the United States without documents is often very high. Unauthorized immigrants are frequently confronted with the difficult decision to migrate across perilous borders in order to fulfill their most basic needs, leaving behind wives, husbands, and children, thereby raising the danger of family breakups and, in the long run, of the unraveling of civil society and culture in their countries of origin. In that sense, while undocumented immigration is on one level a tough public policy issue and on another level an issue of the core principles shaping the identity of the United States, it is most fundamentally an issue of human survival and flourishing. As a way to contribute to crucially important public discussions about these issues, we offer, in the pages that follow, stories that replace narratives associating "illegality" with violence, insecurity, terrorism, and invasion. We tell, instead, complex stories of heartbreak, survival, work, family, and hope among those who are "living illegal" in the United States.

Why Migrate?

Making Sense of Unauthorized Migration

The tiny town of Santa Ana, Mexico, can be found at the termination point of a narrow two-lane paved road that juts from the highway linking the sprawling metropolis of Mexico City to a midsized city called Jilotepec.[1] Where the paved road ends and a network of red dirt roads begins, a small cluster of homes and shops is anchored by the local Catholic church and a grassy town square with a covered pavilion in the center. In 1998, the average monthly wage for a family of seven in this town was 600 pesos—approximately $60—and 70 percent of the population earned less than the minimum wage for Mexico. Yet for those whose trained eyes are familiar with the small towns and villages of this region of Mexico, Santa Ana did not appear impoverished.

Most of the homes in the colonia were flat-roofed, single-story concrete block structures with three or four rooms, a small interior courtyard with outdoor kitchen, and perhaps an interior bathroom. A few were much larger two-story homes with pitched roofs, large satellite dishes, modern indoor kitchens, and multiple indoor bathrooms. Rather than having a courtyard, many had a garage for the late-model pickup trucks in which their owners drove many times over the course of each year to visit "home." The trucks almost always displayed Georgia peaches on their license plates, since most of the owners lived and worked in Atlanta. Of the approximately five hundred residents of this small town (referred to by locals as a *rancho*), very few were working-age men and women. Those who could had migrated *al otro lado*. They crossed the border into the United States, using the only viable strategy available to them for sustaining and maintaining their communities and their families. They went to the "other side" not only to earn a living but also to better the situation of their families and, many hoped, realize their dreams. Most of their dreams were simple: to earn enough to build a home for their family or to open a small shop in the nearby town. Yet these dreams required money, and the cornfields surrounding this *rancho* had long ago ceased to provide the means for earning and saving cash. The migrants came back often, though, in trucks filled with family members, to celebrate births and mourn deaths, to mark rites of passage such as baptisms, and to gather for important holidays of the community: the town's annual *feria* (fair), the feast day of the Virgin of Guadalupe, Posadas, and Christmas.

Since the late 1990s, their visits have become less and less frequent. With few exceptions, the fancy homes lie empty and their owners' shiny trucks rarely cruise the *rancho*'s dirt roads. Homes are still being built, and important community celebrations continue to happen with the support of the "migradollars" sent from Atlanta. Those who send the money still dream of returning to visit family or perhaps to settle down and start the small business they once imagined having in their hometown. But for now, at least, they cannot. The vast majority of migrants from this *rancho*, and from countless others like it throughout Mexico, are unauthorized. As tightened border enforcement has increased the risk and cost of crossing, while economic instability has made their ability to earn a living in *el norte* even more crucial, these unauthorized immigrants find themselves, strangely, trapped inside the United States. For many, this means living thousands of miles from their spouses and children, with the knowledge that a visit could result in detention and perhaps death. For those who were able to bring their families with them, this means that their children know the place they call "home" only through photos and phone calls, through internet searches seeking images and information. Herein lies the first and perhaps most profound paradox of unauthorized immigration from Latin America: unauthorized immigrants are settling, by necessity, in the United States, while the few who have had the good fortune of being offered a route to legalization continue to live their lives constantly crossing borders.

The overwhelming majority of migrants from Santa Ana have settled in Atlanta. They have purchased homes in the city's suburbs and sent their children to the local public schools. They have worked to transform the landscapes of the city, as gardeners, and to build entire neighborhoods of new homes, as construction workers and masons. With migrants from other parts of Mexico and Latin America, they have revived failing business districts, installing in them shops and restaurants that cater to their wants and needs—and that introduce local residents to new flavors and styles. Many fill the pews of the city's churches, as their music spills into the airwaves. Their desire for information relevant to them creates a need filled by new Spanish-language newspapers, radio stations, and television stations. Not only have their investments transformed the contours of the place they call "home," but they have reshaped the places that, often grudgingly and sometimes with outright hostility, "host" them.

Beyond Push and Pull:
Unauthorized Immigration in Context

An estimated 11.9 million unauthorized immigrants live in the United States. They constitute 4 percent of the nation's population and 5.4 percent of the U.S. workforce. Their children, 73 percent of whom were born in the United States and are therefore U. S. citizens, account for 6.8 percent of the students enrolled in the nation's elementary schools. Approximately three-quarters of the nation's unauthorized immigrants are from Latin America, and the majority of them, a total of approximately 7 million people, are from Mexico.[2]

In the sending countries, poverty is endemic and opportunities for upward social mobility are scarce. The United States, on the other hand, represents the promise of a better life, or at least greater access to the resources necessary to get ahead in life. In 2009 per capita GDP in the United States stood at $46,436. In Mexico per capita GDP for the same period was $14,337. In Brazil, per capita GDP was $10,427, and in Guatemala the gap was even wider, with a per capita GDP of only $4,749 in 2009.[3] As glaring as these wage differentials are, they mask even greater differences in the rural migrant sending communities of southern Mexico and Guatemala, where the minimum wage for agricultural workers is approximately $8 per day, though many work for less.

But these figures only tell part of the story. The fact is that wage differentials, crushing poverty, and the desire for a better life are insufficient predictors of migration. If the difference between Latin America's poverty and the United States' wealth were the sole driver of migration, we would see a great deal more immigration from Latin America (and the rest of the developing world) than we currently do. Research on immigration suggests that there is a much more complex set of economic, social, personal, and political

factors that combine to influence who decides to migrate and
when. Perhaps the most significant factors are the ones most
rarely articulated: in our globally integrated world, we must
pay particularly close attention to the economic, political,
and military actions across borders that are taken by migrant
receiving countries such as the United States. In other words,
what are often described as "push" factors (poverty, political
turmoil, and economic stagnation at home) and "pull factors (wealth, political stability, and job opportunities in the
host country) tell only a part of the story, and not the most
significant part.

While push/pull theories would lead to the hypothesis
that the poorest nations are most likely to send migrants to
wealthy nations, the data on global migrations reveal that it
is not the poorest nations but the nations and communities
undergoing development—that is, entering into global economic networks—that are the most likely to send migrants.
Furthermore, they send migrants not simply to the wealthi-
est nations but to the specific nations with which they have
developed durable and sustained relationships through such
processes as commerce, trade agreements, political intervention, military action, and historical patterns of colonization.[4]

Migration is a process influenced by both macro structures, such as the international relationships of production
and trade formed in an increasingly integrated world economy, and micro structures, such as the informal networks
that migrants develop through which knowledge about the
process of migration and assistance to settle in a new destination can be shared. Once such patterns are initiated, they
become largely self-sustaining. In other words, migration
follows migration, and entire communities of origin and destination are transformed in the process.

The forces that have created the unauthorized immigrant
population and that have radically altered such communities

as Santa Ana, Mexico, and Atlanta, Georgia, are complex and difficult to understand. In the United States, they challenge our notions of who we are as a nation, asking us to reconsider questions of fairness and to interrogate the political and economic systems that we largely take for granted. They require us to delve into our own history to gain awareness of how the actions of our government and our consumption patterns and lifestyles inextricably tie us to the immigrant flows that many Americans now decry. Moreover, because these unauthorized immigrants are part of the fabric of our everyday life—we share schools, neighborhoods, and churches with them; they pick the food we eat, build our homes, and take care of our children and elderly parents—they challenge us to understand their stories, struggles, and dreams. Given the current economic crisis, there is a strong temptation to dehumanize these immigrants and to portray them as overwhelming masses of faceless invaders who challenge the principles upon which our country is built. We shall see, though, that the stories of contemporary unauthorized immigrants bear much resemblance to those of other would-be Americans who came at the turn of the twentieth century, though the circumstances shaping their patterns of migration have given them precious few—if any—alternatives to "living illegal."

Importing Labor, Exporting "McMansions":
Understanding the Forces That Propel Migration

In Santa Ana in the summer of 2002, Don Felipe, perhaps the most successful migrant to Atlanta, proudly offered a tour of his recently completed home. The two-story stone home seemed strikingly out of place in its environment, although it would have fit perfectly into one of the new, wealthy suburbs of Atlanta. It was surrounded by a high stone wall and wrought-iron gate, inside of which lived several ferocious guard dogs and grew dozens of fruit trees. The most striking exterior feature of this home was the large, attached two-car garage with modern electric garage doors. The home, with multiple exterior gables, five bedrooms, and two and a half bathrooms, had a contemporary-style kitchen complete with island and breakfast bar. The kitchen opened into a large dining room with carved mahogany furniture and a living room, the centerpiece of which was a large television. Many of the floors in the home were carpeted, a true rarity in the region.

Don Felipe spent his early years in a very simple, three-room stone home adjacent to this grand home, which he built for retirement. In his first home, he shared a bedroom with his seven siblings. Don Felipe had the opportunity to attend school for less than four years. He spent most of his childhood assisting his father in the cultivation of corn, wheat, and beans on the family's *ejido* property. They had cattle and sheep but, particularly in times of drought, the family's earnings from the land were not sufficient. So, like many other young people of his generation. Don Felipe migrated to Mexico City at the age of fifteen, accompanied by his older brother and his sister. His sister basically served as their mother, cooking, cleaning, and ensuring that they stayed out of trouble. She recalled that, as a teenager, "I took care of them, I washed their clothes, I did their ironing, I made their food. Uy, I did a lot! I took care of seven men, cousins and brothers."

Some of these men attended secondary school in Mexico City, but Don Felipe and his brother went to work in a grocery store, partly to finance their brothers' schooling. Felipe soon found a better job working for the Mexican government installing and repairing water meters. He lived for twenty-three years in Mexico City with his wife, who was also from

Santa Ana, returning home for visits at least once a month and supporting his parents and siblings economically. Over the years, Don Felipe earned enough in various government jobs to invest in purchasing a Laundromat. He also bought property, on which he began building a home.

In 1978, when Don Felipe ran out of money to finish the construction of his home, he decided to try international migration. His older brother, on the advice of some friends from a *rancho* in the state of Hidalgo, had traveled to Atlanta the year before. As the first from Santa Ana to migrate to Atlanta and one of the first to travel to the United States, he returned with reports that jobs were plentiful and earnings were good. Hoping to support his family (which now included six children), finish construction on his home, and earn enough money to open another Laundromat, Don Felipe agreed to work for three years in Atlanta with his brother. He stayed in Atlanta for twice that amount of time, and returned in 1984 to purchase another small business. After only eleven months, Don Felipe and his brother found themselves heading back to Atlanta to earn more money.

Atlanta was initiating a period of rapid expansion as it began to draw middle-class and professional workers from around the United States. Though Atlanta's economy was booming, this was during the "lost decade" for economic development in Mexico, when the government was forced to implement a series of economic austerity measures in response to a severe debt crisis. These measures, which were part of the Washington Consensus, sought to liberalize the Mexican economy and open it to foreign investment, producing widespread dislocation, particularly in such small towns and villages as Santa Ana.[5] Not surprisingly, considering the economic situation of Mexico during the years that followed, Don Felipe's businesses suffered in Mexico. His older sons, nephews, and eventually wife and daughters all joined him in Atlanta.

Don Felipe used his entrepreneurial skills in Atlanta as well. He initially worked as a laborer in construction, but soon established a small business as a stonemason who subcontracted for large construction firms. Over the years, Don Felipe's business employed dozens of young men from Santa Ana. Don Felipe, along with a few others who migrated as undocumented workers before 1986, was able to attain legal status in the United States through the amnesty provisions of the 1986 Immigration Reform and Control Act. Eventually he became a citizen of the United States, and he used the family reunification provisions of current immigration law to help his wife and children become citizens as well. Don Felipe and his family, in a sense, settled in Atlanta. He bought a small ranch-style home in the suburbs and worked hard to develop his business.

For fifteen years, Don Felipe worked building homes for the wealthy in metro Atlanta: "They're houses that are just for very wealthy people, because there are houses worth $7 or $8 million . . . with twelve bedrooms." Don Felipe lived modestly in Atlanta, but when he began construction on his retirement home in Santa Ana, in which he intended to live for about half of each year, he flipped through the magazines bearing images of homes like those on which he had worked for years in Atlanta until he found one that particularly suited him. He hired a group of men still living back in Santa Ana to build a replica next to his family's ancestral home. The new home bears witness to the hardships that he endured and the eventual successes that he achieved.

Residents of Santa Ana often joke that, before the 1980s, no one from their town had heard of Atlanta, and certainly no one had been there. Norma, a young woman who migrated

to Atlanta in the late 1990s from Santa Ana, explained how
much the situation has changed:

> Now, many people, almost the majority, have some-
> one that lives in the United States, which makes them
> economically solvent, because there's really not much
> work in the town. . . . I think it was just a bit before
> 1984 . . . it was a little before '84, because many of my
> cousins, friends, they all lived [in Santa Ana] but some-
> one began coming to Atlanta and from there, well they
> all started running to Atlanta, since there's so much
> work, and so many people began coming to Atlanta.

Santa Ana residents, like the residents of *ranchos* and *pueblos* throughout Mexico who had once relied on internal migration combined with farming as an economic survival
strategy, found that the "migradollars" earned through
international migration had become a necessary source of
economic advancement.

Although Santa Ana did not have a history of international migration, other regions of Mexico have been characterized by a long history of circular migration through
well-developed migration networks between Mexico and
the United States. During the *enganche* period (1900–29), a
number of factors fueled migration: the disruption caused by
the Mexican Revolution and its aftermath, the expansion of
large-scale farming in the United States, and the labor shortages created in the United States by the restrictions of contract labor from China and Japan. During this period, labor
recruiters actively sought Mexican workers to fulfill labor
demands in the United States. This was followed by an era
of mass deportations (1929–41), when the economic depression fueled restrictionist policies combining voluntary depar-
tures, formal deportations, and organized repatriations. It is

estimated that 20–40 percent of the Mexican population in the United States returned to Mexico during this period.[6]

In 1942, during World War II, the United States instituted the *bracero* program, a program that would reinvigorate flows of migrants from Mexico and also shape the course of future migrations. The program provided for direct government contracting of labor to fulfill demands for workers during World War II and its aftermath. It established flows of temporary workers who were authorized for short-term labor in the United States. Farm owners in the United States quickly realized that through the personal networks of their *braceros*, they had access to a pool of laborers who would be willing to work for lower wages as unauthorized immigrants. They used *braceros'* social networks to actively recruit undocumented workers from Mexico. Thus, the *bracero* program created pathways and networks for unauthorized temporary workers as well.[7]

Mexico's own internal development, which included the redistribution of land, became a factor encouraging emigration during this period. For the first time, many potential migrants in Mexico had access to arable land, but they lacked the capital they needed to make such land productive through the purchase of tools and seed. In the absence of a sophisticated banking system in Mexico to provide such capital, the *bracero* program and the demand for unauthorized migratory flows that accompanied it proved to be "a godsend."[8] In small agrarian communities throughout Mexico, migrant income became a key source of capital and began to replace local labor as a source of sustenance. Agricultural workers from Mexico developed streams of migration that continue to flow, albeit as much larger rivers, to this day.

The *bracero* program established, on a much smaller scale, precisely the types of connections, both macro and micro, across national boundaries that would come to characterize the ensuing era of global economic integration. The program facilitated the expansion of large-scale agriculture in the United States while also creating profound transformations in migrant workers' communities of origin, as the capital to which they had access through their labor could be invested in those communities. While the program offered legal pathways for migration to a few, it also established a range of signals to those without legal means for migration, making clear to them that migration was a viable option, and perhaps the only option, for those who wished to participate in the economic, cultural, and social transformations occurring around them. Furthermore, potential migrants began to see wage labor in the United States as a strategy for earning capital and for investing in development projects "at home."

The mechanization of cotton and sugar beet farming in the United States, combined with the growing civil rights movement and opposition from organized labor, eventually led to the end of the program in 1964. During the decade that ensued, Mexico, like other Latin American countries, followed an economic policy of import substitution, relying increasingly on its own rapidly developing manufacturing sector rather than exporting raw materials and then importing manufactured goods from wealthier nations like the United States. Rapid industrialization, coupled with slow growth of agricultural production, pushed forward processes of urban migration inside Mexico. By the middle 1970s, though, the Mexican economy was straining under the weight of slow revenue growth from manufactured exports. In 1976, Mexico reached a loan agreement with the International Monetary Fund (IMF) and implemented the first of many austerity programs, which reduced government spending on social welfare as a means to service external debt. It was during this period that Don Felipe and a handful of other adventurous entrepreneurs from Santa Ana decided that they too would seek investment capital by migrating to the United States.

In subsequent years, often termed the era of the "Mexican miracle," a development boom ensued, bolstered by the discovery of vast oil reserves in Mexico and by huge loans, made primarily from U.S. banks, on the assurance of those reserves. In the early 1980s, oil prices softened significantly, and the Mexican miracle turned into a disaster. On August 15, 1982, Mexico fired the "shot heard around the world," announcing that it could no longer meet interest payments on its foreign debt. The nation entered into an agreement with the IMF that would have profound consequences for poor and working-class Mexicans: the peso was devalued sharply, cutting into the wages of working Mexicans, and the cost of a basic food basket rose from 30 percent of the minimum wage in 1982 to 50 percent in 1985. Then, on September 19, 1985, a devastating earthquake hit Mexico City, intensifying the already dire circumstances for poor Mexicans.[9]

Until this time, migration between Mexico and the United States had continued steadily—primarily in the form of circular migrations of young men from communities with a long-standing connection to the United States, in many cases through networks established during the *bracero* program. But now a turning point had arrived. In 1986, the United States passed the Immigration Reform and Control Act (IRCA), which aimed to reduce the number of undocumented immigrants by sanctioning employers and increasing border security, but it also included a provision (the LAW, or Legally Authorized Worker, program) that offered amnesty to long-term undocumented immigrants and another (the SAW, or Special Agricultural Worker, program) that offered legalization to undocumented agricultural workers. More than two million Mexicans took advantage of IRCA's legalization provisions, and they soon began to petition for their family members to join them as permanent legal residents of the United States. Though IRCA aimed to reduce undocumented immigration, Mexican migration continued to flow north after 1986, prompting policy makers to focus ever more keenly on the border as the key to stanching the flow of unauthorized migration.

At the same time as the United States was working to clamp down on unauthorized migration, the nation was entering into ever more intimate economic relationships with Mexico. The increasing economic integration of the United States and Mexico was signaled first by Mexico's entry into the General Agreement on Tariffs and Trade (GATT) in 1986, and the country's subsequent participation in the North American Free Trade Agreement (NAFTA) in 1994. The austerity programs that accompanied this shift in Mexico produced a rise in unemployment and the dissolution of social safety nets. As the United States pursued investment strategies entailing the relocation of production to free trade zones in Mexico's interior, local economies in Mexico experienced severe disruption. The results were initial internal population displacement from rural to urban settings, generally followed by international migration. Furthermore, for the first time, significant numbers of women, who were the primary wage earners in free trade zones, entered into migratory labor streams.

Over the past twenty-five years, the United States emphatically has promoted economic integration with its southern neighbor through free trade and has aggressively asserted political and military influence over the nation, particularly with respect to the growing problem of the international drug trade. The federal government also has passed a series of immigration policies aimed at radically reducing flows of migration. The 1986 Immigration Reform and Control Act, the Immigration Act of 1990, and the 1996 Illegal

Immigration Reform and Immigrant Responsibility Act all increased resources for border enforcement and implemented several other strategies for curbing unauthorized immigration, including sanctions on employers who hire undocumented workers. In short, the United States has pursued contradictory policies. These policies aim simultaneously to open and to close the border: goods and capital flow with increasing ease, while migrant labor is radically restricted.[10]

These contradictory policies have altered migration patterns from Mexico, as economic integration disrupts local and regional economies and pushes people to seek work elsewhere. For instance, the small town of Santa Ana and countless others like it throughout Mexico had not been a part of earlier waves of migration to the United States. Until the early 1980s, when the economic integration of the United States and Mexico began to intensify and spread throughout the country, these had been simple agrarian communities, where farmers worked small plots of land to raise corn to sell. As Don Felipe and his brothers had, family members often spent periods of time earning additional money working for wages in nearby cities, but these were intended to supplement earnings from agriculture.

Yet, during the last quarter of the twentieth century, residents of this town—and similar towns throughout Latin America—experienced a dual process that would change their economic lives. First, because of corn subsidies being implemented in the United States, they found that they no longer were able to earn money on the international market for the corn they grew in Santa Ana. Second, because of profound changes in the economic relationship between the United States and Mexico, including the implementation of NAFTA, their small communities were, for the first time, being altered by international capital investment and the construction of factories in which locals worked for wages on products to be exported to the United States. These changes thrust small cities and towns surrounding Santa Ana into a modern system of capitalism, shaking up local communities and disrupting the former survival strategies of those who would become migrants.[11]

As the case of Don Felipe and his small hometown of Santa Ana reveals, the inaccessibility of credit for many families in Latin America over the past forty years has made sending a migrant to the United States an important strategy for making capital investments in land or other income-generating enterprises. In many of the small agricultural villages of Mexico and Central America, survival may be possible, but upward social mobility is extremely difficult. In such scenarios, migration is a viable option to improve earning potential. When migration from such a small town or village begins, it sets into motion a series of changes in the local economy that are difficult to reverse, and those who remain behind increasingly rely on remittances sent by emigrants.

The Shifting Geopolitics of Migration

Mario, a young Guatemalan immigrant in Jupiter, Florida, explained his decision to migrate: "I'd like to buy a little land, build a house, and help my siblings . . . I'd like to help my siblings go to school or buy them a little land so they can work there . . . I hope to stay four more years so I can accomplish that." Mario is from Jacaltenango, the municipal head of the department of Huehuetenango, Guatemala. Jacaltenango covers an area of approximately 220 square kilometers encompassing a number of smaller *aldeas* near the border between Guatemala and Mexico.[12] Jacaltenango and its surrounding areas saw significant action during Guatemala's civil war, particularly during the 1980s and 1990s. As David, another young man from Jacaltenango also living in

Jupiter, poignantly exclaimed, "They say Guatemala is the country of eternal spring, but I have never seen that spring since I was born."

Like the story of Don Felipe and his *compadres*, Mario and David's stories cannot be understood without reference to the significant structural forces shaping opportunities for them and other young men in their community. Just as the economic integration of Mexico and the United States shaped migration patterns decisively, so did Guatemala's dense political and military integration with the United States, specifically through the U.S. Cold War policy of containment in Central America. In 1954 the CIA orchestrated the overthrow of democratically elected Guatemalan president Jacobo Arbenz. Arbenz had made the "mistakes" of enacting a far-reaching land reform program that threatened the interests of the American-owned United Fruit Company and including some Communist Party members as informal advisers in his government. The U.S.-sponsored coup brought an end to Guatemala's short-lived democratic experiment and ushered in a series of authoritarian military regimes supported by the United States. In Guatemala, as in the rest of Central America, successive U.S. administrations framed military dictatorship as a necessary evil to prevent Communist inroads in the region. Nevertheless, the repression of peaceful political dissent and the refusal to implement social and economic reforms fueled guerrilla movements in El Salvador, Guatemala, and Nicaragua against military regimes.

Efraín Rios Montt was president of Guatemala during one of the deadliest periods of the civil war (1982–83). A born-again evangelical Christian and retired officer from the Guatemalan army who received support from churches in the U.S. Christian right movement, Rios Montt launched a counterinsurgency campaign to suppress support for the guerrilla groups in the rural areas of Guatemala. As part of this campaign, entire villages were destroyed and tens of thousands of people, especially the rural Maya, were killed, disappeared, or forced to become refugees. As the anthropologist and Mayan refugee Victor Montejo recalls, "The army's intent was to kill all suspected guerillas, and all Mayas were suspect." [13] The army created "model villages" structured to resemble strategic hamlets used in the Vietnam War. Tens of thousands of displaced Maya were forced to leave Guatemala. The persecution and displacement of the Maya during the civil war played a major role in the eventual chain of migration to the United States. Thousands of Maya fled Guatemala to refugee camps in Mexico, and others went to the United States and Canada. Some of the Maya who fled Guatemala during the civil war due to political persecution were later able to adjust their status in the United States by claiming refugee status. Later they sought to bring family members to join them.

Three important pieces of U.S. immigration policy during the 1980s and 1990s affected Guatemalans who migrated to the United States: the Immigration Reform and Control Act, the American Baptist Churches (ABC) settlement, and the Nicaraguan Adjustment and Central American Relief Act (NACARA). IRCA affected Guatemalans much as it had Mexicans in the United States. Almost sixty thousand Guatemalans who were in the country before January 1, 1982 (as well as some agricultural workers who came to the United States after that date), adjusted their immigration status under IRCA's provisions.

Some Guatemalans who did not adjust their status under IRCA had fled Guatemala due to the war and sought refugee status in the United States. Yet, the Immigration and Naturalization Service routinely dismissed the cases of many Guatemalans seeking asylum in the United States. This situation ultimately led the American Baptist Churches to file suit against the INS, charging the asylum status was being denied to Guatemalans (and other Central Americans) because the United States did not openly oppose the strongly anticommunist government at the time. In 1991 the ABC case was settled, and the INS agreed to revisit the cases of thousands of Guatemalans whose asylum claims had been denied. In 1997 the Nicaraguan Adjustment and Central American Relief Act was signed into law, further addressing the cases of Guatemalans and other Central American refugees. Section 203 of NACARA granted to Guatemalans who had registered for benefits from the ABC settlement prior to 1991 or had entered the United States before 1990 the right to apply for permanent resident status.

Despite the signing of peace accords in 1996, the pattern of migration from Guatemalan regions that had little previous contact with the United States was firmly established by the year 2000, when the price of Guatemala's main export, coffee, began to decline dramatically. Guatemala entered a deep economic crisis.[14] Though the initial migrants left Guatemala escaping the violence of the war during the 1980s and early 1990s, most Guatemalan migrants to the United States today are motivated by the same set of factors that influenced Mario and Don Felipe. The International Organization for Migration (IOM) reports that in 2009, 91 percent of Guatemalan emigrants left because they were either looking for work or for better pay, while less than 1 percent were traveling to escape violence.

Current estimates on the number of Guatemalans living in the United States vary between 980,000 and 1.3 million, nearly one-tenth of the entire population of Guatemala. Guatemalans have established communities in traditional migrant-receiving locations such as Los Angeles and

Houston, but increasingly they have also settled in nontraditional migrant destinations ranging from Florida to Iowa, Georgia, Arkansas, Delaware, Kentucky, Tennessee, and the Carolinas.

Linking Economic and Geopolitical Forces

Brazilian immigration has been shaped by a combination of economic and political factors that bear similarities to those influencing immigration from Guatemala and Mexico. During the 1980s and 1990s, as Brazil emerged from a period of repressive military dictatorship, the country embarked on a wide-ranging process of economic restructuring, seeking to implement the Washington Consensus. This economic restructuring included a series of fiscal packages that, among other things, devalued the currency and froze bank accounts, drastically eroding the purchasing power of middle-class Brazilians. By contrast to the Mexican and Guatemalan cases, the earliest Brazilians who made the decision to migrate came from the professional and middle classes and experienced downward mobility. Adriana, a Brazilian migrant to Atlanta, explained: "In the U.S. you have to be prepared to do things that you never thought you would do. I started in a car wash, even though I have a master's in nutrition and used to work at a hospital in Brazil."

In particular, professionals on a fixed salary and those working for the state, which was substantially downsized in the effort to deregulate the economy and make it more competitive in the global markets, saw their possibilities of economic mobility severely curtailed. Under these conditions, migrating to the United States became the crucial strategy through which Brazilian professionals could maintain their middle-class lifestyle, even if such migration meant that they would be unable to continue to work in their professions.

For Mario, Don Felipe, Adriana, and many others, contemporary migration is just as much a result of intersecting historical forces of political and military intervention, development, and capitalism as it is of poverty and wage disparities. As the principles and practices of free markets stretch farther into the rural areas and Mexico, Central and South America, migration should be an expected by-product. Simply put, capitalism has expanded in the region of the Americas through increasing political, economic, and military interdependence. This economic model requires that people find a way to accumulate some capital for investment, and migration is one way to get it. Most unauthorized immigrants come to the United States not because of lack of development but because their own communities have been inserted into a global capitalist economic system, disrupting traditional economies and structuring new opportunities and challenges. These macro forces combine with micro forces—specific social networks and relationships—to drive migration.

Migration Following Migration: Understanding Migration Patterns from the Ground Up

A complex set of forces steers individuals toward migration. While poverty is a serious problem in Latin America and the lure of higher potential earnings in the United States is strong (per capita GDP in the United States is 344 percent higher than in Mexico and 892 percent higher than in Guatemala), factors of supply and demand alone do not fully account for migration. Access to social networks, the process of development and the spread of capitalism, financial deprivation relative to families with migrants in the same community, the need to diversify risk, and the growing inaccessibility of land (and general investment capital) to families that do not receive remittances are all powerful forces driving migration.[15] Ultimately, when enough people from a single area make the choice to migrate, a network of micro connections forms, and this network perpetuates further migration. The economic, social, and family connections that span sending and receiving communities become a conveyor belt, sending the factors that motivate migration back to the sending communities and sending new migrants themselves into the receiving communities.

Returning to the story of Santa Ana and the small town's increasing connections to Atlanta, we can see how emerging patterns of migration look from the ground up. One of the young men whom Don Felipe invited to work in his growing stonemasonry business was Berto, the middle son in a family whose Santa Ana home was adjacent to Don Felipe's. Berto made his first trip to Atlanta in 1992, shortly after the birth of his daughter, in hopes of earning enough money to finish construction on the home he was building adjacent to his parents' home. His neighbor and family friend, Don Felipe, had assured him that a job would await him upon his arrival in Atlanta. So Berto crossed to the United States in a rather uneventful journey. Initially, his wife and young children had remained behind, but in 1998—after six years of waiting, during which Berto had been able to establish his own small stonemasonry business—they decided to cross the border to join him. Berto's younger brother Oscar also decided to cross with them.

In San Juan, Berto's parents live in a small, traditional-style home in the shadows of Don Felipe's American-style house. Their property encompassed not only their home but also two other small vacant houses—in various stages of construction—belonging to sons who lived and worked in Atlanta. Berto's father supervised construction on Don Felipe's grand home and also on the small residence that Berto was sending money from Atlanta to build. Most of the sons, living and working in Atlanta, had not been available to help with these construction projects. Yet a decade after Berto's initial migration, in December 2002, they and their sisters reconverged on their family home to celebrate the Feast of the Virgin of Guadalupe and the return visit of two sons from Atlanta.

The festivities were elaborate and lasted well into the morning hours. After spending the following morning cleaning up, Berto and Oscar's father called all of the children to a large table on the modest home's patio. Sipping *pulque*, a traditional drink made from fermented cactus, the family discussed strategy. In this family of six children, four were living and working in Atlanta. They negotiated together who would remain in Santa Ana, who would travel to Mexico City to work, and who would return to the United States. They decided together that Oscar would stay in Mexico, seeking work in the city, while Berto, whose family was by now well established in Atlanta, would return to the United States and continue to send money to support the extended family's collective endeavors.

This pattern of migration, often described as "chain migration," is very common, and it reveals the role of social capital and social networks in shaping decisions to migrate and patterns of migration. Through his social networks and his connection to Don Felipe, Berto was able to lower the cost of his own migration by increasing the likelihood that he would find a good job in Atlanta. Once he had successfully migrated, his wife, Norma, and his younger brother Oscar also migrated. Norma and Oscar now had gained access to the migrant network through Berto, who not only was able to provide guidance and financial assistance for the trip but also received the newcomers in Atlanta, further lowering the cost of migration for them.

Like Don Felipe, this family eventually used migration to Atlanta as a way to acquire investment capital to start businesses in Mexico and to keep them afloat if the economy took a turn for the worse. Berto, his brother, and his sisters all invested some portion of the money they earned in Atlanta toward a family enterprise: the construction of a small apartment complex in the city of Jilotepec. The enterprise provided his father and brother-in-law, who remained in Santa Ana, a source of work and income, and it also served as an investment in their extended family's future. In other words, they used migration to facilitate their success as capitalists. Being a successful capitalist also requires that you insure your investments when possible, and migration diversifies risk for families seeking to ensure their futures.

As their small gathering made clear, migration is indeed a rational decision. Yet it generally is not an individual decision. The decision to migrate most often is made by families and communities that calculate together how best to survive and to thrive in the context of structural forces that profoundly shape their options. But migration also results from shifting worldviews and changing imaginative landscapes. When successful migrants such as Don Felipe build new and distinctive houses in their home communities, they reconfigure horizons and possibilities for the young men and women in those communities. For young people in migrant-sending communities, evidence of the success of previous migrants also serves as a powerful motivation to migrate.

Julio, a young Guatemalan migrant in Jupiter, Florida, explained how this process impacted his decision making: "I came because I was not seeing any of the money from my work and I could see the progress that the people who had migrated were making. They had fixed their houses, they had more money, and I could see it and that's why I came." The impact of money that can be earned working in the United States is evident to the entire community, where differences between families with and without migrants are clear, even to young children. Until recently, these incentives proved particularly appealing to young single men, but they increasingly propel women, both single and with families, into migration streams. Doña Rosa, a Guatemalan business owner in the Atlanta area, remembers how her children influenced her decision to migrate: "[My daughter] would tell me, 'Yes, Mama, go, go and send us shoes, send us a TV, send us this and that . . . We all agree, Mom, you should go, you understand? We all agree.' " When Doña Rosa's youngest child was twelve years old, she finally bowed to this pressure and made the decision to migrate.

Working at the Bottom: Segmented Labor Markets and Unauthorized Laborers

Even as we carefully attend to the macro and micro forces shaping emigration, we should not lose sight of the fact that migrants come to specific destinations in the United States because there exists a demand for their labor. If indeed there is a demand for their labor, why do these migrants live and work *unauthorized* in the United States? In 2010, the renowned immigration scholar Tamar Jacoby spoke at the Woodrow Wilson International Center for Scholars, addressing contemporary issues of immigration and immigration policy in the United States and explaining a significant disjuncture between our immigration policy and our current economic and demographic realities. Jacoby explained that the most significant factors shaping immigration from Latin America to the United States are the profound demographic, economic, and educational shifts in our country and in the region. Jacoby highlighted three structural factors that impact supply and demand for immigrant workers. First, U.S.

fertility is now below replacement value, meaning that there are fewer native-born people of working age available to enter labor markets. Second, 75 million baby boomers are on the verge of retiring, which will create an overwhelming demand for further service sector workers. Third, U.S.-born adults are achieving unprecedented levels of education. In 1960, half of the working-class men in the United States were high school dropouts. Currently, that figure is less than 10 percent.[16] The demographics of our working-age population have fundamentally changed. Jacoby argues that our immigration policy has ignored these shifts and the demand for immigrant labor created by them.

Jacoby calculates the demand for work-related visas in the United States as 1.5 million per year, but the United States only grants 1 million. This leaves an annual deficit of half a million, which tends to be filled by unauthorized workers. Jacoby makes clear that the costs of unauthorized immigration have to do primarily with this gap: from deaths on the border to demands on emergency rooms and schools, most of the cost side of the equation of undocumented immigration relates to the differences between what our economy needs and what the United States allows each year in terms of visas.

The demographic factors Jacoby describes create a demand for specific kinds of labor in the U.S. economy: flexible low-wage employment. Put simply, many migrants come to specific destinations in the United States because our economy creates a large demand for people to mow our lawns, clean our dishes and bathrooms, work bottom-end construction jobs, and fill a niche of other service and short-term labor needs. These migrants come without authorization, at least in part, because—despite demand for their labor— there is an overwhelming shortage of visas available for the kinds of work that they do. For the native born, who have increasing levels of formal education, these jobs have become undesirable because they represent low status and prestige and fewer opportunities for upward social mobility.[17]

We often hear the accusation that illegal immigrants are "stealing jobs" from young people in the United States, but most unauthorized immigrants are working in segments of the economy that the native born want to avoid.[18] This dynamic has been described as a segmented labor market: at the very bottom of the job market exists a set of jobs that pay poorly and are viewed as undesirable by the vast majority of the native-born population.[19] The very jobs that bear a social stigma for the native born become the niche market for unauthorized Latin American immigrants, for whom these jobs acquire a very different set of social meanings. While a U.S.-born teenager may be embarrassed to take a job picking vegetables, plucking chickens, or cleaning hotel rooms, a migrant from Latin America may see in such jobs a path to upward social mobility. Unauthorized immigrants are highly represented in this job sector.[20]

Don Felipe exemplifies this trend. Although he had worked his way up to become a business owner in Mexico City, he was willing to enter at the bottom of the construction industry as an unauthorized worker in the United States to maintain his dream. While his job in Atlanta did not put him at the top of the social prestige ladder in Atlanta, Don Felipe's situation was much different in Santa Ana, where his house stands as a testament to his achievements and high social status. Young men and eventually women and families followed him to Atlanta not only because they desired opportunities to work their way up as he had but also because they knew that such opportunities would be available.

By the time his young friend Berto arrived in Atlanta, a significant demographic transformation was under way in that city, one that clearly demonstrates how labor demands in the segmented labor market shape patterns of immigration.

During the decade of the 1990s, the foreign-born population of Georgia increased by 232 percent. More than 60 percent of that change was attributable to the immigration of Latin Americans to Georgia. Between 1990 and 2008, the population of people living in Georgia who were born in Latin America increased by 930 percent.[21] Most of that growth was centered in the Atlanta metropolitan region and was precipitated by an announcement made on September 18, 1990, strangely enough, in Tokyo.

On that day, Atlanta's far-fetched dream of becoming the "next great international city" was thrust into the realm of reality by Juan Antonio Samaranch, the president of the International Olympic Committee. Surprising the world, he announced that the 1996 centennial Olympic Games would be held not in their Athens, Greece, birthplace, but instead in the little-known U.S. city of Atlanta. Observers from around the world undoubtedly pulled out their maps to find the city, but Atlanta launched itself into a frenzy of celebration. By 1992, when Berto decided to make the journey to Atlanta, the city had shifted from gleeful celebration to frantic preparation. Soon thereafter, several international and local observers announced that Atlanta was poised to fail as the venue for the 1996 Olympic Games, as construction and renovation were running well behind schedule.

Jerry Gonzalez, the head of the Georgia Association of Latino Elected Officials, explained, "Leading up to the Olympics, the call went out basically saying that 'we're not going to be able to get all of the jobs done and all the sites and venues completed before the Olympics' schedule starts.' That's when things got desperate and I think that's when people were recruiting immigrants to come here."[22] In a desperate search for laborers to complete the preparation for the Games, the Metropolitan Olympic Committee and city and state officials, off the record, contacted Teodoro Maus, the consul general for Mexico in Atlanta. They begged him to get the word out about the city's labor shortage.[23] News began to travel through established networks such as those between Atlanta and Santa Ana, and an increasing number of migrants crossed into the United States with Atlanta as their first destination. Some found work in construction projects directly linked to the Olympic Games, but many others worked to build the infrastructure for the rapidly growing metropolitan area, which was drawing professionals from throughout the United States, thereby propelling an even greater demand for low-end service and construction workers to care for their children and elderly, maintain their lawns and homes, build and renovate their offices, serve their meals, and clean their dishes.

Teodoro Maus explained in a 2003 essay:

Atlanta woke up one day, somewhere in the mid-nineties, to find itself a truly international city. For a long time, Atlantans kept telling visitors "Atlanta is becoming an international city." One day it did. It did because it suddenly became the magnet for new immigrants—most from south of the Rio Grande—that came to work, as other immigrant groups had done before them, hard and honestly in the most difficult, unattractive jobs. And jobs there were. It became almost like a self-fulfilling prophecy: People came because there were jobs available, and their presence and buying capacity expanded the job offers, making more jobs available. With them came an internationalization of products that were brought to serve their needs and requirements.[24]

These workers were prepared to take "the most difficult, unattractive jobs" in the segmented labor market. In so doing, they not only fulfilled labor demands but also themselves created jobs, especially in the many businesses that developed to serve their desires for food, products, and information that catered to them. Yet, despite having been recruited informally to meet Atlanta's labor demands, potential employers did not offer them the visas they would need to live and work legally in the United States. Atlanta's unauthorized population began to swell, and—as Teodoro Maus has gone on the record to explain—immigration officials simply looked the other way.[25]

As we will see in the chapters that follow, during the years in which immigration officials "looked the other way," so to speak, such families as Berto and Norma's became increasingly settled and established in Atlanta. For Norma, Berto, and their two children, the initial transition to living as a family in Atlanta was difficult, but they quickly learned to navigate schools and neighborhoods. During the housing and construction boom, demand for Berto's labor seemed insatiable, and as the professional classes also swelled in Atlanta, Norma developed a thriving small business cleaning private homes. Both of them employed other workers from Santa Ana, as well as young men and women they met in Atlanta. Their children enrolled in local schools and, after a short struggle to develop English fluency, found themselves being named to the honor roll and, perhaps ironically, being chosen for citizenship awards at their local public schools. In 2001, Berto and Norma had a third child, who is a citizen of the United States.

In many ways, their story has been the typical immigrant success story: hard work and commitment to family have allowed them to better their lives, contribute toward the well-being of their extended family and community in Mexico, and offer expanded opportunities to their children. Yet, in sharp contrast to Don Felipe and his family, they have not been able to become citizens of the United States, and they are unable, though willing, to participate fully in the economic, political, and civic life of the United States. As Norma once explained, they feel as if they live "neither here nor there." Their unauthorized children, who are fully integrated into life in the United States and have not visited Mexico since they left Santa Ana, face a series of dead ends. They and the 65,000 unauthorized students who graduate from high school annually are completing secondary education prepared to participate fully in the economic and political life of the United States, and they already contribute significantly to American social, cultural, and civic life.[26] But, as we will see in the chapters to follow, these promising young people face an uncertain future.

Don Felipe and Berto represent two very different unauthorized migration trajectories: Don Felipe came to the United States unauthorized but was granted amnesty in 1986, and he and the members of his family eventually became citizens of the United States. Berto, Norma, and their children were drawn to the United States for many of the same reasons as Don Felipe, but they had—and continue to have—no options for adjusting their status to live legally in the United States. Challenging many of the assumptions we have about those who "live illegal" in the United States, Berto and Norma have no desire to circumvent the laws of this nation. For instance, both have obtained tax identification numbers, which allow them to pay federal income tax despite their inability to obtain social security numbers. Why, then, have they not found a way to adjust their status and become permanent legal residents of the United States? Why, at some point during his eighteen years living and working in Atlanta, did Berto not take the initiative to "get in line," even as he and his wife have undertaken significant efforts to abide by the laws and customs of the United States in many other ways? It is to this question that we now turn.

"Getting in Line:"
A Glimpse into United States Immigration Policy

"Why can't they just go home and get in line? Why don't they just fill out the paperwork and do it the *legal* way?" This, perhaps, is the most vexing of all the questions posed about the phenomenon of unauthorized immigration. Immigration critics often make reference to a "line" that "illegal" immigrants should wait in so that they can do things by the book, according to the United States' rule of law. In debates over immigration reform, a path to legalization is termed "amnesty" because it would allegedly allow immigrants to skip to the front of this line. The "line" refers to the legal means available to people who desire to move to the United States from Mexico, Guatemala, Brazil, or anywhere else. But such opportunities are profoundly limited. For most, including Norma and Berto, there simply is no line available.

Those who desire to live and work legally in the United States must obtain a visa.[27] There are two broad categories of visa. The first is employer-sponsored work visas, which are divided into five categories. Most of these visas are reserved for professionals, people—such as computer scientists or professional baseball players—with special skills and extraordinary abilities. Clearly, these visas are out of reach for the hundreds of thousands of undocumented Mexicans, Guatemalans, and Brazilians who come to the United States to work in the segmented labor market each year. In 2008, the occupations with the highest share of unauthorized immigrants were farming (25 percent), building maintenance and groundskeeping (19 percent), construction (17 percent), and food preparation and serving (12 percent).[28] With the exception of farming, these types of employment would fall into the category of "unskilled labor," a category for which a meager handful of visas are provided.

The second and more likely way that an immigrant from Latin America might come to live and work legally in the United States is through the process of family reunification. Family visas are divided into four priority levels. The first priority is for unmarried sons and daughters of U.S. citizens. The second is for spouses and unmarried children of legal permanent residents. The third is for married sons and daughters of citizens. The fourth is for brothers and sisters of adult U.S. citizens. The Department of State publishes a monthly bulletin summarizing the availability of visas for family reunification and work purposes. According to the January 2011 bulletin, family-sponsored visas for Mexicans are "oversubscribed" and thus visas "are available only for applicants whose priority date is earlier than the cut-off date listed." [29]

For Mexicans falling into the first family-sponsored category (unmarried sons and daughters of U.S. citizens), the cutoff date in January 2011 is January 1993. For those falling into the second category (spouses and minor children of permanent legal residents), the cutoff date is April 2005, unless those unmarried children have reached adulthood. For adult unmarried children of permanent legal residents, the cutoff date is June 1992. For Mexicans falling into the third category (married sons and daughters of citizens), the cutoff date is October 1992, and for siblings of citizens, the cutoff date is December 1995.

These dates are evidence that the line is very long and very slow. Waiting six to nineteen years to obtain a visa often proves unrealistic for families living separated. The wait times for spouses and minor children of permanent legal residents, in fact, has decreased significantly in recent years. In the late 1990s and early 2000s, rather than waiting a decade or more to be reunited with their immediate family members, many spouses and minor children of legal permanent residents made the decision to migrate to the United States before being granted permission. When they make such a decision, they join the ranks of the unauthorized. In an attempt to discourage such practices, the U.S. Congress enacted legislation, as part of the Illegal Immigration Reform and Immigrant Responsibility Act of 1996 (IIRIRA), that would impose a ten-year penalty on those who had accumulated a year or more of unlawful presence in the United States while waiting to reach the front of the line. In other words, when these unauthorized immigrants finally are given notice that they would be eligible to apply for a visa, they are issued orders to return to their country of origin, with a ten-year bar on their reentry.

In Santa Ana, the very few potential migrants who have the opportunity to become legal residents of the United States are the immediate family members of earlier migrants who had arrived in the United States by the early 1980s, and whose status was adjusted through the amnesty provisions of the 1986 IRCA or SAW program. Most of them are wives and minor children of such workers, and they face the difficult choice of waiting in an extraordinarily long line or of entering the United States without authorization and facing a steep penalty. How did this system emerge? On what values and priorities is it based? And what does it tell us about the United States' tumultuous history of immigration?

Today's Migration in Historical Context: The Intersection of History and Policy

"My grandfather was an immigrant to this country, but he came here *legally!*" We often hear this claim in public debates and forums addressing the issue of immigration reform. In some cases, the speaker goes on to characterize today's unauthorized immigrants in an extremely negative

light, as criminals, welfare recipients, or sneaky invaders intent upon getting a free ride on the backs of American taxpayers. Yet even when such characterizations do not follow
the initial proclamation, the claim functions to insulate the
speaker from the criticism that he might be anti-immigrant.
After all, if his grandfather was an immigrant, how can he be
biased against today's immigrants?

But why is it that this person's grandfather could come
to the United States legally while such a high proportion of
immigrants today are unauthorized? When we say that the
United States is a nation of immigrants, we mean simply that
the nation was built through fluid processes of immigration.
During the vast majority of the history of the United States,
borders remained, for the most part, open. In the nineteenth
and early twentieth centuries, as America was emerging as a
new global economic and political power, the United States
took in three-fifths of the world's immigrants.[30] The "grandfather" to whom this bold proclamation refers was likely
among the immigrants who arrived during the period before
1924, when the category of "illegal immigrant" did not exist.

The development of the category of the illegal immigrant,
the closing of the national borders, and the creation of the
Border Patrol to enforce those borders are all fairly recent
phenomena. They emerged in the context of rising nativism
in the 1920s. Like the contemporary outcry to get tough on
unauthorized immigration, the enforcement policies adopted
in this period were strongly shaped by an emerging economic
crisis, but they also were fueled by concerns that immigrants
from certain regions of the world were unassimilable—too
different to incorporate into the life of the nation.

After the initial waves of immigration from Britain and
western Europe, each ensuing wave of immigration to the
United States has raised concerns about the cultural, religious, educational, and ethnic makeup of new immigrant

groups. From the 1840s through the 1860s, reaction to the influx of Catholics from Ireland and Germany led to the growth of the "Know-Nothing" party, which framed its platform in terms of anti-immigrant and anti-Catholic propaganda. The mid-1800s saw riots break out over the issue of immigration; Catholic churches were burned and priests were attacked as hostility toward Catholic immigrants surged.[31] At the time, the fear was that the large influx of poor, rural Irish and German Catholics would undermine the Anglo-Protestant core values of America. Similar arguments are now being made regarding Mexican immigration. We often hear claims that Mexican immigrants' perceived refusal to abandon Spanish and their continued espousal of the authoritarian, corporatist values that are part of their Hispanic-Catholic culture threaten to unravel the unifying fabric of American society.[32]

The concern that certain forms of immigration threaten the nation's most deeply held values has long shaped immigration policy. In the late 1800s, when the federal government began to develop restrictive immigration policy, it started with a law that prohibited people accused of being convicts and prostitutes from immigrating. The federal government's role was enhanced with the passage of a series of laws between 1887 and 1891 that granted the Treasury Department authority over immigration policy. The Chinese living on the West Coast also became the object of concerns about immigration. Chinese immigrants had been relatively well received during the gold rush, but as gold became more scarce and the economy took a turn for the worse, animosity toward them increased, culminating with the 1882 Chinese Exclusion Act. This act, which was not repealed until 1943, severely curtailed immigration from China.[33]

In 1907, the Gentlemen's Agreement between the governments of the United States and Japan emerged as an informal agreement to integrate Japanese children into schools—predominantly in the San Francisco area, where a large portion of the Japanese in the United States had settled. In return, Japan agreed to stop issuing passports to Japanese citizens who aimed to emigrate to the United States.[34] Once again there was fear that, given the foreignness of the newcomers' language, religion, culture, and appearance, they would change America for the worse. Nativists raised the alarm of an impending "yellow peril."

With the Chinese Exclusion Act and the Gentlemen's Agreement, the United States was now well on the way to an era of much more restrictive immigration. When it comes to immigration policy, politics tends to encourage strange bedfellows. In the late 1800s and early 1900s, those who favored restricting immigration included both "scientific" social reformers and the sort of conservative xenophobes who had made up the Know-Nothing movement and the Ku Klux Klan—whose platform was heavily anti-immigrant, anti-Semitic, and anti-Catholic during the first half of the twentieth century. Fueled by scientific "evidence" and driven by theories of social Darwinism and eugenics, restrictionists argued for literacy tests and quotas to reduce or deter further immigration from races and ethnic groups deemed "inferior." On the other side of the issue, conservative capitalists and foreign policy internationalists favored more open immigration laws, the former because it supplied cheap and flexible labor and the latter because it fit with the goal of spreading U.S. influence elsewhere in the world. Presidents Cleveland, Taft, and Wilson each vetoed restrictionist immigration measures in 1896, 1913, and 1915, respectively. But in 1917, Congress produced legislation requiring a literacy test and aimed at restricting southern European immigrants from entering the country.

The Immigration Act of 1924 (preceded by the Temporary Quota Act of 1921) was a victory for restrictionists. It set new numerical limits on immigration that were based on "national origin." Taking effect in 1929, the 1924 act set annual quotas to just 2 percent of the nationality counted in the 1890 census.[35] The law aimed explicitly to return the ethnic makeup of the United States to pre-1890 contours, when the nation was comprised primarily of Western and Northern Europeans. Asians were virtually barred from immigration under this law, with few exceptions. However, there were no numerical restrictions imposed on immigration from the Western Hemisphere. This reflected the continuing demand for Mexican labor in agriculture.

Immigration, which had already significantly slowed during World War I, dropped precipitously with the passage and enforcement of the new legislation. Not surprisingly, emigration came to surpass immigration in the United States during the Great Depression, and the United States entered into an anomalous period in its history: four decades characterized by low rates of immigration.

By the early 1960s, the United States was in the midst of the civil rights movement, and the overtly discriminatory nature of the national origin quotas began to come under attack in Congress. The Hart-Celler Act of 1965 (also known as the Immigration and Nationality Act and Amendments or INA) shifted the course of and the rationale for immigration policy. The INA tied admissions criteria to family reunification and to special vocational skills, rather than narrowly focusing on national origin. The conventional wisdom is that Congress opened the floodgates to Latin American immigration with the passage of the INA, but this view distorts the reality of post-1965 migration.

Without question, the Hart-Celler Act changed the ethnic makeup of the United States, but it did so primarily by opening immigration from the Eastern Hemisphere (and Asia in particular) and by reserving 80 percent of visas for family reunification. The 1965 act established for the first time an annual quota of 120,000 for the Western Hemisphere, and subsequent annual limits of 20,000 for each country in the region. Prior to the passage of the INA in 1965, immigration from the Western Hemisphere (and from Mexico in particular) was regulated at border crossings, but it was not numerically restricted by federal law. In other words, the 1965 law played a significant role not only in changing the face of the United States, by opening Asian migration and by increasing chain migration through family reunification, but also in establishing the image of the illegal immigrant from Latin America. By establishing quotas and suspending the *bracero* program, which we discussed above, new laws ensured that Mexicans, and also Central and South Americans, who desired to work in the United States, had to seek alternative ways to enter, even though work opportunities were available. Thus began the era of unauthorized migration from Latin America.

The personal decisions that many Latin Americans make to go to *el norte* are strongly shaped by changes in U.S. immigration policy. But as we have demonstrated, post-1965 patterns of immigration also have been shaped profoundly by global, regional, and transnational processes in which the United States plays an important role. These have ranged from U.S. interventions to contain the spread of Communism to implementations of the Washington Consensus: economic policies and prescriptions that advance a certain form of capitalism. Unauthorized immigration is not simply a micro process—it is not simply a choice that specific individuals make to break U.S. laws or to take advantage of the system. It is also a macro process—a product of the systems. The phenomenon of contemporary unauthorized migration emerges in a dynamic interplay between individual and family survival strategies, government policies, and the shifting dynamics of the global economy.

Conclusion: Immigrants *Are* American History

"Once I thought to write a history of the immigrants in America. Then I discovered that immigrants were American history." These words, first written by the historian Oscar Handlin in his groundbreaking 1951 book *Uprooted: The Epic Story of the Great Migrations That Made the American People*, offer an important reminder to those of us who prefer to take a short view of American history. The nation-building process of the United States has relied profoundly upon wave after wave of migrants both voluntary and—as in the case of African slaves—forced. Immigrants and their descendents have played key roles in building the infrastructure, economy, and culture of American society, and they will likely continue to do so in the future. The very groups who were considered "threats" to American society at the turn of the twentieth century now make up part of what is considered mainstream U.S. culture. Their stories are the story of the American dream.

It is difficult, though, to shake the sense that the United States is facing an immigration crisis of unprecedented proportions. The terms we hear and see in the media contribute to this sense. We frequently hear that we are facing a "flood" of illegal immigration, an "invasion of illegal aliens," a "rising tide of humanity," or even a "reconquest" of the southwestern United States. These metaphors are quickly linked to "overburdened" school systems and health care facilities, "unprecedented demands" on welfare and other social services, rising crime, and other negative alleged repercussions of immigration. If we think about the period when most of our media commentators, politicians, and baby boomers were born (during the age of restrictive immigration prior to 1965), this "siege mentality" about immigration is somewhat understandable. But the fact is that the period from

1924 until 1965 was actually an aberration in the history of immigration to the United States. The higher levels of immigration we experience today are much closer to the norm of U.S. history, and the doomsday scenarios about immigration have proven wrong before.

History also gives reasons for optimism. Despite fears of the "yellow peril" or of Vatican conspiracies to take over the government, and in the face of persisting racial inequalities and tensions, American society has shown a remarkably creative capacity to incorporate successive waves of newcomers. Looking back to the arguments used against immigrants and immigration at the turn of the twentieth century, it would be easy today to dismiss them as misguided and overtly racist, or as simply another episode of nativist hysteria. However, these arguments—then and now—are based on real, dramatic changes that generate uncertainty, insecurity, and anger among the native-born population. Given the current climate of economic uncertainty and geopolitical turmoil, it makes sense to ask not only about the future of the United States as a political and economic world leader but also about the kind of society we want to be. But it is one thing to have a rational debate about these questions and another to sweep away any meaningful and constructive engagement by invoking the dehumanizing specter of the "illegal alien." At the core, arguments swirling around immigration reform are about the politics of difference.

Changes in U.S. immigration policy since 1965, and the increasingly global reach of our economic, political, and military actions, have created dense connections—bridges across which immigrants travel. These changes have meant that our newest immigrants come from different places and that a larger portion of them are unauthorized, but we have every reason to believe that they too can incorporate into the life of the nation if provided the opportunity to do so. Taking the long view, we also can expect that the broad forces impacting immigration, which we have outlined in this chapter, will shift again.[56] This is not to say that unauthorized immigration is not a problem for the United States. A country in which nearly 4 percent of the population lives in fear of civil authorities and cannot participate in civic life does have a fundamental problem. Prior waves of immigrants successfully lived and transformed the American dream because they were able to participate in and contribute to this nation's civil society. In the next chapter, we explore the difficulties faced by unauthorized migrants in negotiating daily life in the United States, while also striving to maintain connections to the reasons they came—their homes, their families, and their communities.

2

People in Motion

Life Crossing and Across Borders

During the summer of 2002, a group of women crammed into the dimly lit living room of a rented duplex at the corner across from the elementary school in Jupiter, Florida, to talk about their journeys from Guatemala. The duplex was home to six men from Jacaltenango, Guatemala, but it served as a central meeting place for the migrant community, as the backyard was large and abutted the parking lot, where there were no neighbors to disturb. Over the years, the backyard had hosted a significant number of *quinceañeras*, *fiestas*, and other community meetings for the Guatemalan community in Jupiter. On this summer day, as each woman spoke, the others would join in to add details, clarify, or reference their own individual experience. Claudia was among the first to tell her story.

Claudia had been living in Jupiter since 1995, but she had been thinking about coming to the United States for some time before then. She and her husband, Wilberto, had family living in the United States and, like most Jacaltecos, they had heard about Jupiter through the neighborhood grapevine. But there were complications that delayed their original plans. As Claudia explained:

> When my daughter was born, my husband had the opportunity to migrate, but my daughter was born

premature at seven months, so it was difficult for me to take care of her by myself. She weighed seven pounds, two ounces and required special care, so it was too difficult for me alone. My mother-in-law, who lives in Mexico, had come to visit us, and she told my husband that she had everything ready, the coyote and everything. He said, 'Yes, Mom, I want to go, but I cannot leave my wife and daughter like this,' so somebody else went instead. So finally, in 1994 we left Guatemala, but to go to Mexico. My husband went to work at a banana plantation and after a little while, because my mother-in-law was helping me out with my daughter, I thought I also could work in the banana plantation, so I did. We worked from 6:30 a.m. to 7 p.m., Monday through Friday and we saw our daughter on the weekends. It was like that for about one year, until we were able to gather enough money for my husband to make the trip to the United States. It was all well planned. Thank God he made it. He had Mexican papers through his mother. He rode on a truck and in about fifteen days he made it to the United States.

It wasn't long before Claudia followed her husband to Jupiter. Like many spouses of migrants, Claudia was concerned that her husband would not approve of her decision to cross the border, so she tried to keep him in the dark about it. During her trip through Mexico, however, circumstances forced her to fill him in:

Three months later, I didn't ask him, the idea just popped in my head. I didn't want him to worry, so I told him I needed money for something else, I don't even remember what I told him. I didn't want him to worry until I was at the border. So I spoke with my mother-in-law and she supported my idea. She said, 'That's good, *mija*, I will take care of the girl, don't worry.' So like that, I put myself in the hands of God and wished myself the best of luck. I decided to leave on a Thursday. It was the eighteenth of December. I spent Christmas on my way north. I thought to myself: 'If I take a truck, it's going to take a very long time,' and I knew a little bit how things worked in Mexico, so I decided I was going to try to get across Mexico by plane. I took a plane in Tapachula. It was a four-hour flight to Mexico City. I did not know anybody there, and I didn't have a whole lot of money, but I had to take a taxi. In the taxi, I was robbed and left without any money. So, out of necessity, I had to call my husband and tell him that I needed money. He said, 'Okay, I will send the money to my mom's house.' I said, 'Sorry, but you're going to have to send the money to Mexico City.' He said, 'What are you doing there?' So I told him that I had decided to go to the United States. So he sent the money to a hotel, where I stayed for two days. Then I took a plane to Tijuana.

But getting to Tijuana was only half of the battle for Claudia; the most harrowing portion of her journey was yet to come. Despite the fact that she had networks of support and her husband waiting for her at the other end, Claudia faced many more obstacles along the way.

In Tijuana I got in touch with my sister-in-law who lived in Los Angeles. My sister-in-law knew someone who could help me cross, and she got in touch with him for me. We had to walk all day and all night to cross Tecate Mountain to make it to San Diego. This was in 1995, on December 22 or 23. That year was one

of the coldest winters. We started crossing in Tecate.
I remember we lost three people there, because of the
cold. They froze. The snow kept falling. I remember I
was wearing four pairs of pants and tights underneath
that. In Tecate they have a sensor. It's a camera that will
detect anything over 1 meter of height. I'm not tall. I'm
only 1 meter and 55 centimeters tall. But those 55 centimeters . . . I had to crouch down. We had to crawl a
lot, too, because of the patrols and the helicopters that
are around. Our pants got worn down to the skin. It
was hard, with the cold and everything, but I was lucky
and with the help of God, I crossed. They picked us up
at 5 a.m. in San Diego the next day on a truck from a
landscaping company. There were twenty-four people
in our group, and the space in the truck was so tight you
couldn't breathe. They put all of us in that truck. We
were in the truck for two hours, but it felt like an eter-
nity. We made it to San Diego and we were in a house
until night, when they called our family members to
pick us up. For me, it was my sister-in-law that came
to pick me up. Back then, crossing cost $400, in 1995.
So they paid for that. Crossing the border took approximately eight days. I consider myself very lucky and my
trip relatively easy. There are people who risk so much
more than I did on their way through Mexico. Crossing Mexico means a lot of suffering for many people.
I was lucky to do it on a plane. I crossed Mexico in no
time. Other people have to cross in a truck, on a train,
or walking even.

As horrific as Claudia's experience was, she had the benefit of flying through Mexico. Many other women are not
so fortunate. Another woman in the room, Rita, had a very
different journey through Mexico:

For me, it was a difficult trip. In Comitán [a city near the Mexico-Guatemala border] they put us in the cabin of a bus . . . the cabin where the driver is supposed to sleep. The space is supposed to be for one person, but they fit eight of us in there: four looking one way, four the other way. I don't know how many hours are from Guatemala to where we were going in Mexico. I think eighteen or twenty, I'm not entirely sure. That whole time we were there . . . we could not breathe or anything. On top of it, the other driver came in. They have two drivers and one is supposed to rest while the other drives. He came to where all eight of us were and there was no air . . . There was a little fan, but it was not sufficient. We were all so hot, all wet because it was so hot. Some people even vomited. They're smart because they have bags ready. . . . They already know so they have bags for when people need to vomit, they just gave them a bag and then the other driver throws the bag outside. Others had to go to pee because they been holding it for so long, almost twenty hours. The men just went right there, they would pass a container around and then just throw it outside. But the women, we had to hold it from Comitán until the capital. We were all there, sick. They threatened us to not come up even if we had no air because the passengers were there.

From Mexico City, Rita and her group went on another bus to Matamoros, near the U.S.-Mexico border. Rita's journey through Mexico had been harrowing, but her passage to the United States was only halfway complete. Rita went on to explain how she finally got across to the United States:

We had to cross the Rio Bravo with another coyote. A lot of us didn't know how to swim. I didn't know how to swim, so the coyote had to help me. He took me under his arm and helped me cross. A lot of people who didn't know how to swim tried. . . . They would hold on to the coyote's foot and try, but it was very hard. One person nearly drowned. In Matamoros they had told us that we needed good clothes to cross, so we had to go and buy new clothes, new shoes, but we had to cross the river in our underwear. You lose your embarrassment, your *vergüenza*, because you want to live. You had to take everything off, because it was harder to cross the river wearing clothes. We had put our clothes in bags so we could get dressed across the river. Get dressed, put shoes on, and start walking. We made it to Texas.

After crossing the river into Texas, there was still more ground to cover. Rita knew her limitations and had planned for a trip that did not involve walking through the desert, but in Texas she found that she had no choice in the matter:

We were there for two days, in a place without air conditioning. It was very hot and there were twenty of us. . . . They had lied to us because they told us that we weren't going to walk in the desert, but then after two days in that place, they told us we would have to walk two days and two nights. A girl from Honduras kept fainting along the way, and I also fainted. Thank God there was a nice young man in our group. I had told them ahead of time that I could not walk that far. I was traveling with my sister and my brother-in-law, but he was taking care of his wife, so we spoke to the nice guy and asked him to look after me if I fainted. When I fainted, the guy carried me until we got to a place where there was water. We would walk and faint of thirst, and then we would rest when we got somewhere

where there was water. A girl from Honduras, she fainted a lot. She kept fainting and she even got lost for a little while, but some people in the group went back to find her. And we walked like that for two days and two nights until we made it to Houston. By the time we got to Houston we had crossed two rivers: the Rio Bravo and another river that was very muddy. . . . We would sink into mud with every step. In Houston when the car came for us, we were soaked. Our clothes were soaked. Then the cramps started and our feet were swollen from walking so much . . . and then we came here.

Unauthorized immigrants are often portrayed as opportunists who want to come to the United States to take advantage of the generosity of Americans. However, as the testimonies of Claudia and Rita show, if there is a calculus to immigration, it is infinitely more complex than push-pull theories of wage differentials would suggest. The stories that immigrants tell again and again are of great sacrifice and hardship. For many, the decision to come to the United States, while necessary to ensure the survival of their families, is extraordinarily difficult and fraught with danger. This is a human reality that we need to take into account in our conversations about immigration. It is a reality that is many times obscured by the uncritical use of the term *illegal* and by the one-dimensional portraits painted of those to whom the term is applied.

The path of Claudia, Rita, and many other unauthorized immigrants who have arrived in such new immigrant destinations as Jupiter in recent decades is littered with obstacles. They face challenges at each step of the way: crossing borders, settling in new destinations, and living their lives constantly building and maintaining connections to their place of origin. Understanding these obstacles and the ways that unauthorized immigrants overcome these challenges us to broaden the boundaries of public discourse on what it means to "live illegal" in the United States. As we will see, the stories of these migrants shed light on the profoundly contradictory impacts of border enforcement. They also reveal the shortcomings of claims that unauthorized immigrants come to the United States seeking easy access to money and services and that they resist integration into U.S. society.

Migration may bring benefits to individuals and their families and communities of origin, but it often comes at a high cost and risk on both sides of the border: families are separated, children are left vulnerable, communities are torn apart by new economic divisions, and the journey may involve physical injury and even death. For the unauthorized, "living illegal" means living with fear as a constant companion. This may come as no surprise. Typical media portrayals of the unauthorized focus on fear of apprehension and deportation, and our immigration and border policies indeed traffic in such fear. Yet, as we will see, the fears and anxieties of the unauthorized are much more complex, and in fact more profoundly and universally human, than we might assume.

Crossing: Dangers, Debts, and Duties Across Borders

The years in which Claudia and Rita crossed into the United States were marked by a significant shift in U.S. border policy. The Border Patrol was founded in 1924, when a period of heightened anti-immigrant fervor swept through the nation. Still, border enforcement was minimal for much of the twentieth century. Indeed, from the end of the *bracero* program in 1965 until the passage of IRCA in 1986, the United States operated a "de facto guestworker program" in which "border enforcement served a symbolic purpose" but did not deter undocumented border crossings.[1] Migrants from Mexico and Central America, the vast majority of whom were young men, engaged in circular migrations much like Don Felipe's early journeys, chronicled in Chapter 1. These men traveled to the United States to work for periods of time and then returned when work no longer was available or when duties to family and community called them home. The informal policy of fluid borders began to change in 1986, with the passage of IRCA, but the most significant changes came into effect in the early 1990s, just as Rita and Claudia were preparing to cross.

The 1990s marked the beginning of increased focus on border enforcement and security. There were two fundamental changes regarding border policy during the Clinton administration: first, the budget allocated for border protection was drastically increased, and second, manpower was focused on key popular crossing points.[2] The first operation with a heavy focus on border security and enforcement was Operation Hold the Line in 1993, which focused on a twenty-mile stretch of the El Paso area border zone. In 1994, Operation Gatekeeper continued along the same enforcement path, focusing on several stretches along the San Diego area. Operation Safeguard (1994) focused on selected Arizona border zones, and Operation Rio Grande (1997) focused on the Rio Grande valley in Texas.[3] All of these operations had similar strategies, stressing increased numbers of Border Patrol agents, the use of technology such as infrared cameras to detect crossers, and an information database to keep track of repeat offenders.[4]

The Bush and Obama administrations continued to follow these strategies. For example, while the number of Border Patrol agents was 3,965 in 1993, by 2006 there were 12,349 agents[5] and by 2009 there were 20,119.[6] The budget allocated for immigration enforcement, especially border protection, also has increased significantly. In 2004, under the Bush administration, the total budget for immigration enforcement was $9.5 billion.[7] By 2010, under the Obama administration, the budget had escalated to $17.2 billion.[8]

In May 2009, during his testimony to the Senate Judiciary Committee's Subcommittee on Immigration, Border Security, and Citizenship, Douglas Massey, an expert in migration from Mexico to the United States, noted the marked increase on border-focused policy, stating that "from 1980 to 2000, the number of Border Patrol agents increased 3.7 times, linewatch hours rose by a factor of 6.5, [and] the agency's budget increased by a factor of 12."[9] The increased focus on border enforcement jumped to a new level in 2001 as a result of the events of September 11. Massey noted that, despite the fact that none of the 9/11 hijackers entered the United States through the Mexican border, "border enforcement nonetheless rose exponentially after September 11, with the border patrol budget increasing 95 times its 1980 level and the number of line watch hours rising 111 times. After 9/11 deportations also began a marked increase, rising from just 11,000 in 1980 to some 350,000 in 2008, breaking old records last set during the mass deportation era of the 1930s."[10]

Ironically, the period of heightened focus on enforcement has corresponded directly with the largest growth in the unauthorized population in the history of the United States. Though estimates vary, demographers suggest that there are approximately 12 million unauthorized immigrants living in the United States today.[11] Building walls and closing popular border crossing points has made crossing the border much more dangerous and costly—but it has actually done little to halt unauthorized migration. A recent joint publication of the American Civil Liberties Union (ACLU) and the Mexican Commission for Human Rights (MCHR) reported that in 2009, on the deadliest sections of the U.S.–Mexico border, the risk of dying was seventeen times greater than in 1998,[12] and that "from 2000 to 2008 the unauthorized population grew from an estimated 8.4 million to 11.9 million."[13] Why hasn't the focus on enforcement and security slowed down unauthorized migration? Primarily because enforcement-only policy does little to change the factors that cause migrants to come. The most significant change that comes with greater border enforcement strategies is that the cost of migration increases markedly. While this may deter a small number of potential first-time migrants, the larger effect is that migrants who formerly circulated regularly between the United States and Mexico will now stay in the United States. As Douglass Massey explained in his testimony to Congress:

This shift in behavior occurred because our militarization of the border increased the costs of crossing it from $600 to $2,200 in constant dollars while also increasing the risk of death while having no effect on the probability of apprehension. Given the higher costs and risks of border crossing, fewer migrants left; but those who did still got across because the odds of apprehension did not rise. Once inside the U.S. they hunkered down and stayed longer and in larger numbers to avoid experiencing the costs and risks again. In sum, it was because of a decline in return migration and not an increase in entry from Mexico that the undocumented population ballooned during the 1990s and made Hispanics the nation's largest minority a decade before demographers had predicted. If return migration to Mexico had remained at its pre-1986 levels, we would have had nearly 2 million fewer undocumented Mexicans settling between 1980 and 2005. This is the reason Mexico dwarfs all other countries in the unauthorized population.[14]

In short, border militarization does not deter immigration; instead it increases deaths during crossing, elevates the cost of smuggling, and in fact increases the number of undocumented migrants settling in the United States. In other words, immigration policy intended to reduce unauthorized immigration from Mexico and elsewhere has the unintended effect of adding to the number of unauthorized migrants and shifting migration patterns toward settlement.

"To Make It Across Alive": Crossing Through Mexico

Although the majority of unauthorized immigrants in the United States are Mexican nationals who have had to cross only one international border, a great many unauthorized Latinos, particularly those from Central America, must first make a perilous journey through Mexico. Gathered across from the Jupiter elementary school on that day in 2002, giving their assessments and pointing to similarities and differences with their own experiences, Claudia, Rita, and other Guatemalan women made clear that although they understand the perils of border crossing, potential migrants nevertheless take the risk. Interestingly, they made this point most evident in their discussion of the *first* border they would need to cross—the border between Guatemala and Mexico. While the final trek across the U.S. border took a major toll, the worst part of the journey for Guatemalans was the passage through Mexico.

Doña Juanita had a relatively easy trip. She avoided extreme difficulties, but still experienced profound anxieties as a woman traveling alone. As she explained:

> The biggest risk a woman takes in crossing [into Mexico] is being raped. Coming alone, it's risky. You leave your house in your town and there are people from

other places, people you don't know. I was the only
woman in a group with twenty-two men. I prayed the
whole time. I wasn't thinking of myself, but of my
daughters. Thank God nothing happened. Everyone
said they were my cousins, my family. You always hear
that women get told all sorts of things; thank God that
wasn't the case with me.

Claudia echoed Doña Juanita's point, offering her own insight into the perverse impact of militarized border strategies:

I also think all women experience violence and humiliation at some point along the journey, and verbal
abuse. They are just transporting a human being like
cargo that's paid for. There's a clear objective to make
it across alive. It doesn't matter if you're hurt, or feel
any sort of pain. They do not care in the least bit about
the health of the person they're crossing. It's a deal, a
transaction. You bring me here and I pay you. How you
bring me, under what conditions, nobody cares. The objective is the most important: to get here.

Mexico is a country of transit, with strict immigration
laws and a history of corruption that compounds the danger
and abuse to which Central American migrants are subject
as they cross into Mexico from Guatemala. In 2010, Amnesty International released a report about victimization at
the border with Guatemala, finding alarmingly common
instances of kidnapping, threats, assaults, murder, extortion,
rape, and use of excessive force by coyotes and the Mexican
police. The report explained of the sexual, psychological, and
physical assaults that it documented, "in many cases [these]
would appear at first glance to be the work solely of criminal
gangs, [but] there is evidence that state officials are involved

at some level, either directly or as a result of complicity and acquiescence." Regardless of the identity of the perpetrators, the victims are most often migrants from Central America. In 2009, the National Institute of Migration in Mexico reported that more than 65,000 Central Americans were held in migrant prisons and nearly 63,000 were deported, approximately 4,000 of whom were under the age of eighteen. Furthermore, 3,753 were rescued by members of the Grupo Beta (a humanitarian assistance force),[15] and 737 were found to be injured or mutilated, while 168 migrants were found after being reported lost.[16]

As the women gathered in Jupiter to tell their stories were painfully aware *before* they made their journey, women are a particularly vulnerable group among migrants through Mexico. Estimates from NGOs and other organizations put the number of women who are victims of sexual violence as high as six in ten.[17] As with other types of victimization along the Mexican leg of the migrant journey, officials are often the perpetrators. Amnesty International reported that of ninety women interviewed in one study, twenty-three reported being raped, and of those, thirteen stated that the rapist was a state official. These numbers may easily have undercounted the reality because women were reluctant to talk about their experiences while in detention in Mexico.[18] Beyond rape, women are also subject to humiliation and verbal abuse from the predominantly male coyotes, their fellow travelers, and Mexican authorities.

The stories these women tell demonstrate not only the profound difficulties of crossing but also the fact that U.S. and Mexican policies designed to deter or raise the costs of migration simply did not have the intended effect for these migrants. The factors influencing their choice to come to Jupiter simply outweighed the anticipated risks of violence, rape, or even death. Despite having some knowledge of these risks, the women made the choice to migrate anyway. As the United States undertook policies of increased border enforcement with the intention of deterring migration, the simultaneous economic integration of the region of the Americas (which we describe in Chapter 1) meant that potential migrants were propelled by a broad range of factors into taking the risk. In so doing, they not only risked their lives and health but also incurred significant debt.

"The Loan Hangs over Us": *Increasing Costs of Crossing*

In one sense, the high cost and dangers of crossing provide evidence that the policy focus on border enforcement is having an impact. The impact, however, is not the intended one, as migrants decide to come despite the higher costs and greater danger. Despite their socioeconomic differences, Mexicans and Guatemalans highlighted the fact that their higher debts and the difficulties of crossing were factors that were *keeping* them in their U.S. destinations longer than originally intended. The vast majority initially came with plans to return to their country of origin after a few years of work. But the very first obstacle to that plan was financial.

As the risks of crossing the border increased in the first decade of the twenty-first century, so did the cost. Mexicans in Atlanta report that they currently pay approximately $2,600 to cross into the United States with a coyote. When we spoke to the Jacaltecos in Jupiter in 2002 and 2003, the rate for hiring a coyote to make the trip from Guatemala to Jupiter was between $4,000 and $6,000. Migrants often acquire large debts in order to finance the high cost of crossing the border. Some are fortunate enough to have a family member in the United States who can help them with the money, but most have to resort to local *prestamistas* (informal lenders).

These *prestamistas* usually loan money at high interest rates, up to 10 percent monthly.[19] Miguel, a young man from Jacaltenango, explained his experience with the loan: "We borrowed part of the money there . . . we borrowed $1,125 from an aunt. She charged interest of 8 percent. By the time we were done paying it was $1,986.00." Women are often the ones who shoulder the burden of debt, not only because they are usually the ones who borrow the money (for their sons, husbands, etc.) but also because when men migrate and send the money back, it is the women who must manage the money and stretch every dollar to support the household and make loan payments.[20]

Concepción was one of the women in Jacaltenango whose husband had migrated but whose family had yet to reap any of the promised financial benefits because of the debt. Concepción's daughter had become ill and needed major surgery. Her situation was particularly dire, as she now faced looming medical bills on top of the cost of her husband's migration:

> In our case, we spent a lot of money for him to go—we spent $9,931. So now we have to pay the coyote. We still haven't finished paying. I go drop off all the money he sends to pay the coyote. Everything he sends in a month goes towards that. So now I go to work to try to support my baby and my little girl. I go clean houses. I cannot save any money; the money has to go to too many different things. It is hard. . . . I had a difficult time with my daughter. We could not borrow money to get her better, so my husband went to a different town to borrow money to go north—to get the money to cover the expenses. We haven't been able to cover them yet. The loan hangs over us. All the money goes to debt. He tells me to take a little for my expenses, but I only keep about $25.

As Concepción explained, remittances are often insufficient to cover both living expenses and the debt incurred to migrate. Only after migrants have been able to cover the debt they incurred can they begin to invest and spend remittances as they planned. In Concepción's case, the story did not have a happy ending. Her daughter died in the hospital, and Concepción was hospitalized herself just as her husband was about to leave for Jupiter. By the time he finally arrived in Jupiter their debt load had become unmanageable. Although they initially viewed migration as the only solution to their debt problems, in the end it simply compounded the problem.

The experience of Concepción's family was not the exception. While some of the migrants in Jupiter had paid their debts, the vast majority of the more recent arrivals were still working on it—some of them well past their initial planned return date of three or four years after arrival. Unexpected expenses at home (such as Concepción's medical bills), high interest charges from the *prestamistas*, and the high costs of living in new urban destinations all made it more difficult than anticipated for migrants to pay down their debts. Migrants who may initially have intended a short stay in the United States (engaging migration as a form of investment, as we describe in Chapter 1) often find that they are burdened with financial debts and duties to protect and support those in their sending communities. Dire circumstances have prompted them to leave home, despite their awareness of the dangers they would face. They have survived the perilous crossing, but many more obstacles stand in their way as they struggle to settle in new destinations.

Settling:
The Challenges of Daily Life in New Destinations

When Claudia and Rita finally ended their long journeys, they joined the growing number of immigrants arriving in new cities and regions of the United States that have only begun to receive Latin American immigrants in the past three decades. The duplex where Claudia, Rita, and the other Jacaltec women gathered is located in the heart of Jupiter, Florida, a coastal city on the northern edge of Palm Beach County, less than ten miles north of West Palm Beach. In Palm Beach County, Latinos constituted 7.7 percent of the population in 1990, 12.4 percent in 2000, and closer to 17 percent by 2010. According to 2000 census data, Jupiter's 2,881 Hispanics or Latinos made up 7.3 percent of the city's population.[21] Although figures from the 2010 census are not yet available, the most recent American Community Survey figures show a marked increase since 2000. The 2006–8 American Community Survey lists 7,682 Hispanics or Latinos in Jupiter. They make up 14.6 percent of Jupiter's population, twice the 2000 estimate.

As a popular vacation destination, Jupiter (like most of south Florida) experienced a major housing and construction boom that began in the early 1990s. Guatemalan and Mexican immigrant laborers are the majority of workers in the construction, landscaping, and golf course maintenance industries. In the years prior to the 2006 opening of the El Sol Resource Center (a day labor center that matches workers with employers) hundreds of day laborers could be seen each day, crowding the sidewalk and parking lots in front of apartments, waiting for contractors and private individuals to arrive and offer work. Most of these individuals are relatively recent immigrants from Guatemala and Mexico, and approximately one-quarter of them come from the town of Jacaltenango and its surrounding areas in northwestern Guatemala. Thus, Jupiter's migrant population is comprised predominantly of indigenous Maya.

In the southeastern United States, Jupiter is one among many "new destinations" for migrants from Latin America. The flows of migration from Mexico and elsewhere in Latin America traditionally moved through Texas, California, Arizona, and New Mexico and to "gateway cities" such as Miami, Chicago and Los Angeles. These patterns began to shift significantly after the 1986 passage of the Immigration Reform and Control Act (IRCA), which combined with changing labor demands to draw immigrants away from traditional gateway cities.[22] Another important factor that contributed to the emergence of new destinations for immigrants was the deterioration of the features that had previously attracted them to such traditional destinations as California. After an economic downturn, a drastic increase in anti-immigrant sentiment (embodied in legislation such as Proposition 187), and increased militarization of the border, discouraged immigrants, many of whom had been able to adjust their status through the amnesty provisions of IRCA, moved to other regions of the country, most importantly the South.[23] Once established, they began to invite friends and family from their places of origin to join them, and the informal networks of migration that we describe in Chapter 1 created new paths for immigrants directly from Mexico, Central America, and South America into such new destinations as Jupiter and Atlanta.

As a consequence of these changes, Latino immigrant proportions have declined in traditional destinations, while such states as Georgia, Nebraska, Iowa, and North Carolina have experienced exponential growth in Latino population.[24] According to the 2000 census, seven of the ten states showing the fastest rates of Latino growth in the nation are located in the Southeast, with North Carolina, Arkansas, and Georgia leading the way with growth rates of 394 percent, 337 percent, and 300 percent, respectively. In Cobb County, Georgia, a suburb of Atlanta, the Latino population increased 399 percent between 1990 and 2000.[25] Latinos as a proportion of the population increased from 1 percent in 1980 to 11 percent in 2007, while the non-Hispanic white proportion of the population declined from 94 percent to 60 percent during the same period.[26]

These statistics tell us something important about the changes associated with contemporary unauthorized migrations. Unauthorized immigrants are arriving in cities and towns, particularly in the U.S. Southeast and Midwest, that do not have a tradition of immigration and that have, until very recently, either been relatively ethnically homogenous or have been characterized by the politics of black and white. Many of the tensions and fears relating to immigration have as much to do with these new dynamics as they do with the process of immigration itself.

"Everything Is Different Here; Life Is Harder": Adjusting to Life in New Destinations

For migrants from rural Guatemala and southern Mexico, the challenges associated with transition to life in the United States are multiple. Cultural, linguistic, economic, and social obstacles face them at every turn. For Mayan Guatemalans, who may speak only the language of their indigenous group, these obstacles are compounded. Armando, who is from Jacaltenango but has been living in Jupiter for several years, explained his experience: "The most difficult thing is speaking English. You have to learn so many things to function well. Spanish becomes of secondary importance. There are many Hispanics, and some services are in Spanish but not that many. The *q'anjob'al* [indigenous Maya] women are the most marginalized because they cannot communicate at all [since many speak an indigenous language but do not speak Spanish]. The children cannot communicate well with their parents anymore because of language." Eduardo, a young Jacalteco living in Jupiter, explained some of the difficulties migrants face with even the simplest of tasks: "We have to do laundry . . . If you don't have a car; you have to ride your bicycle to the Laundromat. There are some Laundromats that are nearby, but a lot of them are far away. You have to find someone who can give you a ride or ride your bike if it's easier because it's just too hard to go on foot. . . . Everyone also cooks and cleans. Everyone knows how to make food, but the food is no good."

Eduardo's complaint about food was echoed by a number of the young migrants we spoke to. While this may seem trivial, it means a great deal to the young men who have never had to fend for themselves before. After a hard day of physical labor that frequently begins before dawn and does not end until well after 5:00 p.m., the complexities of going to a supermarket, getting home with the groceries, and then preparing something edible was beyond the capacity of many of the young men who were newcomers to Jupiter. Many of them described their working days as a fog of work, sleep, and time spent looking for work, with little space or time for recreation or social contact outside their immediate living space.

Most often, what makes migrants endure these long odds and inhospitable conditions is commitment to family. As one young father explained: "The only thing we could do for our children was to come to the United States. My wife was crying and she didn't want me to go, but I had to do it for the kids . . . Here I'm going to work for about three years, I think, and then return to Guatemala because my children need me." Four years after the interview he was still seeking work as a day laborer in Jupiter, his debts not fully paid off as work had become scarce and costs continued to rise. Another migrant father, who was almost crying as he spoke, described the tensions he felt caught in the same predicament: "I just spoke on the phone to Guatemala . . . I was desperate here because everything is different here, life is harder, people are different, what is most difficult is to be far from my wife and kids. The worst thing is that finding work is hard and it doesn't pay well. If only I could be there now, but I can't." The ambiguity these young fathers describe is one of the most striking elements of contemporary unauthorized immigration—the tension between the need to work in one location and the need to support a life and family in another.

Another significant obstacle for many of the young migrants was learning how to deal with institutions such as banks and money-sending services in order to fulfill their obligation to send remittances home. One of the major issues that plague the migrant community is a fundamental mistrust of banking institutions. Because a large number of unauthorized migrants fear that they may lose any money deposited in a bank if they are detained by immigration authorities, they tend to carry their week's pay in cash. This habit has not gone unnoticed in communities such as Jupiter, where migrants have been identified as easy targets by thieves. A 2005 article in the *Palm Beach Post* recounts a series of robberies targeting Guatemalans. The article reports up to fifty victims, most of whom were Guatemalans picked up "for work" along Center Street (where day laborers gathered) and then robbed and beaten.[27]

The perpetrators of this particular string of crimes were eventually apprehended and sentenced to five years in jail, but many crimes against migrants go unreported. Many unauthorized workers also are victims of wage theft. Since the opening of El Sol Resource Center in 2006 (which we discuss in Chapter 5), the problems with wage theft in Jupiter have dropped significantly, but the problem continues in other locations throughout the country.

Don Alfonso, for example, had moved to Atlanta from Immokalee, Florida, because he had been offered a job loading trucks. While he had been promised good wages, Don Alfonso soon found himself making $150 a week working for twelve hours a day loading and unloading trucks. He finally decided to seek help when he was not paid at all: "So that's where I started working in Atlanta. I was working there and one day we had to load and unload trucks all day without any pay. No pay at all that day. When we started working for pay we worked from 6:00 a.m. to 6:00 p.m. for $150 a week. Twelve hours. We had come in a group and people left because we were not making anything. Three of us stayed. . . . Eventually a church helped us."

While almost all the day laborers we spoke to had been the victims of wage theft at one point or another, their most pressing concern was with getting a job in the first place. With a larger debt looming and daily costs growing, the pressure to find work and cut costs is constant. In order to afford shelter, groups of young immigrant men often live together in rented apartments or single-family homes. This leads to problems of sanitation and makes privacy nearly impossible for the migrants. A police officer we spoke to in Jupiter described the living situation in one set of apartments as "submarine" conditions. As he explained it, the residents utilized the beds in the apartment in shifts to sleep. With more individuals than beds, each person had to sign up for a turn to sleep.

In the end, while the fear of being apprehended may not be at the forefront of daily concerns for survival, it brings the cycle of alienation full circle. As we explore in detail in Chapter 3, new destinations for unauthorized immigrants often are sites of hostility, interethnic tensions, and violence toward immigrants, and new laws are making detention and deportation increasingly likely. Being deported would mean losing all the resources invested in making migration possible, and also the great effort invested in the process of settlement. Thus, many undocumented Latino immigrants find themselves pushed into the shadows of society, reinforcing the stereotype that they do not want to be integrated. In a sense, these unauthorized immigrants do not resist assimilation; assimilation resists them. Nevertheless, as we will see, unauthorized immigrants settle, build households, and integrate into often inhospitable communities at remarkable rates and against significant odds.

"Not That I Minded Doing That Kind of Work":
The Experience of Downward Social Mobility

Many unauthorized immigrants not only overcome the hurdles of adjusting to a new society, but they also confront the obstacle of downward social mobility. Middle-class, college-educated Brazilians who migrated during the 1980s and 1990s, decades of political transition and economic instability in Brazil, have ended up cleaning houses or working in construction and landscaping, where they are able to earn more money than in their original professions. Brazilian immigrants tend to have a different profile than their Mexican and Guatemalan counterparts. They have generally higher levels of formal education, and many come from urban areas, where they would be classified as middle-class and lower-middle-class.[28] For example, a study of the Latino labor force that came into New Orleans to rebuild the city after Hurricane Katrina found that Brazilians have an average of

9.7 years of formal education compared to only 7.2 years for Central Americans.[29]

Immigrants who worked as lawyers, teachers, psychologists, and dentists in Brazil typically find work in the service and construction sectors of the U.S. economy. Forty-two percent of the Brazilians we spoke with in Atlanta and in Florida indicated that they earn monthly salaries between $1,400 and $2,000, and 17 percent state that they earn over $3,000 per month. Economic stability, however, comes at the price of not being able to work in the professions for which they trained in Brazil.

As Erica, who came from São Paulo to Atlanta following the 1996 Olympics, explained, "I didn't know that people came from Brazil to clean houses. At first, it was even funny. When I met new Brazilian friends, they asked me if I wanted to work as a maid. And then I would [say]: 'No, no, I'm a psychologist.' But I didn't know better. Not that I minded doing that kind of work. I would do it if it were necessary, and indeed, in the end, I adjusted and ended up doing it."

The experience of downward social mobility also entails adjusting to new living conditions. As one Brazilian immigrant in Florida explained to us, "Many Brazilians come to the United States alone, without their families, and share an apartment with other Brazilians. Often five or six Brazilians share a two-bedroom apartment. They have no space to relax in private. They are here to work and become totally alienated."

Another Brazilian woman expressed strong nostalgia for the home she left behind: "In Brazil, my home was totally different [from here], since it was my family. We all thought and felt the same. So I was bothered when I came to a house where everybody was different. In Brazil, I loved to be at home because I loved to be with my family. Here, everybody has to do their own thing."

These women understood that their downward mobility and difficult living conditions were included in the cost of immigration. When one is undocumented, there are limits to the kinds of opportunities and jobs available, even for those who come with considerable education and training.

"The Woman Has to Work as Much as the Man": *Families Settling Against the Odds*

Largely as a result of the rising risks and costs of traveling back and forth, unauthorized migrants are making the decision to settle somewhat permanently in the United States. While men may initially travel to the United States alone, they frequently are followed by wives and children. In these increasingly settled unauthorized immigrant families, some children may be unauthorized, but many are native-born U.S. citizens. Norma and Berto's case, which we discuss in Chapter 1, is instructive. After they married, Norma and Berto began building a home on the property of Berto's parents in a small rural community in Mexico. The home was not in the center of town and was about a fifteen-minute walk from the household in which Norma was reared and in which her parents and sisters still lived. After the birth of their daughter, Berto decided to travel to Atlanta to earn money for the completion of the home, leaving Norma in a somewhat tense domestic situation with her mother-in-law. Norma very much disliked having to live so far from her own mother. She also resented the fact that Berto's parents discouraged her from working as a street vendor, which she enjoyed doing as a way to earn extra cash. As soon as it was economically feasible, Norma and her children joined Berto in Atlanta.

After arriving in metro Atlanta, women like Norma had, for the first time, an opportunity for economic independence, which also increased their status in the household. Yet they were also expected to continue being responsible for all domestic activities. Men were glad to have their wives join them, since when they lived without women, they had to learn to cook and clean. Norma explained, "Berto says that when he lived with a bunch of guys, their lives were really ugly [*feo*], because there were so many of them, they didn't get paid much, and they had to send all of the money they could to Mexico. They slept in chairs, sometimes, because no one was concerned about buying nice living room furniture or having a nice apartment. They just weren't interested in that stuff." Some men, particularly of Norma's father's generation, had no interest in migrating to work in Atlanta, since "people come back and tell them about how a person is always locked up in his apartment, he has to make his own food, he has to do all those things."

For the men who did migrate, life improved when their wives joined them. First, they had additional income from their wives' work to invest in their household and to send home. Second, they had someone to take over domestic chores. Norma explained: "But for the woman, I think that it's more work when you have your family here, you have to work, watch over your kids, and make food for your husband. And the men, they just go, work, come home, 'Give me some food,' take a bath, and go to bed." In many cases, however, the transition in male and female responsibility was difficult for men to handle. Arturo, also from Mexico, explained in an interview, "Husbands want their wives in Mexico to be in the house, to take care of the kids. And here, we know that in the United States, life is different. The woman has to work as much as the man, and she can't always make dinner at home. So we have to get used to this." Nevertheless, most women chose to work, and they found the opportunity to earn their own money very appealing. It offered independence from their husbands and an opportunity to invest in items that they valued, particularly goods and services for their children. When women work outside the home, they also contribute to increasing economic stability for the household, which allows many unauthorized immigrant families to purchase cars and homes while still sending money and goods regularly to their place of origin.

Norma, Berto, and their children, like millions of other unauthorized immigrants, live perpetually separated from their loved ones "back home." As is typical of many unauthorized families, Norma and the children have not, since their initial migration, risked returning to visit their hometown, and Berto has visited only once. In most cases, family members who remain in Mexico or Guatemala are denied tourist visas because of the concern that visitors will use such visas to travel to the United States, find employment, and overstay their visas to become unauthorized immigrants. Their unauthorized children lack the opportunity to visit grandparents for summer vacation, and their parents and siblings "back home" cannot visit to meet a newborn child or to celebrate a *quinceañera*. They are physically separated by a dangerous border, yet they struggle to maintain close connections to their place of origin through their cultural and religious practices and through the dense social networks that continue to bind them to an increasingly distant "home."

The case of Norma, Berto, and their children is far from extraordinary. Nearly half of unauthorized immigrant households (47 percent) consist of couples with children. This is by comparison to 21 percent of households in which the householder is U.S.-born and 35 percent of legal immigrant households.[30] Inside these households, we see what are called "mixed-status families"—families in which at least one parent is unauthorized. Currently, 8.8 million people in the United States live in mixed-status households—and

more than half of them are U.S. citizens.[31] Almost half of undocumented immigrant heads of household who have been
in the United States for more than ten years own their own
homes.[32] In other words, despite significant obstacles, the unauthorized have made real strides toward realizing the elu-
sive American dream.

We often hear the claim that unauthorized immigrants resist assimilation, thereby posing a fundamental challenge to
the cultural identity of the nation. Indeed, many unauthorized immigrants arrived in the new destinations emerging
throughout the U.S. Southeast with no intention of settling
permanently in the United States. Yet the contradictory impact of border enforcement has shifted these immigrants
into patterns of increasing settlement. Rather than resisting
integration, many of them—and, perhaps more significant,
their children, the majority of whom are U.S. citizens—have,
despite real obstacles, found ways to weave themselves into
the fabric of the communities in which they reside. Not only
have many unauthorized immigrants overcome significant
obstacles to integrate into the lives of their communities, but
they also have demonstrated some of the qualities most valued in the United States: sustained commitment to family
and household stability and consistent willingness to work
hard, sometimes with a loss of social status, to achieve their
dreams.

Living Here but Dreaming There:
The Transnational Nature of Migrant Life

While the difficulties of day-to-day life in new immigrant
destinations such as Jupiter and Atlanta are formidable, some
of the biggest challenges facing unauthorized migrants often
emerge from the heavy burden created by the distance between the immigrants, their families, and their communities

of origin. Tragically, the process of migration that was meant to help poor rural families survive frequently ends up undermining family and village ties, which generates transnational dilemmas and conflicts. To anyone who has been away from loved ones for a significant period of time, feelings of loneliness, nostalgia, and longing for home are certainly familiar. But there is a great deal more at stake for unauthorized migrants and their families, who cannot reunite across borders without facing the profoundly difficult alternatives of either economic failure or more family members in unauthorized status.[33] Thus, many unauthorized migrants are forced to construct their lives in a manner that is both here and there, frequently with an imagined future that brings them back to their hometown to be reunited with their family and community after they have achieved the economic goals of their initial migration.

"The Houses Are Different from Before": *The Impact of Economic Remittances*

Among the many connections that link migrants and their communities of origin, one of the most salient is economic remittances—the money they send home. Remittances not only connect migrants to their homes but also change those homes in ways that exert pressure on migrants to remain in the United States, so that the stream of remittances will continue. In other words, the changes wrought by remittances both drive further migration and pressure migrants to remain in the United States longer, to sustain the evolving patterns of growth and consumption initiated by their remittances. Jacaltenango provides an excellent example. As the quantity of remittances from the initial migrants began to grow during the early 1990s, the price of land and housing in Jacaltenango rose sharply. In turn, more Jacaltecos left for

Jupiter, sending back more remittances and driving up prices even further.

Economic remittances impact sending communities in multiple ways. Carmela, a Jacalteca whose husband is in Jupiter, explained: "Most people invest in building their house . . . but there are other people who misspend the money in luxuries too. They start buying things that are not necessities, like cars and cell phones. But people build their houses too. The houses here are different from before . . . back then they used to be adobe, now they are made out of concrete block." Migrants are also aware of how houses have changed due to remittances. Aureliano, originally from San Vicente (another highland Guatemalan village), arrived in the United States in 1989 and after some years working he was able to build a house in his hometown. He explains how things have changed since then: "I built a two-story house in my community, it was not too expensive, 70,000 *quetzales* back then. . . . Currently you can build something like that for 350,000 *quetzales* if you can get a good deal. Can you imagine? We're talking more than $40,000 or $50,000 now." These changes are visible to the entire community. Two-story houses like Aureliano's are more common, more visible, and increasingly desirable in a community where the only families likely to be able to afford them are those who have members working in the United States.

Young women in Jacaltenango also expressed their desires to have things that their friends with access to remittance dollars had. Sara explained how she felt about girls with families in the United States: "They have money and have the luxury of traveling; they send things from the U.S. and we wish we had that; they send them original clothes and perfumes." Diana chimed in: "For example, I know some girls that have their laptops; I just wish I had one because I don't have the possibility to . . . The way they dress too,

sometimes you can tell it's better clothes and they are showing it off, they wear only gold earrings . . . They have better
things in their homes. We have adobe. On the other hand
they have terraces, American style. They try to show that
now they have better things, they belittle you." Young men
and women like Diana and Sara understand the purchasing
power of remittances in migrant-sending communities, and
articulate a desire to migrate themselves if possible. For the
migrants who risked so much and work so hard to produce
those remittances, this was hardly the impact they anticipated when they began their journeys.

"Go to El Norte *to Learn How to Be Men":*
Social Remittances and Changing Attitudes

While monetary remittances are generating change in
migrant-sending communities, social remittances may play
an equally important role in creating connections across borders. Social remittances are new ideas and worldviews that
migrants send back to their home communities. Peggy Levitt
defines these as "the ideas, behaviors, identities, and social
capital that flow from receiving- to sending-country communities." [34] Social remittances have the power to change
value structures and ultimately change the migrant-sending
community by helping determine how money is spent (what
kinds of houses are built, what types of appliances are bought,
etc.). Social remittances, however, can be a double-edged
sword: although they are created through constant contact
and information exchange between the migrant and his
loved ones back home, they frequently disrupt the sending
community in ways that perpetuate the cycle of migration
by changing some of the values, such as family and education, that drove the first migrants to assume the many risks
associated with undocumented migration.

Immigrants living in the United States are exposed to different ideas about such issues as gender roles or the value of saving for retirement, instead of relying on children to support parents in their old age. These travel back to their places of origin. For instance, Berto's mother, in Santa Ana, Mexico, explained, "Mexican men are useless. They have to go to *el norte* to learn how to be men." She described proudly how her sons living in the United States were often sweeping or cooking dinner when she called to talk with them in the evenings. In this small village, the imaginative possibility that "learning how to be men" would entail caring for children, cooking, or cleaning had begun to reshape norms of male gender identity.

Young migrant men in Jupiter often expressed how they were exporting values and ideas they had learned in the United States to their home communities. José, for instance, explained his change in outlook about savings: "I want to be more stable to be able to retire. I want to have a retirement fund. . . . I don't want to depend on anybody. I don't want to depend on my children or my family. I want to earn my own." David, another young man from Jacaltenango, described an instance in which he actively sought to confront official corruption in his hometown because of his experience in the United States:

The good thing is that in this country [the U.S.], for any little thing, the police are there. In our country, if you are in an accident the guilty person can just give the police some money and the police will say that the innocent person was to blame. This last time I visited, I was witness to an accident, and the guy had money and paid off the police, and the police blamed the innocent person. I went and complained about it . . . what did they do? They took my license away. There you can

buy the law . . . there is no law in Guatemala. . . . The
beautiful thing about this country is that there is less
corruption than over there.

Migrants like David and José are changing their own perspective and are sending these new ideas back home along
with their financial remittances. But the social remittances
returning to sending communities are not always perceived
as beneficial to the community. Consumerism, the deterioration of traditional family structures, and a reduced emphasis
on working the land, because migration represents a much
more lucrative option for young people, are also new values
that have reached remote communities in Guatemala and
Mexico. One immigrant in Jupiter lamented that children
in Jacaltenango did not want to wear Guatemalan shoes
anymore. Now that their parents were in the United States,
they only wanted to wear Nikes. He also complained, "Nobody wants to work the land anymore." This sentiment was
echoed by Doña Rosa, an unauthorized immigrant in Atlanta. Doña Rosa sent one of her sons in Guatemala $6,000
to invest in a chicken-raising enterprise. Her son, however,
spent the money drinking and buying other consumer goods,
but he was later able to convince Doña Rosa to invest money
in a coyote for him to cross into the United States instead of
remaining to raise chickens in Guatemala.

Perhaps ironically, the value placed on education has
also suffered as a result of migration. While many migrants
make the journey specifically to be able to provide a better
education for their families, children growing up in migrant-
sending communities see the financial benefits that remittances bring, and they develop awareness that getting an
education may not pay off in the same way. Mario and Vinicio, two young Guatemalan men in Jupiter, expressed the
complexities of education's role. Mario explained that he had

come to the United States precisely to help his siblings go to school. Vinicio described his motivations as the opposite: "It's true, some people may have a degree. They could be teachers, accountants—go to college and all that. Even the college students come here. . . . People get old looking for work in Guatemala, looking for a source of income. That's why I'm here." Thus, while Mario maintained that he would help his siblings get ahead through education, Vinicio explained that he migrated already believing that work in Jupiter would be more lucrative than continuing his education. The community Mario and Vinicio left behind is rapidly changing. Mario's siblings are surely aware of the financial advantage their family reaps from remittances, and they may not value education as much as Mario wishes they would.

"Families Begin to Break Down":
The Impact of Unauthorized Migration on Relationships

In Santa Ana, Mexico, a local priest lamented the change in values that often accompanies migration. Father Mauricio explained that that two of his brothers migrated as undocumented workers to the United States to earn money for the huge fiesta they would sponsor on the occasion of his ordination. They easily earned the money they needed, and they returned for the ordination, but on the following day they left again for the United States. Father Mauricio explained,

> Something that I can share with you is what we observe in this community about the people that migrate to the United States. I have preached on this. Going to the United States, they go out of necessity for money, for work. But then, once they're there, sometimes they no longer work out of necessity, but instead the money that comes to them becomes their "treasure." And,

because of this money, they change their relations with their family. When they start, they're calling their family once a week, but by the end, they sometimes have forgotten their families. . . . It is causing much family disintegration.

While fulfilling family obligations often represents the primary reason for migration, the short-term or long-term separation that migration inevitably causes also generates a great deal of stress on the families of those migrants who live separated from them. The International Organization of Migration reports that 47.6 percent of migrant households in Guatemala faced a rupture in family structure due to migration.[35] Particularly for married couples, the distance can be overwhelming. Women in sending communities fear that their husbands will start new families, while men in the United States fear infidelity by their spouses who remain. Some marriages simply cannot bear the stresses caused by migration.

Aureliano, a Guatemalan immigrant living in Jupiter, was married when he migrated, but he was unable to maintain his relationship with his wife. He explained:

We no longer had a good relationship. We did not speak for six months because back then we did not have cell phones. We had no way to stay in touch. I moved around too. When I was in Jupiter I did not have an exact address so I could not receive letters. . . . It used to take twelve days for letters to get to Guatemala and longer for letters to get here from there. . . . [Our marriage] did not last. . . . We did not communicate and the time came.

The difficulties associated with maintaining family life in a transnational context extend far beyond spousal relations.

The entire family unit is affected in the process. Migrants and their spouses often report difficulties with children that are exacerbated by migration. Adriana, a woman we spoke with in Jacaltenango, explained what she thought of how children were being raised when one of their parents had migrated: "Not well, because there is no one to be correcting their mistakes and they grow however they want to, because their parents' support is not there. Families begin to break down." Diana, a young woman in the same community, explained how her peers who had a migrant parent acted differently from those who did not: "Most of the people who have their parents in the States . . . they have more freedom, they can come into their homes later, and they can hang out with guys. . . . Since parents aren't here, they cannot be aware of what you are doing."

The migrant parents who live separated from their children are aware of many of these changes, and such awareness adds to the anxieties they carry in daily life. A Jacalteco living in Jupiter explained: "In the family there are problems because the kids are going wild." Another young father expressed his exasperation with his situation: "I can send them money but I can't control their behavior from here. What am I supposed to do?" Such parents are left to grapple with the troubling irony that decisions they made to promote the well-being of their children have had unintended negative effects.

"To Have a Better Christmas . . . Back Home": Transnational Civic Engagement

The stresses involved in maintaining a transnational life are significant, particularly when they are combined with the daily struggle to find work and to provide for and maintain families. Re-creating elements of their home life in their new communities serves for many migrants as a way to alleviate these stresses. In the face of the many challenges of everyday life, hometown associations play a critical role in organizing local fiestas and celebrations. In Jupiter, the Maya Jacaltec Association provides a good example. Initially, the organization ran a soccer league and planned small ceremonies to honor the most important religious celebration in Jacaltenango, the fiesta of the Virgin of Candelaria. Each year, as connections with the local university and town representatives grew stronger, the fiesta also has grown in size and importance. The organization also collected funds to send home the corpses of fellow Jacaltecos who had died while in the United States. Over time, the organization became more institutionalized, and formally applied for nonprofit status under the name Corn-Maya Inc. Corn-Maya, in turn, ran the pilot program and fund-raising that eventually led to the opening of the El Sol Center in Jupiter, which we discuss in Chapter 5.

Hometown associations also play a critical role in sending communities. Migrant-funded community improvement projects often are loosely and informally organized across national boundaries. For instance, in Santa Ana, the small village in Mexico that we discuss in Chapter 1, town leaders had tried for many years to build a church in the town square, since, in the words of one leader, "A town without a church isn't a town!" In the late 1970s, the community mustered enough financial resources to build the four walls of the church that stood adjacent to the town square. But very little progress was made. Doña Lupe remembered that during the childhood of her five daughters, they occasionally celebrated mass there, under the open sky. She explained that over the years, the church was added onto "little by little," under the supervision of small groups of laypeople that the town put in charge of raising money for the construction of the edifice.

In 1990, Doña Lupe and her brother-in-law were put in charge of church construction. Doña Lupe explained that, disheartened by the slow progress, "they didn't know whether to continue with it or whether it was going to fall down or what." She then had an idea. Rather than asking for donations from local residents, which had not garnered sufficient funds even for the maintenance of the walls that already existed, they went to those living and working in Atlanta. Using their transnational social and family networks, they were able to get enough donations from those living in *el norte*, as well as from a few fund-raising dances, to finish construction on the church.

Projects often involve migrants from the same hometown who formally organize, forming an association to sponsor development initiatives in their communities. Aureliano shed light on the importance of transnational hometown associations both for migrants and for the community back in Guatemala. He has lived in the United States for almost twenty years, has two American-born sons, and speaks English fluently. Though relatively established in the United States, Aureliano continues to be active in the community back home. As he explained, the migrants from San Vicente have taken on several improvement projects for their town: "Here in Atlanta, the people from San Vicente had a meeting to talk about putting some money together. This was nine or ten years ago. I got involved when they asked me for a contribution for a Christmas celebration. They wanted $5, $10, whatever you could help with. They wanted the money to decorate the town. That was the idea, to have a better Christmas for the town back home. I contributed $50 and that's how we started thinking about how we could divide up projects for the town amongst people."

After the initial push to gather money for the Christmas celebration, migrants from San Vicente who were living in

Atlanta began taking on more projects to improve the general infrastructure of the town. Not surprisingly, the first project was the soccer field, which holds important sentimental value as one of the good memories of home that migrants such as Aureliano hold on to:

> Then we had the idea that we should fix the soccer field. This was about six years ago. Almost sixty people got together to fix up the soccer field. We thought this was what the children were missing, what they would enjoy and they needed to have. When I was a kid I used to go from work in the fields to play soccer. It was about $115 each to fix up the soccer field. . . . Then my brother and other people thought another thing the town needs is public lighting. They invited me to help and I told them that I couldn't go to meetings because I didn't have the time but that I could help with some money. So we were able to get lights for the street . . . Now we're talking about paving the road. We're trying to get $20,000 together for that.

For undocumented migrants such as Aureliano, contributing to the civic life of his home community takes on a particularly vital role. Although he has lived in the United States for many years, his unauthorized status profoundly limits his role as a civic actor in this country. But as a financial benefactor, he can contribute to community projects and religious celebrations, to remain an important contributor in his community of origin.

As these examples illustrate, the process of living transnational lives is shot through with ambiguities for unauthorized migrants. Some critics accuse Latino immigrants of "divided loyalties" and unwillingness to assimilate. These arguments, however, fail to take into account that transnationalism is often a strategy that immigrants are compelled to deploy in order to survive amid global economic changes that they cannot control. Particularly when the society of settlement is openly hostile or when one's immigrant status is precarious, it makes good sense to rely on ethnic networks or to refer back to communities of origin for support and participation. Transnationalism is thus both a form of duty and responsibility to families and communities in place of origin and a way to endure the ambivalences and costs of "living illegal." Living lives across borders helps unauthorized immigrants carve out a place to be in new destinations while also fundamentally changing the communities they come from in ways that may perpetuate the cycle of migration. Yet maintaining involvement in the civic life of their communities of origin is, for many migrants, not just a way to maintain dignity and integrity in the face of the difficulties of "living illegal." It also may, many migrants hope, demonstrate to the United States these migrants' potential as future citizens of the United States. In the words of Amilcar, one young member of the Jacaltec community in Jupiter, "The unity among Guatemalans is essential. We unite with the purpose of showing this country who we are so that they pay attention to us . . . and so we can get our papers."

Living in Fear:
Increased Enforcement and Daily Life

To date, the attention of the United States government to young people such as Amilcar has not been in the direction of allowing them to "get our papers." Despite the fact that both the Bush and Obama administrations pledged to enact comprehensive immigration reform, the most significant immigration-related activity of both administrations has been to step up immigration enforcement. Immigration and

Customs Enforcement reported that in 2008 it had removed 356,739 people from the United States, which represented an increase of 192 percent from 2006 (under the Bush administration), when ICE removed only 185,431 people. More deportation orders were also issued in 2008 (221,085 new orders), an increase of 46 percent over the previous year.[36] These drastic increases in ICE operations coincide with the increase in spending in recent years.

In Jupiter, we spoke with an immigration attorney who put a human face on the impact of increased enforcement. She told us the story of a young Guatemalan woman whose husband had been picked up while looking for work in 2008:

> The young woman had come to the U.S. when she was fifteen and had suffered rape and abuse both during her crossing and after arriving in South Florida. At the time of her husband's detention, she had finally settled down, and they were making a life with each other and their two children, ages two and eleven. Her husband had been without work for a week, so he took the car and their two-year-old son to stop at some businesses and ask about employment opportunities while she went to clean houses. Their eleven-year-old was in school. Later that afternoon, she received a phone call from her husband to tell her he had been stopped by police for driving with an expired license plate. He asked her to come pick him up, but was then forced to hang up the phone. As the young woman pleaded with her employer to give her a ride to pick up her husband and son, she received a second call and heard her son crying in the background. Frantic, she made a third call to her husband's phone, and it was answered by a woman she did not know. The police had apparently passed her child to a bystander who said that she knew the

PEOPLE IN MOTION 99

family—but left the woman with no paperwork or information on where they were taking the child's father. She was able to reunite with her child shortly, but it took weeks for her to find out where they had taken her husband or what he had been detained for. Her husband was injured during a fall at the local jail, and complained that he was never treated for his injuries. After that, he was quickly moved from a local facility to an immigration detention center, and deported within the month. Her children remain traumatized—the two-year-old no longer sleeps well, waking in the night and repeatedly asking for his father. Her eleven-year-old is now in counseling at school. By the time she came to me it was too late to do anything other than document these events.

For unauthorized migrants who run afoul of the legal system, there are very few options. The El Sol Center in Jupiter runs a legal clinic focused primarily on wage claims and other legal assistance. The Catholic Church and other churches and nonprofit organizations also offer legal assistance. But for the most part, by the time unauthorized migrants get caught up in the legal system and enter the federal detention system, it is simply too late to do anything for them. And today more immigrants are getting caught up in that system than ever before.

In 2008, Congress began appropriation of funds for ICE to create the Secure Communities program, intended to streamline the identification and removal of "criminal aliens." Under the provisions of the Secure Communities program, police officers in participating jurisdictions who arrest any person, for whatever reason, are required to send his or her fingerprints to be run through a Department of Homeland Security database so that "criminal aliens" may be identified for a rapid deportation process. Though the program is intended to target dangerous criminals, minor offenders are the most likely to be caught in the process. The National Immigration Forum reports that "there is no check on the motives for bringing a person to the jail. The program is applied by participating jails even where the underlying arrest was based on racial or ethnic profiling or was merely a pretext for checking immigration status."[37] Because there is no standard for whose fingerprints are sent to the Department of Homeland Security for an immigration check, law enforcement is now casting an extremely wide net, and many people who are not dangerous criminals have been affected by this program, including the 5 percent of those arrested who are, in fact, U.S. citizens.[38]

Programs such as Secure Communities spread fear in the migrant community and have many deleterious effects. Beyond the obvious impact of dividing families, such programs seriously undermine trust in local law enforcement and deter immigrants from reporting crimes. A representative of a local service agency in Atlanta noted one particularly onerous effect. Her organization works primarily with migrant women, and she stated that women rarely reported spousal abuse because they feared what would happen if their husbands were to be deported. Although her organization provided what support it could to migrant victims of abuse, she could hardly blame the women, who would be left to fend for themselves in a hostile and alien environment if they were to file charges. Furthermore, women who report abuse also are, in many cases, accused by their abusers of also having perpetrated abuse, which means that they too risk being arrested and detained.

The immigrant detention system into which these migrants are filtered has been subject to extensive criticism. In a 2007 evaluation of the availability of phone services for detainees, the Government Accountability Office (GAO) found widespread problems. The GAO found "systemic telephone system problems at 16 of 17 facilities that use the pro bono telephone system."[39] Concerns raised by members of Congress and advocacy groups resulted in another GAO study of detention facilities in 2008, which focused on compliance with medical care standards. The GAO report found instances of noncompliance with detention procedures in areas of medical care, including "lack of timely response to requests for medical care" and absence of medical requests forms in Spanish in detention centers where most of the detainees speak Spanish. The GAO also found that detainees' "grievances at the facilities . . . visited typically included the lack of timely response to requests for medical treatment, missing property, high commissary prices, poor quality or insufficient quantity of food, high telephone costs, problems with telephones, and questions concerning detention case management issues."[40] These investigations only begin to scratch the surface of the reality of immigrant detention centers, according to the GAO report. Further problems addressed in the report include the "use of hold rooms, use of force, food service, recreational opportunities, access to legal materials, facility grievance procedures, and overcrowding."[41]

Anton Flores, who has spent several years conducting humanitarian visitations with detainees in the Stewart Detention Center in Lumpkin, Georgia, explained to us:

My relationship with the Stewart Detention Center began in 2007 when I read in a Spanish-language newspaper that detainees had engaged in a hunger strike in protest of the conditions there. I had no firsthand knowledge of the conditions; I had never visited any detention center, much less this one—now the largest in the United States—located in a remote, rural, and economically depressed southwest Georgia town. However, after organizing a couple of vigils, I thought it was important to make a connection with the men detained inside. Family members of detainees began to find out about our vigils via the Internet and began to contact me and ask if I could visit their loved one, and so I did.

Now, after countless personal visits and organizing dozens of humanitarian visitations, I know that our acts of resistance are holy acts. Since 2007 I have learned that inside this privately owned, for-profit detention center there have been transgendered detainees held in solitary confinement, two inmates have died, and at least one American has been wrongly detained and deported. Furthermore, the inherent dignity of these men is stripped from them just as easily as their street clothes are stripped off them and replaced with color-coded prison garb for what is a detention center for a civil, not criminal offense. There are no contact visits permitted; my heart breaks every time I see a small child having to visit her father through Plexiglas. In fact, just last week I met a woman who was visiting her husband accompanied by their three-week-old child, a child this man has been forbidden from holding, all because he was an unauthorized immigrant who was driving without a license.

Living without formal immigration status increasingly translates into a life of constant apprehensiveness and extraordinarily difficult decisions for unauthorized individuals. The things that most of us take for granted—driving our children to school, walking through an airport to greet relatives, or qualifying for a job—are major hurdles for those who cannot produce a valid form of personal identification. At the El Sol Center in Jupiter and in the many churches we visited in both Atlanta and Florida, we heard stories from individuals who were left to deal with the aftermath of immigration raids, roadblocks, and traffic stops that led to detention and deportation. Migrant parents keep their children out of school for fear that they might be picked up on their way to or from classes. Pastors and church workers spend large amounts of their time trying to track down members of their congregations who have disappeared into the immigrant detention system. Many of the Guatemalans we met in Jupiter had originally been able to get a driver's license when they arrived in the 1990s. However, after 9/11 and then the passage of the REAL ID act in 2005, few of them were able to renew those licenses, and subsequently a large number lost their insurance, their vehicles, and ultimately their jobs.[42] Ironically, these were the individuals who were most settled, assimilated, and upwardly mobile among the new immigrant populations in Jupiter.

Conclusion: The Bankruptcy of Fear

From border policy to workplace raids and ICE's Secure Communities program, the enforcement side of U.S. immigration policy is negotiated in the currency of fear. Fear is expected to deter unauthorized migrants from crossing the border, keep them from taking jobs, and discourage them from residing in U.S. communities. Yet if there is anything we learn from the stories of unauthorized immigrants, it is this: U.S. immigration and law enforcement systems may traffic in the currency of fear, but when it comes to stopping or changing patterns of unauthorized migration, the strategy is bankrupt.

To be unauthorized in the United States, indeed, means to live in constant fear. But the deepest of the fears is not fear of being deported. Nor is it fear of being caught while attempting to cross the border. It is the fear of failure. Many unauthorized immigrants live haunted by the possibility that they will not find enough work to pay their debts. Among those whose debts are paid, the fear is of the changes wrought by the economic and social remittances they send home: changes in their families, in their communities, and in their relationships. For those who have left their families behind, fear of detention and deportation is only a secondary fear, as it would jeopardize the primary goal of making a better life for their loved ones. For those who have their families with them, the fear of being separated again—or of seeing their children forced to "return" to a place they barely know—conditions every element of their lives.

Despite living in an atmosphere of perpetual fear, countless unauthorized immigrants have managed to carve out lives for themselves in the new destinations they have come to inhabit. From soccer fields to storefront churches, thriving enclaves of Mexican, Guatemalan, and Brazilian immigrants are sustained by connections with communities of origin. In local community colleges and restaurants gather thousands of unauthorized young people who have been raised in and assimilated into U.S. society but who remain outside the formal system. In the next chapter, we explore the ways in which unauthorized immigrants are changing local communities, and we also examine the mutual fears that reinforce boundaries in such communities and that continue to hinder rational discussions about immigration and immigration reform.

3

Living Together, Living Apart

Interethnic Relations in
New Immigrant Destinations

Outside Jimmy's barbershop in the Cobb Shopping Center, a strip mall in Cobb County, Georgia, a sign reads "Corte de Pelo—10 dólares."[1] Easily confused from the outside as just another Latino-owned business, on the inside the barbershop harks back to an earlier time in Cobb County's history. On a particularly slow day in April, Jimmy and his father, two white, native-born southerners, were sitting in the old-fashioned, high-backed barber chairs fitted with hydraulic lifts. While serving up a "Businessman's Cut," Jimmy, the current owner, related how the barbershop was one of the anchor businesses when the strip mall opened in 1967.

> Up here where this El Dorado restaurant is was a deli called Howard's, and he was actually the cook for American Legion. Hallmark office supply was in here, Kirby Vacuum Cleaners, Dr. Norris, which was your dentist, Max Hams owned the drugstore. You had your hardware store. It was just—like I say, it was apple pie and a Chevrolet. Just a little strip mall with all your local things you needed for that era. The only original businesses that are left here with any longevity to them is the dry cleaners and the barbershop.

Jimmy went on to explain how things began to change. "I think the first change that came in here was a gentleman by the name of Orlando opened up a *tienderia* for his Hispanic community and started doing a lot of check cashing and things like those out of there. So they just kind of got spotted and the next thing you know—you turn around twice and it's like a child, they're grown."

The Cobb Shopping Center is a veritable window into the dramatic changes that immigration has brought to Atlanta's northern suburbs. The mall also anchors in place and in everyday life some of the tensions, ambivalences, and hopes that emerge as immigrants seek to carve out their own places to be amid spaces previously dominated by the native born. As immigrants engage in this process, the native born are pressed to reconsider their own position in relation to newcomers, and they begin to ask questions about the impact of new immigrants in their local communities. Examining these questions, which tend to cluster around jobs, schools, and crime, provides a window into interethnic relations in new immigrant destinations and to the ambivalent positions of the native born. Such an examination allows for a more nuanced and realistic portrait of interethnic relations than those we often see painted in the media. Nevertheless, as we will see, restrictive immigration policy implemented at the local level tends to exacerbate tensions, shifting ambivalence into polarized debates that revolve around misunderstanding, anger, and fear.

From Deli to *Tortas*: "Latinization" and Its Impact

When the Cobb Shopping Center opened in 1967, it was anchored by a hardware store, a drugstore, Hallmark office supply, dry cleaners, and a barbershop. Today, only Jimmy's barbershop and the dry cleaners remain. In the past ten years, the hardware store and other small white-owned businesses were gradually replaced by a number of Latino-owned businesses. Except for the dry cleaners, all of the businesses now cater to the growing Latino population in the area. The Latino-owned businesses include a small department store selling clothes, footwear, sporting goods, and household items. There's a *panadería* (bakery) offering Mexican *pan dulce*, pastries, and cakes; several Mexican eating establishments; a *carnicería* (butcher shop) serving up Mexican-style cuts of meat; a dress shop featuring dresses for first communions and *quinceañeras* (fifteenth-birthday celebrations); a pool hall; and a dance hall. Instead of the deli, there's Tortas Locas, a highly successful family-owned chain of Mexican sandwich shops in the metro Atlanta area that offers twenty-two styles of sandwiches and a huge salsa bar featuring more than a dozen different spicy salsas and hot sauces.

The neighborhoods around the strip mall are representative of areas that have experienced the outmigration of whites toward northern suburbs and exurbs and the influx of Latino immigrants. Faced with dramatically changing demographics and a growing Latino market, in 2000 Jimmy and his father decided they needed to hire a Spanish-speaking employee to attract Latino customers.[2]

And we were just sitting here one day and I said, "We've gotta do something." One Hispanic had come in—I said, "We gotta do something, Dad." He said, "What?" I said, "We've gotta start—you know, those people got hair; we've got to figure out something." So the next week, we found us a couple of ladies that wanted to work, and I put an ad in the paper. A lady from one of your better-educated countries, I don't know which one. She came in, she sat around, padded around here for a little while, but she wanted to buy the shop, and

I said no. And by then it was so heavy raw Hispanic at this time, it was over her head. She didn't want to deal with that type of people. She was a little too professional for that.

Jimmy quickly found a Mexican hairdresser who could "understand" the customers, primarily construction workers and laborers from Mexico and Central America. However, as his Latino clientele increased, some of his most loyal customers left.

Our business was falling off, and we were like, you know, the area's getting—it's going down, down, down, down, you know? And we were the dumb ones that stayed, and it's what people thought in the long run as you see now it's kind of coming back, you know? We lost a lot of business. They [white Americans] would come in and you would have a girl up here talking Spanish and all. They would tuck their tail and—I mean, the bank president, we had a lot of influential—we still do have a lot of influential people that trade here. We lost a lot, but now they're—the workforce they're in now, they're begging for that business, you know what I mean? One of the bankers, he left because he didn't like to hear Spanish being spoken. Now you walk in a bank that he's president of and he's got three tellers that speak the languages.

The Cobb Shopping Center is one of many strip malls that dot the landscape in Cobb County and is symbolic of the recent demographic changes and spatial reconfiguration resulting from large-scale immigration to new destinations. The strip mall is also representative of the "latinization" of public and commercial space that has occurred in metro

Atlanta over the past fifteen years. "Latino spaces" in Atlanta are characterized by their bright colors and Spanish-language signage, and are sometimes juxtaposed alongside Asian-owned stores and restaurants. In addition to the strip mall like the one described above, metro Atlanta is home to a number of large Latino-run shopping centers and supermarkets that cater to Latino consumers. In many of these businesses are found a dizzying array of Mexican magazines, Latin American music CDs and movies, and prepaid phone cards with names like Los Tigres del Norte, Dígame, Órale Güey, Mexicanísima, and La Gasolina. One of the most preferred businesses for Latino immigrants is the *carnicería*, offering the cuts of meat so central to local cultures. Besides selling meat, the *carnicerías* function like small supermarkets, offering an array of Latino products. While some of the products, like *frijoles negros refritos* and *salsas picantes*, are manufactured in the United States, others, such as cleaning products and soft drinks, are made in Mexico and elsewhere in Latin America. Moreover, many traditional department and discount stores in metro Atlanta, including Marshall's, Kohl's, and Walmart, are carrying more and more products oriented toward Latinos. Finally, the commercialization of religious icons is also symbolic of the growing Latino presence in Atlanta. At the Plaza Fiesta, a huge Latino-owned shopping center on Buford Highway, Catholic icons, such as the Virgin of Guadalupe, Santo Niño de Atocha, and San Juan Diego, can be found in all shapes and sizes, some complete with bright lights and most—symbolizing the strong outcomes of economic globalization—manufactured in China.

"They're Buying Stuff, You Know?":
The Local Economy and Purchasing Power

The visible changes that Latino immigrants bring to the landscape in new destinations are closely connected with frictions over social and economic resources including city services, taxes, and jobs. At the other end of the Cobb Shopping Center, a Korean-owned laundry has been affected differently by the demographic changes. Sun Hee and her husband bought the laundry in 1986 after working in the dry cleaning business in Detroit for several years. Over the years their principal customers have been military from nearby marine and air force bases, professional people living in the area, and senior citizens. According to Sun Hee, the influx of Latino immigrants into the neighborhoods surrounding the strip mall has driven out Euro-American residents: "Since the Hispanics move in, so they kinda move out. A lot of them paid off their houses, and they sold to the Mexicans and moved to Kennesaw, north of here. They buy the land and build bigger houses." Because most of the Latinos in the area work in construction and landscaping, they do not represent prospective customers for Sun Hee: "They wear clothes just wash and dry, work clothes. They don't wear like a professional suit tie. No, no. They use more coin laundry."

Compared to Jimmy, Sun Hee has no Latino customers and rarely interacts with Latinos outside her business. She emphasizes the negative impact Latino immigrants have had on the surrounding neighborhood:

> They don't follow this society rule, like a common rule; so they just party a lot, so loud music. And also they live one house, so many people live there so they didn't clean up or keep up maintain the yard or house cleans up like, ah [laughs], white people do. I think the

Hispanic people, whoever the leader or advocate have to educate his own people: if you want to live here you have to do . . . when people come over here first immigrants when you go to America you have to do such and such and such; basic rule.

Unlike Sun Hee, who still gets upset with Latinos parking in front of her store when they're frequenting other businesses, Jimmy has seen some positive changes in the Latino immigrant community over the years and equates these with immigrant assimilation. According to Jimmy, the first wave of immigrants consisted mostly of single males; however, increasingly, Latino immigrants are being joined by their spouses and children,

> When these guys first came over and they were—the saloon atmosphere, and drinking, and back on the job Monday, now their wives, their children are here. You went from the shoot-'em-up bang-bang, you know, and they went to work on Monday with a hangover, and now you see them coming in through the week, coming in the sandwich shop, conforming. Like I say, they aren't living in that house, boardinghouse with three different families. There isn't a kitchen big enough for those two women, you know? So you sell your big pickup truck, and we're gonna get a Taurus and rent an apartment over here. And they're putting the child in a safety seat. You know, the man's handing the paycheck to his wife; before it was the barmaid. So now they're adjusted to America. They're having to understand that it's not the Wild Wild West anymore. It's over.

Like Jimmy, other longtime Cobb County residents expressed somewhat contradictory opinions about the impact of immigration on local neighborhoods and the economy.[3] Some noted that as a result of immigration there were more Latino businesses and a growing Latino market, which benefited local businesses: "I think the local economy is fueled a lot by the immigrant population that's been here. I mean in all kinds of jobs, not only jobs, but they're buying stuff, you know." They viewed immigrants as contributing to the economy and noticed that local businesses catered to the immigrant population. One man even suggested that supermarkets that catered to Latinos, such as Food Depot, had fresher food because of the growing number of Latino clients.

Other residents voiced a more negative view of immigrants' impact on the local economy. One man we spoke with made a distinction between earlier waves of immigration and that of today. Immigrants during the 1920s "came through Ellis Island and that made a difference," but immigrants today come "over the walls and through the fences." He claimed that immigrants send money to their native country and consequently do not spend as much of it in the United States. Some residents also noted that the influx of immigrants had led to a deterioration of neighborhoods and communities. They referred to "five families sharing a house" and claimed that immigrants drove down house values in some neighborhoods. One Cobb County resident explained, "I could tell you that I've seen a great deal of immigrants, a person moving into a house in the neighborhood, renting when somebody can't sell it. The next thing you know, there's five pickup trucks there, about ten people living there and it will send the neighborhood down." As longtime residents struggled to make sense of the economic impact of immigration on their neighborhoods and businesses, they also grappled with the impact of ethnic and international diversification. Their impressions were shaped by a complex set of factors and, in some cases, by misperceptions.

Despite claims that Latino immigrants do not contribute significantly to the local economy, research demonstrates quite the opposite. Latino buying power in Georgia increased from approximately $1.3 million in 1990 to over $15 million in 2008.[4] Much of this increase was fueled by Latino immigration. By the year 2013, Latino purchasing power is expected to top $24 million. Georgia's market is considered one of the most attractive Latino markets in the nation along with Nevada and North Carolina. Moreover, a recent study found that if the undocumented workforce in Georgia were removed, the state would lose $7,120 in expenditures per capita, $2,639 in output losses per capita, and $1,699 in income losses per capita (in 2007 dollars).[5]

"The Money Leaves the System":
Taxes and Social Services

Another oft-repeated claim about unauthorized immigrants is that they represent a major burden on social services. People and groups who oppose immigration accuse immigrants of overusing emergency rooms and having a negative impact on the economy. Many Cobb County residents expressed the belief that unauthorized immigrants use services but do not pay taxes: "What I've seen is—I've seen hospital emergency rooms overfilled. I see those people that are using those services not paying for those services. They're earning money, and they're sending it back to wherever they came from, and the money leaves the system." However, a 2006 study found that in Georgia an average undocumented family contributes between $2,340 and $2,470 in taxes (state and local sales and income taxes as well as property taxes). Omitting income taxes, an undocumented family contributes between $1,800 and $1,860 in sales and property taxes.[6] Statewide, undocumented families contributed to Georgia's state and local coffers between $215.6 million and $252.5 million in aggregate sales, income, and property taxes.

Maritza, a successful immigrant from Durango, Mexico, contended that Americans' views about immigrants and taxes were simply misinformed:

> There's a problem that there's a lot of misunderstanding among the American people, now that a lot of misinformed anti-immigrant sentiment has arisen. There are a lot of Americans that believe that Hispanic people don't pay taxes, but the Hispanic people do pay taxes. If you own a property you pay property taxes, if you own a car you pay taxes on the car, and when you buy a pack of gum in the store everybody pays sales taxes. The only difference is that yes, there are legal people that don't do their income tax, and there are people, independent contractors, almost the majority of the people who work in construction, that don't pay taxes on what they earn, but it's not a lot of people in comparison to the number of Hispanic people. But the majority of Hispanic people that work in factories, they have taxes taken out of their salaries.

As with other myths about immigration, immigration policy, especially at the local level, has often been affected by the belief that immigrants are a net burden. For example, in 1994 Proposition 187 in California aimed to restrict immigrants living in California from using social services such as health care and public education. Though Proposition 187 was struck down in court, the idea that unauthorized immigrants are a heavy drain on the system because they overutilize social services remains. Research, however, does not support these assumptions. Going back to California, a 2008 study found that "the average immigrant-headed household contributes a net of $2,679 annually to Social Security, which is $539 more than the average U.S.-born household."[7] In Florida, a 2007 study found that immigrants in that state contribute almost $1,500 more a year than they receive in social services.[8]

These net financial contributions of immigrants, in fact, have to do with how *little* immigrants use social services. On average, an immigrant in the United States receives $1,139 worth of health services per year, whereas a U.S.-born person receives an average of $2,546.[9] Furthermore, rates of emergency room usage are actually lower in areas with large immigrant populations,[10] and qualified migrants are less likely to receive Medicaid, SCHIP, or food stamps.[11] Immigrants use fewer social services, in part, because access is restricted for many of them. Unauthorized immigrants especially do not qualify for many of the social services they are accused of abusing: they are ineligible for social security, TANF, Medicaid, or SNAP benefits. Even some documented immigrants (noncitizen permanent residents) are restricted from receiving some of these benefits.

"We Just Don't Do That Work Anymore": Competition in the Job Market

Another widespread perception is that unauthorized immigrants compete for jobs with low-skilled American workers. However, among Cobb County residents we spoke with, there was little consensus on the issue. Some residents were especially adamant that Latino immigrants were taking jobs away from African American men because they were willing to work for lower wages. Many felt that immigrants were creating an underground economy—meaning they were paid cash for services, were paid less, and did not pay taxes. As one resident of Cobb County explained, "When I think about the impact of immigration I think about, for the African American community anyway, the work that we used to do because we were the hands that built the country. We were the people that did the work—and we just don't do that work anymore."

Other residents noted that because of their reputation as hard workers, Latino immigrants were more attractive to employers. One woman commented, "I think an overall impression is that the Latino population does work very hard. So I do think it's possible that because of their ethnicity, they are taking jobs, and their reputation as hard workers." African American men in particular expressed concern about immigrants directly competing in their job market. They felt that they were constantly being underbid by immigrant workers because immigrants accepted lower wages: "They're taking jobs, not because we don't want to do them but because they're underbidding us. It's illegal what these companies are doing. That's the problem. But they're not going to pay us what we want because they can get away with hiring them." This perception was contradicted by other residents, who thought that immigrants were doing jobs that otherwise wouldn't get done: "I think if you stood on a street corner and took an unscientific poll of people coming by, the general consensus would be yes, they're taking jobs. But I think what we do see is that they're filling jobs that wouldn't get done otherwise." One longtime white resident claimed that, unlike immigrants, African Americans couldn't afford to get paid minimum wage to support their families, as they didn't share their living space with "five other families." "Now there is the downside of the five families in a single dwelling home that none of us like, but who's gonna do the work? Who's gonna do the work today if they're not here?"

Despite the apparent lack of consensus on the street on

whether or not immigrants take jobs away from Americans, in our random telephone survey for metro Atlanta, we found that fully 72 percent of whites and 73 percent of African Americans believed that immigrants coming to the United States "take jobs that Americans don't want." [12] Moreover, an overwhelming majority of respondents described Latino immigrants as "very hardworking" (84 percent of whites and 76 percent of African Americans) and as having "strong family values" (78 percent of whites and 76 percent of African Americans). Most residents described Latino immigrants as having a positive work ethic. One man we spoke with explained, "My son has a lumberyard and he won't—that's all he hires because they [Latinos] work. And they will work—they'll put in their hours and there's no problem. So I think they're probably bringing the level of labor force up." George, a longtime Cobb County resident who is originally from Indiana, compared Latino immigrants' work ethnic with that of native residents:

> Well, I work in a lumberyard—and now almost 90 percent of our workers are Mexican. I'll tell you, they really know how to work. There are a lot of people here who say they are stealing jobs, but that is just not the case. The deal is that they are hungry—like we used to be. But now I can tell you, you drop off the pallets [of wood] for a white crew and they want them just so—'cause they have no plans of finishing that day. But you drop it off for a Mexican crew and they just say put it in the yard—'cause they will be finished that day. I remember when I was growing up and you said "he works like a nigger" and it was a compliment. Now I would kick somebody's ass if they told me that. People just don't know how to work now.
>   I am not a racist. I completely disagree with all the

racists around here. They just don't know how to get
along with people. Down at the yard I am a foreman—
and I show them that I am willing to do the work.
They respect that and treat me with respect. I respect
them back. A workingman has to respect hard work—I
don't care what color your skin is. I have no tolerance
for racism. But I will tell you the truth—both blacks
and whites here don't want to work. And that is why I
have no problem with the Mexicans coming in. Nobody
could afford a house here if we had to pay the blacks
and whites to build them.

The Mexican guys are willing to do piecework—and
they can make money because they will work their
asses off. The black guys and the white guys go to the
bar once it starts raining. Not the Mexicans—man, they
don't go to the bar until the work is done, and then they
stay drunk all weekend. But they are right there for
work again on Monday morning.

Many residents empathized with the conditions of poverty that drove Latino immigrants to find work in the United
States:

When you're making $1.50 an hour and then you
come here, living on a dirt floor with raw sewage running down, you come here and get an apartment with
twenty other people. You've got carpet. You've got air-
conditioning. You've got a television. That's more than
you've ever had in your life. So they were sacrificing
themselves that way because it's not a sacrifice to them
because where they came from, it was so bad that it was
like a luxury to them. That's why they get ahead more
so than us because if the man gives us a job, we want to
get paid for it.

African Americans in particular attributed Latino immigrants' economic success to their drive and ethnic solidarity. One man we spoke with compared Mexican immigrants' drive with his own drive to find any kind of work after recently being released from prison:

> So that drive that I took now that I been out [of prison] was the same thing that made me go to a man's establishment, and I said, "Look, man, I need to work. I'll work seven days a week. I'll work open to close. I'll sweep, empty the garbage and wash the dishes, and you can pay me $2 an hour." He looked at me like I was crazy. But that same drive, getting out of jail, was equivalent to the Mexicans coming over here.

Another resident contrasted what he called Latino immigrants' willingness to "pull each other up" with what he identified as African Americans' own lack of ethnic solidarity. "They'll do that [share their apartment with other immigrants], but you know yourself you ain't gonna let no brother move into your house. What I'm saying is most African American people, we're not gonna let people pile into our house. We like our privacy."

Despite African Americans' mostly favorable view of Latinos' work ethic, these attitudes do not seem to be reciprocal. In our survey, only 15 percent of Latinos described most or almost all African Americans as hard workers. Elena, an immigrant from Veracruz, Mexico, articulates the stereotypes that many Latinos hold about African Americans: "If a black doesn't have a job he runs to the government for help, expects the government to provide for him. In contrast, a Hispanic, even if he has papers to ask for help, he'll first figure out how to arrange his finances to pay his rent, his bills, gas, insurance. We don't run to the government for a check, for food stamps. The blacks receive this assistance while we work to be able to eat. And at work blacks are sometimes lazy while Hispanics work hard." Elena's statement makes clear that stereotypes and misconceptions not only are focused toward Latino immigrants, but also shape Latinos' perceptions of other groups. Such stereotypes hinder interethnic cooperation and contribute to growing tensions in neighborhoods and workplaces.

Not surprisingly, Mexican immigrants challenged the belief that immigrants take jobs away from Americans:

> I imagine that they [Americans] feel like they're the owners of everything around here, because they say that Mexicans come here to take their money. . . . I've heard them say this that we come to take things that belong to them. But it's not like that, because Mexicans come here to work, to do the work that Americans don't want to do. Like in construction, you have only Mexicans doing the heavy work, only Mexicans . . . when you see someone carrying a heavy cement block, it's not the American but always the Mexican.
>
> Imagine if all of us [Mexican immigrants] got together and agreed to leave. The United States would collapse, the economy would collapse, because the Mexican is the one that works in this country, the Mexican is the one that spends more than anyone. Because the Americans put all their money in the bank and only think about themselves.

Studies on the issue of job competition make it difficult to generalize about the impact of unauthorized immigration on the labor market. Some research has found that there is job displacement, particularly among low-skilled African American workers, but the impact is relatively small.[13] Other studies have "found no impact from immigration on African American employment rates."[14] In new destinations such as Atlanta, until the recent recession, Latino immigrants were attracted by the higher rates of job growth compared to more traditional immigrant destinations. These growing employment opportunities benefited not only immigrant workers but also native-born workers. According to a 2005 Pew Hispanic Center report on the impact of Latino immigrants in the South: "There is little evidence that gains for Latinos were accompanied by losses for non-Latinos. Subject to the caveat that resident and job locations may differ, if Latino job growth was a catalyst for job loss among non-Latinos one would expect to observe below-par job gains for non-Latinos in counties with higher job growth for Latinos. But that is not generally the case."[15] Moreover, as to whether Latino immigrants displaced African American workers, the study found that: "Employment trends for black workers specifically also show no signs of job displacement from the rapid influx of Hispanic workers."[16]

Misconceptions about the impact of immigration on the local economy, jobs, and social services can often generate interethnic tensions in new destinations like Cobb County. Not surprisingly, it was easy to find residents who voiced strongly negative attitudes about Latino immigrants; however, it was just as easy to find residents who did not believe immigrants were taking jobs away from Americans, and who expressed positive views about immigrants' work ethic and contributions to the local economy. To complicate matters, many Latino immigrants also perpetuate misconception and stereotypes about native-born workers, and particularly about African Americans. As we will see later, the lack of consensus over these issues provides an opening to politicians at the state and local level to implement restrictive immigration policy.

"You Should Learn Our Language":
Schools and English Proficiency

While economic issues are important, for some critics of immigration, the "culture gap" is the greatest concern when it comes to Latino immigrants. In his influential 2004 article "The Hispanic Challenge," the controversial political scientist Samuel Huntington writes:

> If the second generation does not reject Spanish outright, the third generation is also likely to be bilingual, and fluency in both languages is likely to become institutionalized in the Mexican-American community.
>
> A persuasive case can be made that, in a shrinking world, all Americans should know at least one important foreign language—Chinese, Japanese, Hindi, Russian, Arabic, Urdu, French, German, or Spanish—so as to understand a foreign culture and communicate with its people. It is quite different to argue that Americans should know a non-English language in order to communicate with their fellow citizens.[17]

Huntington goes on to equate the persistence of Spanish language with the failure of Mexican Americans to assimilate and to their lower levels of economic success compared to other national origin groups.

The reality on the ground today, as we will see, is considerably more complex than Huntington suggests. Without a doubt, the demographic changes resulting from large-scale immigration to new destinations are having a significant impact on schools, often generating tension and misunderstanding. For example, in Cobb County, Georgia, the racial/ethnic profile of children in public schools has changed dramatically over the past fifteen years. In 1995, Euro-Americans accounted for 78.5 percent of public school children, followed by African Americans (15.7 percent), Asians (2.7 percent), and Latinos (2.2 percent). By 2010, Euro-Americans accounted for only 45.5 percent of the total, followed by African Americans (31 percent), Latinos (15.8 percent), and Asians (4.8 percent). In other words, in fifteen years the school district went from being an overwhelmingly majority-white district to a majority-minority school district.[18]

While much of the growth in minority enrollment was the result of the influx of African Americans toward a city that is perceived as a center of black economic and political power, as well as of immigration, white flight was also important. Although Cobb County's white population did not grow as fast as the Latino and African American populations, it still grew at a significant rate during this period.[19] Nevertheless, the overall number of white students fell from 62,873 in 1995 to 48,492 in 2010—a decline of 23 percent.[20] Some Cobb County residents with school-age children expressed concern about how their children would fare inside a predominantly nonwhite classroom: "I didn't even send my daughter to—I took her over to the public school and my daughter looks a lot like me—blond hair, blue-eyed little girl—took her over there, and this was—now she's fifteen, so—but she would have been the only little blond-haired, blue-eyed little girl in the class."

Not only did the native born express concerns about their children's potential minority status in the classroom, most Cobb County residents also viewed immigration as having a broadly negative impact on the quality and performance of the schools in the county. Our survey found that only 31 percent of African Americans and 26 percent of whites believe that Latino immigrants "do very well in school." Overall, women were particularly critical of immigrants' impact on education. They were concerned that school resources being used for ESL classes could have been used for their own children or children with special needs. One woman explained, "So I think in terms of impact, we've certainly seen the diversion of the tax resources to folks who perhaps are not even contributing as taxpayers since they're getting paid under the radar and yet they're being fully served."

Residents also believed immigrants were bringing down schools' standardized test scores. They stated that teachers "end up educating to the lowest level" because immigrant students are not fluent in English. They also pointed out that immigrants were constantly moving and that this negatively affected graduation rates. One resident explained,

> When we've got U.S. legal citizens who are having to cut their prices in order to stay alive and pay their bills and educate their children, and then—as you pointed out—in the school system we end up educating to the lowest level in the class because if they teach too high skills and training, the ones who can barely speak English can't keep up, and so they wonder why the test scores are going down so badly, I have a concern that that's part of the problem.

Echoing these sentiments, another resident complained, "We're failing not because we're not teaching the kids. It's because of how immigration has affected us so drastically."

However, a few residents with whom we spoke noted that it was not a specific ethnic group that was lowering the quality of education because white children also misbehaved in school. Some even pointed to the positive impact of immigration on local schools—children were being exposed to different cultures as a result of the presence of immigrants in Cobb County. As one explained, "You can broaden your kids' horizons. Now, even the schools—you've got ESL students in the schools. You've got different kinds of teachers in the school. You're able to be more diverse now than years ago. We've been arrogant where we say we only speak English. We don't speak nobody else's language, and it's about time that we have a second language. Just reality—some things change. That's reality."

The issue of language is a source of tension between some native residents and Latino immigrants. It can also serve as a barrier to greater understanding between native residents and immigrants. For example, in our survey we found that 53 percent of African Americans and 52 percent of whites believe that Latino immigrants "keep to themselves and don't try to fit in." Some residents found it rude when Spanish-speakers used Spanish at work or businesses, and they believed adult immigrants should have to learn English. They also thought that there were too many accommodations for Spanish-speakers, giving them little incentive to learn English. As one resident explained, "I think that when I'm in the business that everyone here should be speaking English to me and around me so that I know what's going on and I'll feel like I don't—like I'm being left out or there's some secret conversation going on that I can't participate in." Expressing concerns about the expanded public use of Spanish, another asked, "As long as you have to push a 1 or a 2 on a phone call for English or Spanish, we're accommodating them. What's their motivation to learn English?" Many residents associated English-language acquisition with becoming American. They stated that English proficiency for immigrants was important but did not want the government to be "catering to them." As one woman explained, "I think that if you're going to come into our country, you should learn our language. Just like I said if I would go to their country, they'd probably expect me, if I were to live there, they'd probably expect me to try to learn their language."

Some residents claimed that immigrants' low level of language proficiency was the main reason they refused to enroll their children in schools with a large immigrant population. They were also concerned about the government using resources to teach immigrants and pointed to family members or relatives who were immigrants and had to struggle to learn English: "Everybody else had to learn, and no one made accommodations, and I think that's probably why my family or relatives are successful." Meanwhile, some residents were conflicted about immigrants' English-language proficiency. While not being offended by immigrants using Spanish at work and in public places, they agreed that immigrants needed to learn English. A few even advocated for Americans becoming bilingual: "My take on it is people just have to realize it's reality. Spanish people are here, so you're going to have to be bilingual."

A lay leader at a Catholic church in Cobb County with a growing Latino congregation offered an interesting perspective on the issue. While he accepted the idea of the church offering services in Spanish, he was very critical of Spanish being used in public places outside the church: "I think the mass should be in Spanish. Because as Catholics, the church must give to its parishioners, to its individuals, their needs. Whatever that is. We aren't here for the church, the church is here for us. Now when we step outside the sanctity of my church, as a U.S. citizen, I have a completely opposite opinion of that. Absolutely. But not when I'm here in the church." The issue of language is also a source of frustration for many Latino immigrants. Several Latino students related to us that teachers and school officials often discouraged them from speaking Spanish.

The whole "Don't speak Spanish, or you'll get in trouble. Don't speak Mexican." They tell you not to speak Mexican, and I'll be like, "Excuse me, I'm not Mexican."

And I think if you understand the long run, because, I mean, technically, we're a hot commodity wherever we go. It's like, "Oh, we're bilingual," but if you're trying to stop us from being bilingual at an early age, you're trying to make us feel ashamed for the fact that we speak Spanish, and I resent that.

Instead of encouraging bilingualism in an increasingly globalized world, some educators and public officials continue to insist that students' main "handicap" is speaking Spanish, despite studies that demonstrate the benefits of bilingualism.[21] In fact, when controlling for other variables, fluent bilingualism has a strongly positive impact on early academic achievement among the children of immigrants, while limited bilingualism "has a consistent, powerful, and negative effect on early academic achievement."[22] The reason may be that limited bilingualism, usually the result of forced language immersion, can lead to the loss of parental languages and greater potential for parent-child cultural conflict.

Despite these studies, immigration opponents continue to insist on viewing bilingualism as an obstacle to learning or a source of cultural conflict. Huntington goes so far as to warn that if these demographic trends continue, "the cultural division between Hispanics and Anglos could replace the racial division between blacks and whites as the most serious cleavage in U.S. society."[23] In a similar vein, many Cobb County residents warned of the deterioration of public schools as a result of the influx of immigrants in the county. Such warnings echo the nativism that arose during earlier waves of immigration and is often rooted in persistent stereotypes about Latinos. Nevertheless, the impact of Latino immigration on schools cannot be simply dismissed. School resources in Cobb

County have been strained because of the dramatic demographic changes that have created the need for additional ESOL (English for Speakers of Other Languages) instructors, translators, and support services for immigrant children and their parents. In other words, Cobb County residents have legitimate concerns regarding the quality of their children's schools. At the same time, Latino immigrants can demonstrate their sensitivity to these concerns by becoming more involved in their children's schools, thereby dispelling some of the stereotypes that fuel discrimination and hostility.

"This Country Can Hit You Where It Hurts": Discrimination and Crime

Between Sun Hee's dry cleaners and Jimmy's barbershop we found Rosita's Mexican *panadería*. Rosita is from Mexico City, where she met and married her husband at the age of seventeen. Her husband came alone to Atlanta in 1996, and she followed a year later with her three children. They both found work in an Italian restaurant and, after three years, had saved enough to open the bakery. Until recently Rosita and her family continued to work at both the restaurant and bakery. "We arrived to work at the restaurant in the morning and my children were here [at the bakery]. We arrived to the bakery at four in the afternoon, and the children went to work in the restaurant, and we stayed here till eleven, twelve at night." Business was so good that Rosita and her husband left the restaurant, opened another bakery nearby, and bought a house a few years ago. Despite living *el sueño americano*, because of their unauthorized status neither Rosita nor her other family members have been able to return to Mexico since arriving in Atlanta thirteen years ago. Rosita's father-in-law died a few days after they opened the first bakery, but her husband was unable to return to Mexico for the funeral: "We had just opened the bakery four days before it happened, we opened the bakery on April 10, my birthday, and my husband's birthday is April 14. We were going to celebrate my husband's birthday when we received the news that his father had died. The bakery dates back to his father's death. Believe me, this country can give you a lot, but it can also take away a lot, it can hit you where it hurts." Rosita and her family dream of the day when she and her family can adjust their legal status: "We're hopeful that there will be some kind of immigration reform. I spoke to the lawyer next door and she said, 'There's going to be something.' I told her, 'Look, all I want is a permit to be able to leave and reenter to see my parents.' That's all we ask for, no? A permit to leave and reenter."

Like Rosita, many of the immigrants with whom we spoke were not demanding any special treatment and would be satisfied with something far short of comprehensive immigration reform. One Mexican immigrant in Cobb County explained, "Since I'm not from here, I know that sooner or later I'll have to return. I'm not demanding that they give me papers—if they give me my papers, fine—but I'm only asking that they allow me to work, allow me to get a driver's license or some kind of permit so that I don't have to walk around with this tension every time I see the police, imagining that they're going to stop me or something." Another echoed these sentiments: "We bought a car, but we're always afraid because of the license. We don't go out, only to church and to work and to buy food. But to go out with the children—we can't because they're also afraid to go out. When they see a policeman they get scared and start to get nervous: 'Papi, I don't want them to take you away.' Sometimes I tell my wife that I would be happy with just a work permit."

The hopes of Rosita and other immigrants like her have fallen on deaf ears in places such as Cobb County, where anti-immigrant sentiment is palpable. These sentiments take many forms, ranging from very public expressions of opposition to unauthorized immigration to more subtle forms of discrimination that immigrants experience in their workplaces, at businesses, and in the classroom. Furthermore, anti-immigrant sentiment is often exacerbated by federal, state, and local policies that target unauthorized immigrants.

Anti-immigrant hostility was on full display at the annual Fourth of July parade in 2008 in Cobb County. Spectators could hardly fail to miss the bright red convertible that served as the float for the North Atlanta Chapter of the Minuteman Civil Defense Corps. Wearing T-shirts that asked "Where's the Fence?" participants marched alongside a sign reading, "Secure Borders, Job Protection, English Only, Safe Neighborhoods, Good Schools." The Minuteman Civil Defense Corps, a vigilante group organized to patrol the U.S.-Mexico border, has expanded its reach throughout the United States, making its presence felt and its message heard in regions, such as suburban Atlanta, that are far from any U.S. border or coastal boundary. Cobb County also is the home of the Dustin Inman Society, one of the nation's most vocal and activist anti-immigrant organizations. Their members can be found milling about virtually any gathering to promote immigrant rights, bearing signs with their signature statements: "Say No to Georgia-fornia" and "Kick Me, I'm a Citizen." Their founder, D.A. King, is recognized in the local media as an "immigration expert," yet his rhetoric is radical and inflammatory. As reported by the Anti-Defamation League, he wrote in a July 2004 article,

> We have become sadly acquainted with the absolute and brazen disregard for the law that comes from the third world horde that is allowed to swarm over our border with Mexico. . . . It is clear that when the mostly

Mexican mob illegally "migrates" into our nation, it
brings with it the culture of lawlessness and chaos that
is responsible for the very conditions that they flee in
the rapidly deteriorating example of Democracy without the rule of law that is Mexico.[24]

King enjoys a close relationship with the sheriff of Cobb
County and has been highly influential with political leaders
at the state level. King's rhetoric echoes that used by many of
those who argue for enforcement as the main or even the only
strategy to resolve the complex problem of unauthorized immigration. For example, Arizona governor Janet Brewer supported the passage of Senate Bill 1070, which mandates local
law enforcement agencies to check the immigration status of
any person if there is reasonable suspicion that she or he is in
the country illegally, because she wanted to "protect every
citizen of Arizona" from what she described as a rising tide
of violence coming across the U.S.-Mexico border.

Though many people disagree, I firmly believe it represents what's best for Arizona. Border-related violence
and crime due to illegal immigration are critically important issues to the people of our state, to my administration and to me, as your Governor and as a citizen.
There is no higher priority that protecting the citizens
of Arizona. We cannot sacrifice our safety to the mur-
derous greed of drug cartels. We cannot stand idly by as
drop houses, kidnappings, and violence compromise our
quality of life. We cannot delay while the destruction
happening south of our international border creeps its
way north.[25]

Recent studies indicate that the perception that unauthorized immigrants are connected with crime is at odds with

reality. Despite an ongoing drug war that has claimed the lives of thousands of Mexicans, violence at the border and across Arizona is down.[26] If anything, it is immigrants who are more likely to be victims of violence. And the threat of violence does not stop at the border. Immigrants are frequently the target of racial epithets and anti-immigrant statements in their daily life. In an area of Cobb County with several Latino-owned businesses, a sign outside a local bar, Mulligans, often displays inflammatory comments. For instance, after the passage of Arizona's SB 1070, the sign read, "Hell Yeh Arizona, Send Them Wetbacks Home! Anchor Babies & All! If U Can't Feed Um Don't Breed Um!" The bar also garnered national attention when, in the months preceding the 2008 presidential election, the owner began selling T-shirts bearing an image of Curious George and the slogan "Obama '08."

Lupe, a young Mexican woman, described her painful awareness of how the owner and patrons of Mulligans feel about unauthorized immigrants like her: "There's this guy who has a restaurant and always puts stuff outside . . . like 'Immigration Agents Eat for Free' . . . Last week he put something that said '12 Million Immigrants, Don't Forget to Pay Your Taxes!' . . . He puts every racist comment that you could think . . . he puts signs about black people and Latinos."

While Lupe found the signs outside the restaurant disturbing, they were not her greatest concern. Like many of her peers, Lupe's greatest worries had to do with her ability to pursue her education and the fears she lived with on a day-to-day basis about being picked up by immigration authorities:

> I want to get a college education. I'm working on it. I'm going to a technical college right now, that's what I can afford. With the laws now they charge me international

tuition ... so that's four times what somebody pays from here. Because of my academics ... they haven't been great, but I do have a decent GPA, still my status doesn't allow me to get scholarships, but I'm still working on that. ... I just hope that things get better here, especially for students. I don't like it when people judge us ... for the things a few people have done. There are people like me who are trying hard ... trying to make friends. There are students who work full-time and all the money goes to school. We spend everything for school. They charge us four times what a regular student who has a low GPA would pay.

She described that periodically news spreads through her neighborhood in Cobb County that the local sheriff's office has set up roadblocks. She then refuses to leave home and spends days indoors, putting her life, her work, and her education on hold.

Discrimination against Latino immigrants takes both overt and sometimes more subtle forms. In Cobb County we spoke to a number of college-age immigrants who had come to the area as children. Their parents had come as unauthorized immigrants, and consequently they also had no papers. Most of them were working in service industry jobs in local restaurants. They were raised in Cobb County, had all of their schooling in the United States, spoke English fluently, and by all practical measures were fully assimilated into the community. Yet they were limited by their immigration status and by the not-so-subtle forms of discrimination they had experienced in the Cobb County school system. As Lupe explained:

I was lucky that I didn't have any problems ... some of my friends did in class. There was this math teacher

who . . . one of my friends came late to class and she
made a comment saying that "You know Mexicans
always come late" or "You know how Mexicans take
things like they're just easy" and my friend . . . he
was really pissed. They went to talk to somebody, they
never did anything . . . It was really uncomfortable. I
was lucky that teachers never picked on me like that
because they'd say things like "Oh you don't look Mexican," and I was like "Okay, how's a Mexican supposed
to look?"

Lupe went on to explain that she had been stereotyped by
the teachers and administrators in the school system, which
limited her options:

Something that I didn't like was that as an immigrant
when you come here they expect you not even to graduate, just to drop out of school . . . they didn't have this
before . . . now they divide you . . . so they have kids
who will obtain a college prep diploma which will allow them to apply for a four-year college . . . and then
you have this other group which is supposed to get the
tech-prep diploma. The difference is that you don't take
two years of a language and you don't take an extra year
of math or science. Well, because I came here and didn't
know the language, I needed to focus on learning and I
needed to take all the classes required for me to graduate. And I couldn't take a foreign language, not even
Spanish . . . They do allow some people to take Spanish, but I wanted to take something else. . . . I wanted
to learn something else and I wasn't able to do that,
not even to take some electives I wanted . . . graphic
design . . . they gave me the chance to take some of

them, so I took classes related to education: psychology, sociology, intro to teaching, and child development.

Latino students from Kennesaw State University (KSU) in Cobb County shared similar experiences:

> I feel like sometimes, specifically for the people that are coming in, they have lower expectations for all of them academically. "Okay, we're just going to put them on there [English as a Second Language, ESL]," and there's no plan to put them into the regular classes. It's just, "Keep them there. Let's graduate them at a lower expectation," because all of them are on the tech route. They're never on the college route, and some of them have the capability, but they never put it in front of them, "Hey, learn the language first, and we'll work you onto the college road."

One KSU student related how her two children, although born in the United States, were initially placed in ESL classes: "I have two kids and . . . just because of the last name, they put them in ESL. First conference, they asked me, 'Well, tell me about the children. When did they come into the States?' I was, like, 'They were born here. They're bilingual.' My daughter, at this point, they had to take her out of ESL because she doesn't need it. So, I mean, they just put us in those places where they don't even assess if we really do need it or if we don't."

Another student told how many teachers automatically think Latino students are involved in gang activities. "Well, it's just the fact that—I guess you could say in the Spanish culture and in the Mexican culture, they have these T-shirts, for example. My sister's in high school right now. She has these T-shirts that have drawings on them with old English and stuff like that. Automatically gang-related. I don't think so, because my sister is far from being gang-related. But at the same time, in their eyes and what they see, she's the typical gang member."

The association between Latinos, unauthorized immigration, and crime is pervasive in Cobb County. This became evident in a conversation we had with a waiter about the research project. Wondering what we were doing in Cobb County, the waiter, an older gentleman from Greece who spoke with a thick accent, began to ask exactly what it was we were studying. When we told him that part of our research was about the lives of unauthorized immigrants from Latin America, he began to turn red and nearly screamed, "What the hell for? Those damn people are here spreading their gangs and crime. I'm tired of paying all my taxes so they can use the services and then steal the stereo out of my car. We should send them all back home!"

From public meetings to newspaper articles and letters to the editor, over and over we are bombarded with the notion that immigration leads to crime and that unauthorized immigrants in particular are associated with crime. The fact is that immigrants are often unfairly associated with high rates of criminality. Although not the majority view—in our survey we found that 26 percent of African Americans and 36 percent of Euro-Americans believe that Latino immigrants significantly increase crime—it is pervasive enough that public figures such as Sheriff Joe Arpaio and Governor Jan Brewer of Arizona often frame the issue of immigration in terms of crime, arguing that strict immigration measures are meant to keep the country "safe" from "criminals." A recent tragedy in Virginia involving the death of a Catholic nun in an accident caused by an unauthorized immigrant from Bolivia driving under the influence prompted immigration foes to demand stricter enforcement of federal immigration laws. The day after the crash, Virginia's attorney general, Ken Cuccinelli II, "issued an advisory opinion concluding that police have authority to inquire into the immigration status of any person stopped or arrested, similar to the Arizona immigration law that is under federal court review."[27]

This type of immigration policy, however, is based on a faulty notion that immigrants, especially unauthorized immigrants, are more likely to be criminals than the rest of the population. The fact is that immigration, including unauthorized immigration, does not lead to more crime. On the contrary, crime rates in the United States have declined since the mid-1990s, at the same time that unauthorized migration has doubled. This is true both at the national level and in cities with high levels of unauthorized immigration. The incarceration rate for young men is much lower for the foreign-born (0.7 percent) than for the native born (3.5 percent).[28] The incarceration rate for Mexicans is on par with the rest of the foreign-born population, while the rate for Guatemalans is actually lower. The findings of a study published in 2008 by Robert Sampson, chair of the Sociology Department at Harvard University, go further, stating that "the estimated probability an average male living in a high-risk neighborhood without immigrants will engage in violence is almost 25 percent higher than in the high-risk immigrant neighborhood, a pattern again suggesting the protective rather than crime-generating influence of immigrant concentration."[29] Sampson suggests that because immigrants who come to the United States are a selective group, the cultural aspects they bring with them are conducive to lower rather than higher rates of criminality.

Although public discourse about unauthorized immigration is rife with references linking immigration and crime, unauthorized immigrants are more likely to become victims than perpetrators of crimes in their communities. In Jupiter in 2007, a sixteen-year-old girl and her nineteen-year-old boyfriend were arrested for robbing three Mayan immigrant men at gun- and knifepoint. One victim was stabbed and another beaten over the head. During her confession, the young woman reportedly told police that she "has a problem with illegal immigrants and doesn't know why they are in this country."[30]

A similar incident occurred in Georgia. On a February evening in 2004, four high school students picked up a fifty-four-year-old day laborer living near Canton, Georgia. They took him to a remote spot, where they ordered him to pick up trash as part of the job they had hired him to do, but then proceeded to attack him, leaving him beaten and bloodied. They stole the $260 cash in his wallet and left him lying in a pool of blood. Just one day before, another migrant from the same area had suffered a similar experience. Ultimately, seven Cherokee High School students were arrested in connection with the series of beatings. Canton's assistant police chief was quoted as saying "at least one of them was going around school bragging about robbing and beating up Mexicans."[31]

These are not isolated incidents. The FBI has reported a 40 percent increase in hate crimes against Latinos across the southeastern United States since 2003.[32] In 2008, among hate crime victims who were targeted because of ethnicity in the United States, 64.6 percent of the victims were Hispanic.[33] In 2009, the Southern Poverty Law Center released results from a survey of Latinos living in the South, finding that 68 percent of respondents had suffered racism in their daily life.[34]

Why is it that the image of immigrants as criminals persists despite evidence to the contrary? The answer has to do with persistent stereotypes and attitudes about Latino immigrants and the unauthorized. Attitudes toward immigrants are driven, to a large degree, by negative feelings toward groups that are racially or ethnically different from one's own.[35] Especially for whites living in the South, issues of race continue to be salient. As Latin American immigrants move into areas that have been racially homogeneous to perform the service and construction jobs that middle-class people require to maintain their quality of life, and in search of the very same things that the native born want (affordable housing, safe neighborhoods, and good schools) racial differences and tensions are bound to emerge. While racial and cultural prejudice is not the only factor that drives attitudes toward immigrants, it goes a long way toward explaining why such attitudes continue to pervade public discourse about immigration. A recent study found that "racial context by and large relates to Americans' public opinion on immigrants and immigration policies."[36] Racial concerns are salient especially for whites and deeply affect views of immigration and immigration policy. These concerns are often exacerbated by the polarizing and polarized discourse that mass media and politicians use when they talk about unauthorized immigration.

Policing Immigrants at the State and Local Level

The anti-immigrant climate in Cobb County and across the state has provided a fertile terrain for a string of laws passed by the Georgia legislature to clamp down on unauthorized immigration. Approved in the summer of 2006, SB 529, the Georgia Security and Immigration Compliance Act, denies state benefits to undocumented workers, requires employers to withhold 6 percent of wages from workers who cannot prove their legal status, and authorizes state and local police to enforce federal immigration laws. Additional restrictive laws have been passed since SB 529, including

SB 350, which increases penalties for unlicensed drivers, including fines of up to $1,000 and jail time for first-time offenders.

In the absence of federal immigration reform, Georgia is one of many states that have taken matters into their own hands. The number of bills introduced in state legislatures dealing with immigration issues has increased dramatically during the past few years. According to the National Conference of State Legislatures, in 2007, 1,562 bills related to immigration were introduced nationwide, and 240 were enacted in forty-six states, triple the number passed in 2006. And just in the first half of 2009, more than 1,400 bills were introduced nationwide. For example, Oklahoma passed a law in 2007 that made it a felony to provide shelter for or to transport unauthorized immigrants, and in 2008 Mississippi passed a law making it a felony for an unauthorized immigrant to hold a job.[37] At the local level, many cities and small towns have sought to deal unilaterally with the problem of undocumented immigration by passing a host of draconian ordinances, such as limiting the number of tenants that can live in a housing unit, denying driver's licenses to those who do not have the proper documentation, or penalizing employers who hire unauthorized workers.[38] In the metro Atlanta area several city councils have passed ordinances prohibiting day laborers from congregating on street corners. For example, the city of Marietta, the county seat of Cobb County, passed the following ordinance in 2010:

> It is unlawful for any person or organization to pick up or hire day laborers or for any person or organization to solicit temporary employment as a day laborer except as otherwise permitted by law, on the streets, sidewalks, parking lots, public property or public rights of way within the city limits of the City of Marietta. It shall

also be unlawful for any person to seek temporary employment as a day laborer except as permitted by law
on the streets, sidewalks, parking lots, public property
or public rights of way within the City of Marietta.

In 2007 Cobb County became the first in Georgia to sign
up with the Department of Homeland Security's 287(g)
program, which permits state, county, and local police law
enforcement agencies to enter into agreements with ICE to
perform certain immigration functions, such as "screening
inmates at local jails and state prisons for immigration status, arresting and detaining individuals for immigration violations, investigating immigration cases, and working with
ICE on task forces to address immigration-related crimes." [39]
The 287(g) program offers three models: (1) the jail enforcement model, which authorizes local incarceration officers to
conduct immigration checks on individuals detained on state
criminal charges; (2) a task force officer model, which authorizes law enforcement officers to perform immigration-
related enforcement on the streets; and (3) a hybrid model
that authorizes both jail and task force functions.

The first memorandum of agreement (MOA) under the
287 program was signed with the Florida Department of Law
Enforcement in 2002. As of August 2010 there were sixty-
nine active MOAs across the country. [40] The overwhelming
majority of jurisdictions that entered into 287(g) agreements
were areas that had experienced high rates of growth in their
Latino population between 2000 and 2006. [41] Following Cobb
County, three other counties in Georgia signed MOAs with
ICE (Gwinnett, Hall, and Whitfield). The 287(g) program
has been criticized for encouraging police to engage in racial
profiling and undermining trust between immigrant communities and local law enforcement. Not surprisingly, the
Major Cities Chiefs Association and the Police Foundation

have both found that local law enforcement participation in the 287(g) program has harmed community policing efforts.[42] Not only does it divert resources toward immigration enforcement, but it also deters unauthorized immigrants from reporting crimes.

The GAO issued a 2009 report on the 287(g) program that was critical of a number of elements, including the lack of documented program objectives and an absence of supervision and oversight in holding participating agencies accountable for carrying out the purpose of the program.[43] Although participating agencies are responsible for tracking data and reporting to ICE, in twenty of the twenty-nine MOAs reviewed by the GAO, "ICE did not define what data should be tracked or how it should be collected and reported."[44] In addition, although the goal of the program was to identify and remove unauthorized immigrants who had committed serious criminal offenses, "participating agencies are using their 287(g) authority to process for removal of noncitizens who have committed minor crimes such as carrying an open container of alcohol."[45]

During 2008, Cobb County's participation in 287(g) resulted in the start of deportation proceedings against 3,180 people, 69 percent of whom were arrested for minor traffic offenses such as driving without a license.[46] In adjacent Gwinnett County's first year of participation, which ended on November 16, 2010, immigration detainers were placed on 3,034 inmates, 93 percent of them Latino. Of the charges placed against those inmates, 21 percent were for ICE's high-priority crimes, such as child molestation and aggravated assault, but 45 percent were for traffic violations other than driving under the influence.[47] Perhaps the clearest demonstrations that implementation of 287(g) agreements has veered from the original intent have been several cases in neighboring Hall County, in which men were arrested by the Georgia Department of Natural Resources (GDNR) for fishing without a license and subsequently placed in deportation proceedings. For instance, the *Atlanta Journal and Constitution* reports that on May 25, 2010, a twenty-five-year-old Honduran named Josue Castro, who was married to a U.S. citizen, was approached by a GDNR officer. The article reports, "The officer asked Castro if he was fishing, to which he replied, 'No.' The officer then asked him to open his trunk, which contained a fishing pole and a dead fish. Because Castro could not show a fishing permit, the officer began to issue him a citation. 'He showed the officer an ID from his church with his address on it, and his wife . . . showed the officer her Georgia driver's license, with the matching address,' [his attorney] said. 'But they called Hall County PD anyway.' " [48] Because the Hall County Police Department had a 287(g) memorandum of agreement with ICE, they were able to initiate the process of deportation for Josue Castro.

Responding to some of the criticisms raised in the GAO report, in 2009 the Obama administration introduced some limited changes to the 287(g) program to standardize MOAs and provide stricter federal oversight, and to refocus on serious criminals and move away from arrests for minor offenses. Also, because of thousands of civil rights complaints against Sheriff Joe Arpaio of Maricopa County, Arizona, ICE rescinded his task force authority under the 287(g) program, and the Justice Department began a formal investigation of civil rights complaints against the sheriff. Arpaio's case demonstrates that while there has been a great furor over the passage of SB 1070 in Arizona, the nationwide 287(g) program, which gives local enforcement some of the same powers and thus carries a similar potential for abuse, has not received sufficient attention. Moreover, enforcement programs such as the 287(g) program only exacerbate existing social tensions in such new destinations as Cobb County.

Despite only enjoying jail enforcement authority under its MOA with ICE, the Cobb County Sheriff's Department carried out extensive roadblocks and raids of apartment complexes and various places of employment and business. These activities were clearly not what was intended under the 287(g) program. According to an ICE fact sheet about the program: "The 287(g) program is not designed to allow state and local agencies to perform random street operations. It is not designed to impact issues such as excessive occupancy and day laborer activities. In outlining the program, ICE representatives have repeatedly emphasized that it is designed to identify individuals for potential removal, who pose a threat to public safety, as a result of an arrest and/or conviction for state crimes." The situation became so difficult for immigrants in Cobb County that in the fall of 2007, Western Union began offering a service for $40 to families who received a phone call from a relative who had been picked up by the immigration authorities. When a family received a cell phone call from someone who had been picked up, they could bring the phone to Western Union and the company could tell the family member which jail or detention center the call came from and offer a ten-minute call to that institution to try to locate the family member.

Suely, a Brazilian who recently arrived in the area, explained that with these changes, settling in Cobb County is "like going to the unknown." She continued, "Imagine those who don't come with any knowledge of the situation, who are undocumented . . . and are fearful of anything that may happen to them. The only option is to close up [se fechar] and often to exaggerate the dangers that they hear through the grapevine. This happens often when one hears that the police are setting up roadblocks. Then the community goes crazy, desperately phoning up their relatives and friends to avoid that street, with fear that they will be picked up."

Jorge, a construction worker from Guadalajara, Mexico, described the climate of fear resulting from the implementation of the 287(g) program in Cobb County:

> You walk around feeling like you're a criminal. When I'm driving and see the police behind me, instead of respecting them or trusting them or something, I'm constantly looking at them in the rearview mirror, trying to avoid them; I don't trust them now, I fear them. If things continue like this I may have to move to another state where things aren't as bad. Because here if you're Hispanic, you probably don't have a license, and even if you do, they'll still stop you even though you don't commit a traffic violation. When they stop you they'll ask for your license and insurance. If you ask why they're stopping you, they'll say because you don't have a license. But how do they know whether you have a license or not? For the simple fact of stopping you, you're finished. They say that the United States is the country of liberty, there's the Statue of Liberty, but liberty for whom? There's liberty for you but for us there's nothing.

Similarly, a Latino student at Kennesaw State University related how her cousin had been a casualty of the 287(g) program: "Here what they have, they implemented ICE along with Cobb County, and you get pulled over, you don't have a license, you're going straight to jail. And, like, it happened to my cousin not too long ago. He was driving without a license, because he can't get one. So, three weeks later, he was in jail. He was deported. And it's like Monopoly. You don't pass—you know, straight to jail. You don't collect $200, none of that good stuff."

Although he is uncomfortable with the heavy-handed

application of the law, Jimmy, the barber at the Cobb Shopping Center, sympathizes with the Cobb County sheriff's decision to enter into a 287(g) agreement: "[The sheriff of Cobb County is] a personal friend of mine. You know, I spoke with him not long ago, and he said, 'Jimmy,' he said, 'Tell them folks in that community I'm not out to bust their chops.' He said, 'But they're breaking the law, come to my jail, I got a job to do.' And by God, he's right. I think we needed to weed out a lot—the end is gonna be a good thing for the ones that want to conform to the ways."

Somewhat surprisingly, Rosita's daughter Gloria, who manages the family's other bakery, also empathizes with the predicament of local police. Unlike her mother, Gloria speaks English fluently and often had police officers as customers when she waitressed at the Italian restaurant and now at the bakery. When she asked some of her police officer friends about the traffic stops and detentions, they answered: "Since it's my job, I have to do it; as a person, I have nothing against them, I have nothing against you, you're my friend. I know that many of them are good people, hard workers; they come to this country for no other reason than to have a better life, not because they like to be here and leave their family behind." According to Gloria, despite their involvement in detaining potential unauthorized immigrants on the streets around the bakery, the police have never asked about her immigration status. Instead of fearing the police, she likes having them as customers and feels that they provide an added layer of security. When asked if this scared off her immigrant clientele, she responded that she reassures her clients that the police are only there to visit her bakery and not to make trouble.

Sun Hee thinks that while more restrictive policies may have a negative impact on the local economy in the short term, over the long term they will have a positive effect:

Economy-wise . . . not just our business but in general . . . yeah, they spend a lot of money; more than the, ah, middle class. Because when they make money, they spend a lot. So since the Cobb County has the new rule, you know, the harsh rule to pick up the illegal immigrant and send them to their country, I think that was the last year, October, it started; since then it really obviously changed. Yeah, yeah. Reduced a lot of Mexicans. So that's why the business is losing. I think that in the long-term future it's good but I guess just the short-term economy-wise it hurts. In big picture, like say in big picture that is good thing to do, I think, because you have to follow the rules.

In contrast, many Mexican immigrants claim that the 287(g) program and other restrictive policies are having a negative impact on the local economy. Because of the climate of fear in Cobb County, some unauthorized immigrants are moving away, and those that remain are more wary of going out to stores and local businesses, and less willing to make large purchases:

It's affecting the economy a lot, a lot of people are scared . . . I noticed that a lot of people have moved, they've moved to other towns where there aren't these types of detentions. I'm a real estate agent and have been affected a lot because so many people are afraid and they're not buying houses anymore. Before, even if they weren't legal, people were buying houses, and now they're not. This affects the economy throughout the country, not just in this state, but all over the country and especially construction. There's no longer the demand in construction, there's no longer the housing sales, and factories are closing their doors.

Look at how the economy is—it's coming down, there's no work, no money, no nothing. But why? Because the Mexican was the one buying the houses and now that everything has stopped, there's no construction and the Mexican isn't buying houses. They [Americans] don't understand that the economy is collapsing because the Mexican is afraid, he's afraid of everything, because when he goes out on the street, at any moment the police can pick him up and take him away, and everything he has here he'll lose, because they're saying if they stop you and you don't have a license, they'll take away your car. Now there's this law in Georgia and [Americans] not realizing that they need Mexican labor. The work that the Mexican was doing isn't getting done because of the fear that at any moment they can pick you up and throw you out of the country. [Americans] don't see that because the Mexican lives in fear the economy is going down. Now the government wants to require everyone to have a license that is valid throughout the whole country. If this comes to pass, imagine what would happen to us.

Despite the impact of increased enforcement of immigration laws at the local level, most Cobb County residents are unaware of the Cobb County Sheriff Department's decision to work with ICE or of recent state laws meant to clamp down on unauthorized immigrants.

Moreover, many residents have no idea of how limited the legal opportunities are to migrate to the United States. George, a longtime resident of Cobb County, empathizes with immigrants wanting to better their quality of life in the "land of opportunity" but can't understand why immigrants from Latin America arrive without legal status: "Just get your visas, get your permit, do whatever and just come

here and work and establish yourself here legally." Another
Cobb County resident assumed that acquiring a visa to travel
to the United States was a straightforward process. This
woman, an African American, believed that immigration
law favored Mexican immigrants: "If you're from Mexico
you do not have to have a work visa. But if you're from any
other country, Turkey or whatever, you can't even come in
the United States unless you have a visa, so if they're—if
they don't want to become a citizen at least require them to
have a visa. And they're not required to do that."

Like most Americans, Debbie—another longtime resident of Cobb County—wrestled with the issues surrounding
unauthorized immigration. She understood that population
growth in Cobb County was linked to the need for workers: "Well, obviously Cobb County's growing and I see the
traffic . . . but I have seen a difference in the population in
certain areas, and I've been in Cobb County since '94. . . .
And I have seen many of the construction workers. They
are, what I assume, is Hispanic. And by that, I do not know
if they're from Mexico or Central and South America. But
I've seen them work hard. I've seen them work long hours."
She also expressed a deep concern for the way in which Latinos were treated in her local community, particularly in the
court system:

> I had the opportunity to go to court with my son, who
> had actually, at the Kennesaw State University, been
> given a ticket for not stopping at a stop sign. And I went
> to Kennesaw court with him. And I was extremely
> embarrassed by the way a gentleman of Hispanic ori-
> gin was treated in that court. He was belittled. I was
> ashamed. I was embarrassed for the court system. . . .
> The gentleman had a ticket for driving a car with a li-
> cense tag on it that was not his license tag. It was his

buddy's license tag. But seven of them needed to get
to work that day, and only one car would start. And he
was—they asked him to see a driver's license. He had
a legal driver's license. The judge literally made a dramatic "I need to circle the calendar." Then he asked
for proof of insurance, and the gentleman had insurance. . . . I don't know if the gentleman was actually
here legally or not. He spoke very little English. He
had cleaned up as best he could to come to court, and
probably 30 percent of the people in that court were of
Central and South American heritage.

She went on to explain, though, that although she was embarrassed by the way this man was treated in court, she also
sympathized with concerns about unauthorized immigration:

But I also must tell you that in my community, when
I see the grounds crews and the workers and so forth,
I always wonder if they're here legally, and that's an
extremely important thing to me, whether you're pink,
green, yellow, blue, black. My daughter-in-law is from
the Czech Republic, and she's here legally. And she
followed all the rules and came here when she was allowed. As a matter of fact, she has taken time to learn
the language, time to legally work here, and it's cost her
a lot of money, energy and time and frustration. She's a
very talented young woman.

   And I have major concerns about the population in
Cobb County using the services in the emergency rooms
with no real right to be here, and using public services.
As someone who has strong faith in God, I struggle with
these feelings. I believe everyone should have medical
care. I believe everyone should have a roof over their
head, and I believe everyone should have something to

eat. But I find myself, when I see groups, wondering and I don't know much of that is what I read in the newspapers, what I've seen on TV, homeland security issues. I don't know. But I know that it's really become an issue with me the last two or three years.

Debbie expressed a deep ambivalence as she tried to reconcile misconceptions about unauthorized immigrants, which are fueled by the media portrayals that shaped her awareness, with more broad ethical concerns about fairness and basic human necessities, concerns that are at least in part informed by her strong religious faith.

Jimmy and Sun Hee also hold somewhat conflicting views on immigration and immigration reform. Jimmy is sympathetic to those unauthorized immigrants who are hardworking and have set down roots in the community. On the other hand, he would like to see those with criminal records returned to their home country. He also has concerns about the mechanics of such a program:

> They're here now, and you can't let a baby suck on a titty for so long and then just throw it out. That doesn't work. But the ones that can be screened—I sat here and thought, how do you screen these people? Where do you start? They're gonna be so intimidated they're not gonna step up beyond here, if you're here illegal what are you gonna put a chip in my ass and see what happens? So that's gonna be the big question. How are you gonna do it?
>
> Like I say, we don't want American criminals, we don't want Hispanic criminals, we don't want Russian criminals, I mean, the ones that are robbing and stealing and selling drugs, get them out of here. The ones that want to work, give them a pass. Give them

a temporary pass. You can stay here so long. And then you got a record of them.

In Sun Hee's case, the fact that she came to the United States legally appears to have influenced her views on unauthorized immigrants. Even so, she seems to agree that it would not be practical to deport unauthorized immigrants who are already in the United States. She explained, "Yeah, whoever comes from . . . I'm not saying . . . I'm legal immigrant that's why I am not saying that, it's but, I guess, country is the same as our individual household, the same way. Yeah, we have to set the rules. We have to follow the rules." When we asked whether she was advocating for a return of unauthorized immigrants to their home countries, she laughed and replied, "Yeah, I'm not going to say about the people who's already here, but I am just saying that whoever trying to come over here later . . . From the future. And I hope they can just follow the rules and then no more problems."

Conclusion: Seeking to Bridge Differences

Back at his barbershop, Jimmy continued to wrestle with the issue of unauthorized immigration:

> But I still understand there's gotta be some kind of reform. These people are willing to drive, and if you get them some license, they'll put insurance on the vehicle, then you don't have the hit and runs and people left. You know, they're in a box. We needed them for this boom construction bit, and once it died out it seemed like, "Oh, hell, let's run 'em back out." But there's still a lot of work going on. My daughter works for a roofing company. Her boss—he nets, brings home $200,000, $300,000 a year. Once he doesn't have the labor to put

those roofs on, he's gonna raise hell about something, and you get ten of those guys raising hell, they can put a sheriff in a box.

As Jimmy's comments demonstrate, on the street, attitudes toward Latino immigrants are not as categorical as they appear in the media. There are indeed frictions and stereotypes on all sides, including from Latino immigrants, many of whom characterized African Americans as "lazy" or "dangerous." However, there are also positive perceptions, expressing admiration for the work ethic and group solidarity of recent Latin American immigrants and some sympathy for the plight of unauthorized workers. And while many have taken their children out of Cobb County's public schools in reaction to the changing demographics, a few see the exposure of their kids to other cultures and language as a positive impact of immigration.

Given the ambivalent attitudes toward Latino immigration, even authorized Latino immigration, it is imperative that we go beyond the simplistic sound bites that have hitherto tended to frame the public debate on the issue. It is essential that we understand the complexities of local encounters such as the ones taking place at Cobb Shopping Center, encounters that are now occurring not only in traditional immigrant gateway cities but also in places such as Siler City, North Carolina, Omaha, Nebraska, and Garden City, Kansas. Through these encounters, the native born may learn about the historical, political, and economic conditions that have compelled people to risk their lives and cross a dangerous, heavily militarized border, just as immigrants can come to know the values, fears, and expectations of the communities that are receiving them. Immigrants may realize that while they contribute to the economy in many ways, building the infrastructure, paying taxes, and consuming, they also pose challenges to underresourced school districts, for example. Such an understanding may in turn lead to more parental involvement in schools, thereby enriching public schools rather than weakening them. Failure to place these uncertain encounters front and center will allow the polarizing discourse to continue, potentially magnifying tensions, prejudices, and misunderstandings at the local level and increasing racial distancing. These encounters, however, require spaces where a true exchange of experiences can take place beyond the superheated language that has become attached to the notion of illegality. We turn in the next chapter to religious congregations, which have been among the very few organizations on the local landscape to carve out space for such exchange, and in some cases to create opportunities for immigrants and the native born to bridge differences and build new forms of understanding and collaboration.

4

"Picking Up the Cross"

Churches on the Front Lines

It was a sunny, warm Sunday morning in October 2007, and the members of Ray-Thomas Memorial Presbyterian Church in Cobb County, Georgia, were gathering for a highly anticipated event.[1] For months the church sanctuary had been under renovation, and this morning's worship service would be their first time worshipping together in the new and improved space. The endeavor they would undertake on this morning, though, was not nearly as simple as inhabiting renewed space. It was an experiment in multicultural worship, and one with very few precedents in new immigrant destinations such as Cobb County. As the pews of the large sanctuary filled to their capacity of six hundred on this morning of celebration, the members of four relatively distinct congregations sat shoulder to shoulder. The church's original congregation, which had built the church in the late 1970s, constituted a significant minority of those in these refurbished pews. They were joined by a small but very active Portuguese-speaking congregation composed of recent immigrants from Brazil, many of whom were unauthorized immigrants. The majority of those gathered to worship on this day, though, were of Korean background. Some were members of a Korean-language congregation, primarily first-generation immigrants. There was also a young group of Korean Americans who had a thriving Korean E.M. (English ministry) church. All four of these were setting out on this day to become, somehow, one church.

The pastor of Bethany, the Korean immigrant church that had very recently joined Ray-Thomas, came forward to announce, "Welcome! This is a glorious day!" He was followed by the pastor of the Brazilian congregation, who offered a prayer: "Lord, thank you for this day, the day we don't have to wait to get to heaven to worship in all languages. We do it here and now."

As the almost two-hour worship service unfolded, every aspect was simultaneously translated, on several large screens around the perimeter of the sanctuary, into three languages. The service moved seemingly effortlessly between contemporary Christian pop, classical chancel choir music, and praise songs with a Brazilian samba beat. The sermon was given by a white pastor who had spent decades working in China and North Korea. When he came to the podium and began to speak in flawless Korean, members of the congregation literally gasped. He began by saying, "Hallelujah— that's the only word I can think of that needs no translation." Referring to the passages from the Bible that had preceded his sermon and to the three languages in which they were read, he announced, "If we read about ten more languages, I'm sure we'd be getting close to the church in heaven. I'm sure that God is pleased today, very pleased."

His sermon focused on the power of the Holy Spirit as a fire of reconciliation, a fire that can burn away prejudice, bring forgiveness, and unite all into one body. Using the metaphor of a jeweler, he described the Holy Spirit's fire as able to shape a jewel, "a beautiful thing for all the world to see." He called upon the congregation gathered in the pews to go out together as "a walking jewel," but he made clear that the Holy Spirit's fire of reconciliation would not "melt"

differences: "When you go out, wouldn't it be wonderful
to go out as Brazilians, Koreans, and all kinds of mixed-up
Americans and share the world? Let's go out together! . . .
In God, there is no color; in God there is no race. God wants
to bind us together as one. . . . May people walk out and say
these must be [people of] God because only by God's power
can Korean and American and Portuguese and second and
third generation come together." The members of these four
congregations, indeed, walked out together on that morning.
They joined for a shared meal and celebration and then embarked on the challenging task of becoming one church.

Reflecting later on her participation in the service, the
twenty-two-year-old daughter of the English congregation's
pastor explained, "To be surrounded by three languages
all singing to the glory of God is the most overwhelmingly
moving worship experience I'd ever experienced."[2] The
nineteen-year-old son of the pastor of the Korean church
added, "I think it's the greatest thing. It's a little picture
of what heaven might be like, to be honest."[3] Members of
Ray-Thomas and Bethany Presbyterian churches understand the irony of this claim. They are well aware that although Cobb County, Georgia, may not be a hell, it is one of
the most difficult places in the United States for new immigrants to live, and particularly for unauthorized immigrants.
Eileen, a founding member of the church who has lived in
Cobb County since the 1970s, explained, "Cobb County in
particular is a scary place for immigrants, especially immigrants who are here without papers. I mean, it's very, very,
very scary. Very scary."

In parts of the country that are plagued with increasing
conflict, fear, and insecurity, daily life can be "scary" for both
immigrants and the native born, who face changes they don't
fully understand. Yet something remarkable is happening in
the midst of these changes, and it is happening in perhaps

surprising places. Churches are devising innovative strategies to face fears head-on, deal with their consequences, and seek a way forward that rejects the politics of fear. In many churches throughout the United States, we find a microcosm of the transformations occurring in the neighborhoods and cities that surround them—the same transformations that have fueled the nation's debates over immigration and immigration reform. Rapid demographic change has generated sharp social and political tensions, and—in ways that have not yet been widely understood or appreciated—churches are among the only places where these are being addressed effectively. Moreover, churches increasingly have put themselves on the front lines of a broken immigration system, both managing the fallout from that system's inadequacies and dealing with the precarious situations in which unauthorized immigrants now find themselves. In many ways, of course, churches are unique spaces, in which members may be guided by principles that are distinct from those of the nation. Yet churches also form a significant part of the fabric of American civil society. And, in places where that fabric threatens to be torn apart by the tensions surrounding unauthorized immigration and interethnic encounters, these religious organizations are devising creative strategies to stitch the fabric back together. The solutions that some churches seek to the problems they confront serve as powerful exemplars for the broader American community, and for this reason they demand our attention.[4]

La Luz del Mundo:
A "Holy Supper" Beyond Borders

On the evening of August 14, 2008, every inch of grass on the expansive lawn outside La Luz del Mundo (The Light of the World) Church in Cobb County, Georgia, was covered by cars bearing license plates not only from Georgia but also from North Carolina, South Carolina, and Tennessee. Having arrived from throughout the Southeast, the faithful were packed inside the large sanctuary to celebrate the most holy day of the year for the members of this Pentecostal church. In truth, though, very few actually *wanted* to be in this Cobb County sanctuary. The faithful longed to be in Hermosa Provincia, the international headquarters of their church, where members gathered every year to celebrate the Santa Cena (Holy Supper). Annual pilgrimage to this sacred space in Guadalajara, Mexico, was, in fact, a requirement for all members of the church. All were expected, as a fulfillment of religious obligation, to join in the Santa Cena—at least, all who were able.[5] The men and women who packed into the pews and aisles of this Georgia sanctuary were among the many who were *not* able to make the journey. For most, their inability stemmed from the fact that they were unauthorized immigrants, and the risk and cost of a pilgrimage requiring them to traverse the U.S.-Mexico border were too great.

More than six hundred men and women gathered in the church on that evening in the absence of their pastor. As a religious worker, he had been granted a work-based visa and thus had been able to travel back to Mexico with his family for the Santa Cena. Rather than focusing attention on the empty pulpit, congregants turned their eyes toward a huge screen, in which the events in the Hermosa Provincia were being webcast live from Guadalajara. The faithful waited in silent anticipation for their living apostle, Samuel, to appear on the screen. When he did, they called out with wails of joy and sadness, raising their hands in the air, swaying, and crying. Quite remarkably, in spite of their distance—or perhaps because of it—they were swept fully into the emotion of the moment.

Tadeo and Estefania were likely among those in the pews

that night. They had met at the Santa Cena in Guadalajara eleven years prior, married shortly thereafter in Mexico, and then crossed the border without authorization and with great difficulty. They settled in Atlanta and began to build a family. When they first arrived, Tadeo, a high-school graduate, worked as a janitor in a large department store. Friends from his church, whom he calls *hermanos* (brothers), soon helped him to find better work in construction, and by 2008 he was working as a construction foreman, responsible for more than a hundred workers and earning more than $600 a week. He and Estefanía purchased a spacious, comfortable home just over a mile from the church, and they lived there with his parents. Estefanía developed a small business that caters specifically to the women in her congregation and in other Latino Pentecostal churches in the area. She began sewing and then selling to *hermanas* (sisters) stylish long skirts that conform to the requirements of modesty for female members of this and other Latino Pentecostal churches in the area. Her home-based business has done well, and she and Tadeo are economically stable and well established in their home and church. When they are not working, Tadeo, Estefanía, and their children often can be found at church, which they attend almost daily for prayer groups and other activities. For them and for many other families who attend La Luz del Mundo in Cobb County, the church offers networks of support that help members negotiate daily life: find work, address legal issues, learn about places to shop, and access transportation.

Luz del Mundo (LDM) was founded during the 1920s in Guadalajara, Mexico. The church's leader, Samuel Joaquín Flores, is the son of LDM's founder and is considered an apostle by church members. The church has a global reach, with approximately 7 million members, mostly in Mexico and Latin America, but also with a significant membership (approximately 60,000 members) in the United States. The LDM church in Atlanta was founded in 1987 by Mexican immigrants and with the support of church leaders from Guadalajara and Houston. Today the church has approximately six hundred members. Eighty-five percent of its members are of Mexican origin, 13 percent are Salvadoran, and the rest include Colombians, Guatemalans, and Hondurans.

The LDM church has successfully put down roots in large cities and small towns throughout the United States, while also connecting its members to their place of origin in Mexico in a number of ways. Members have access to a constant flow of information from the regular visits of church members and leaders from Mexico. Because the LDM in Atlanta is able to congregate a large number of members several times during the week, the church serves as a place where immigrants can build relationships of trust and mutual support and a sense of belonging.[6] The church also serves as a key source of referral and information regarding jobs, housing, day care, and legal assistance. Several church members are legal residents or citizens who own businesses that often employ other church members. The church serves as a safe space, set apart from the challenges of daily life, and also establishes dense networks of support, assisting immigrants in adjusting to life in the United States.

Luz del Mundo, like countless other immigrant congregations throughout the United States, plays a significant role in shaping immigrant participation in American life. These churches may not provide opportunities for interaction with the native born or work actively to confront the political and social issues facing unauthorized members. Yet these churches are among very few spaces in the local community in which unauthorized immigrants can gather together to engage in the activities that they themselves have deemed important. In so doing, they develop skills and confidence as civic leaders.

In some ways, the experience of unauthorized Latino immigrants in La Luz del Mundo and other immigrant congregations parallels that of many black churches in the Jim Crow South. As they were for African Americans in the period of segregation, these churches serve as centers for cultural, social, and economic life, and they provide strong sources of identity and meaning in the face of discrimination and marginalization.[7] As is the case for most unauthorized immigrants living in the United States, the members of La Luz del Mundo have few opportunities in their schools, workplaces, or neighborhoods to develop leadership and engage in civic life. Yet their churches provide security, community, and opportunity for such engagement. As they develop projects and endeavors together, and as they stand before large groups to lead a prayer or offer a testimony, immigrants in these churches develop the confidence and skills necessary for participation in American public life. A group of women in La Luz del Mundo, who participate together in a women's prayer group, demonstrated such potential when they joined the 2006 immigrant rights marches and boycotts in Atlanta. These women are part of a religious organization often viewed as socially conservative, apolitical, and profoundly limiting of opportunities for women. Yet, in the safe space of their church, they developed the willingness and capacity to then step out together and engage in direct political action.

Sagrada Familia: A "Heart Transplant"

On October 28, 2000, a small but committed group of immigrants from Mexico and Central America sat together in the pews of a church bearing the cumbersome name of Sagrada

Familia of the Advent Lutheran Church. The strange name spoke to the recent history of this small Latino congregation, which had transitioned in the past year from being a nested congregation sharing space with the Advent Lutheran Church to being an independent congregation that finally had earned the opportunity to have the space of the church to itself. Perhaps the most notable thing about those in the pews of this church was their youth: young single men and women who had migrated recently sat shoulder to shoulder with new families. Babies and toddlers filled the air with their cries as the pastor struggled to speak over them to make his weekly announcements: He reminded those gathered of the Halloween party that would be held in the fellowship hall of the church later that evening. He also announced that the church would host a Thanksgiving potluck dinner. He asked that each family bring a dish from "our culture," such as mole, tamales, or enchiladas, and that single men bring ice cream, drinks, or bread. Pastor Rodrigo also wanted to ensure, though, that someone would bring traditional Thanksgiving foods: "turkey and pumpkin pie" since "it's not Thanksgiving without these!" He then reminded all to join other members of the congregation downstairs for coffee and fellowship.

By organizing such activities as Halloween parties for the children of the congregation and Thanksgiving potluck dinners, the pastor of Sagrada Familia actively worked to introduce his small congregation of young immigrants to U.S. customs and norms. The members of this church enthusiastically embraced such endeavors, and—as the elaborate haunted house they would construct for the Halloween party later that day demonstrated—they worked hard to learn about U.S. traditions and incorporate into U.S. society. Yet they also appreciated the space of their church as an intimate environment in which they could gather with their closest friends and simply be themselves. They had struggled to earn this opportunity, but they would face many more struggles in the decade to come, as their members, many of whom were unauthorized, felt the impact of local immigration enforcement measures and their small church began to come apart.

The Lutheran Church of Sagrada Familia (Holy Family) was established as a mission of Advent Lutheran church in 1998. Advent Church, which was founded in 1959 and celebrated its final worship service in 1999, had a forty-year history that closely mirrored the history of the suburban Atlanta town in which it was located. Advent experienced what John, the organist, described as its "heyday" in the 1960s, with a vibrant young congregation, a Sunday school, and a large youth group. John also recalled that this was when the area "was on the cutting edge of being a middle-class, suburban-type neighborhood." By the 1980s, though, members of the church had begun to relocate into the more remote suburbs of Atlanta, and the congregation began to experience a gradual change as the community around it shifted into economic decline.

Although the congregation reduced in size to no more than a few dozen members, Advent weathered the changes in the community into the 1990s, when this suburban Atlanta town began to see rejuvenation as a result of immigration. Abandoned apartment complexes filled with refugee families, failing strip malls filled with Mexican *carnicerias* and Asian groceries, and a large empty warehouse adjacent to a public rail station converted into a huge, thriving Latino Catholic mission. During this time, Advent Church began to see immigrants come through its doors. The aging Anglo congregation added a handful of members from Jamaica, Liberia, and Puerto Rico. One Puerto Rican member urged the pastor to consider outreach to the local Hispanic community, and in 1992, he started a kids' club that attracted dozens of Latino children but failed to incorporate their parents into the congregation. In the late 1990s, the congregation of Advent and the Southeastern Synod of the Evangelical Lutheran Churches in America (ELCA), located in Atlanta, began to take an interest in "multicultural outreach." The new bishop, Ron Warren, who took office in 1995, appointed what he described as a "mission transformation team" to create "a major shift in what we were doing based on a vision called 'Living the Great Commission.' " Once limited to African American communities in the Southeast, multicultural outreach would focus on the increasing number of immigrants living within its boundaries, and particularly Latinos. Advent Lutheran Church was a logical place to begin living this Great Commission, since it was a "dying congregation" and it was located on Buford Highway, in the heart of "multicultural" suburban Atlanta. With the help of the national mission offices in Chicago, the bishop identified Pastor Rodrigo, a Panamanian who had been working with a Mexican American congregation in Houston for twenty-five years, and invited him to establish a "Hispanic mission church" in the building of Advent Lutheran Church.

Pastor Rodrigo agreed, and in April 1998 he founded Sagrada Familia with the help of his wife, Reina, a Mexican American who was originally from Monterrey. Rodrigo and Reina quickly filled the pews with children and young families for Sagrada Familia's Sunday services. The newcomers' presence was a source of joy for some members of Advent, who were thrilled to witness young families attending their church. Nevertheless, the general mood was tense. There was very little interaction between members of the two churches, which were "like separate worlds," in the words of one Sagrada Familia member. When Advent members did address the immigrant newcomers, it was often to scold their children for running in the halls. Pastor Rodrigo was never invited to officiate at English services at Advent, and he was put under strict orders not to make any changes in the sanctuary, never to use false flower arrangements, and not to place the Spanish hymnals permanently in the pews.

Less than a year after the founding of Sagrada Familia, the pastor of Advent Lutheran Church died unexpectedly. Unable to muster the resources they would need to hire a new pastor, the members of the church (who by this time numbered less than thirty) decided to allow Advent Lutheran Church to close. As the bishop explained, their decision initiated a "heart transplant." As the phrase suggests, the operations were long and difficult. Advent members would agree to leave their church only if the synod could assure them that the land would not be sold. In the words of Terri, the longtime church secretary, Advent members feared that "we'd wind up getting another Asian mall or another something like that" on the former church's property, "and we just couldn't stand the thoughts of doing that." Rather than giving the property to Sagrada Familia, Advent members decided to put it in the care of the synod, and they also stipulated that their church's name remain on the large sign adjacent to Buford Highway, resulting in a somewhat cumbersome, bilingual sign reading "Parroquia Sagrada Familia of the Advent Lutheran Church."

Beatrice, an African American woman whose husband was the mission developer for the Southeastern Synod of the ELCA, began attending Sagrada Familia and assisting the pastor soon after the church's founding. She evocatively described what happened next:

I saw the death of that church [Advent], and I saw the emergence of Sagrada Familia. And how it happened was in . . . the physicality of the church itself. . . . Before, in the building, it used to be a fear to touch anything because the Anglos would come down on your head. The air-conditioning, everything was controlled by them. So we just had more people there, so that meant it was hotter. They kept the temperature at a particular level, so people just gritted their teeth. . . . That transition was something! . . . Everything that had been sitting there in that church for years, tossed it out. Got some new things going. So the transition from white Lutheran to Hispanic Lutheran was really something to see.

Beatrice described later how, through his actions, Pastor Rodrigo was in a sense saying, "This is my home. I will make it my home." Miguel, a young newlywed and an immigrant from San Luis Potosí, Mexico, was present for the transition. He explained that this was the most important event in the short history of Sagrada Familia. "The most important thing, in my opinion, was when the Americans moved to another church and left us the church especially for Hispanics. I think this has been the most important thing."

As a teenager, Miguel moved to Atlanta from a town near Acapulco, Mexico, in the late 1990s. Two years later, he married Olinda, his high school sweetheart from Mexico, and she followed him to Atlanta. When they began attending Sagrada Familia, they were a struggling young couple with an infant. Miguel worked in construction as a welder, and Olinda washed dishes in a seafood restaurant. They had begun attending the church because they were lonely and experiencing trouble in their relationship. When they asked at a local religious bookstore, the owner told them about Sagrada Familia. They became active in the church, and as they assumed a wide range of responsibilities helping the pastor and his wife, they also were mentored by the pastor, and their relationship deepened and matured.

During the decade to follow, the congregation of this church remained very small, with no more than fifty people in attendance each week, but it was filled with young singles, newly married couples, and young families that offered a great deal of energy and time toward building and maintaining their congregation. A new pastor came to the church, a vivacious Puerto Rican woman, and she also committed fully to helping the members of this small community to live their faith and to support one another through the crises and changes they experienced.

Among the most active members of the church were three sisters. Laura, the oldest, came to Atlanta from San Luis Potosí, Mexico, in 1989 to work as a live-in domestic. She left that work after marrying and worked as a housekeeper. Two of her younger sisters, Marta and Rosa, joined her in metro Atlanta in the late 1990s. Both worked in domestic or housekeeping jobs that Laura found for them before they left San Luis Potosí. Each of these sisters was very different: Marta, confident and intelligent, worked hard to learn English and find a way to improve her status in the United States. Rosa, her younger sister and best friend, often let Marta do the talking for her. She was reluctant to do anything at the church that required public speaking, but she loved to sing, and she quietly organized many of the activities at Sagrada Familia. Laura rarely made eye contact with people she did not know well, and her posture was hunched. She had suffered in her short life, having been abused and then abandoned by her husband, but she had two small boys who treated her with adoration. Over the years, she assumed increasing amounts of responsibility at Sagrada Familia, and as she did so, her confidence slowly returned, and she began to carry herself with more assurance.

Marta explained why Sagrada Familia was a good church to call home: "It's the same as the Catholic Church, but I like it because here one can—how do you say?—participate more! Because one participates more and feels more affection between the few people that there are. . . . Because here there's affection, like a familiarity . . . It gives me so much peace, tranquility." As a small "family," Sagrada Familia was the kind of local religious organization in which a participant could greet those in surrounding pews by name. Over the years, this small group of young families at the church became increasingly close and, in a sense, grew up together. Marta married and had three children. Her husband, Raul, became an active leader in the church, and was elected the head of the council of lay leaders for the church.

By the end of 2008, though, Raul had been detained for driving without a license in Cobb County, and Miguel and Olinda had made the difficult decision to return to Acapulco. Their pastor, at the edge of despair, explained that they refused to live in constant fear and persecution. She described how, although they missed their close-knit community at Sagrada Familia, they were working hard to be able to stay in Mexico. This small but thriving church once again found itself on the brink of collapse, and its pastor and lay leaders have struggled to learn how to navigate the prison system, find legal representation for church members, and deal with the emotional trauma of a small congregation in disarray. Sagrada Familia Lutheran Church had become a home, a place to both take refuge and learn about how to incorporate successfully into the broader society. Yet the home was not immune to the changes occurring in the surrounding community, and it soon began to dissolve under the pressures that its unauthorized immigrant members faced.

Reflecting on changes in the local community, Wilmer,

an unauthorized immigrant from El Salvador who came to metro Atlanta in 1995, explained:

> In my opinion, fifteen years ago everything was easy. For example, if you get arrested for no driver's license or a violation, your status wasn't involved at all. The police give a ticket, you pay for the ticket, and you get out of jail. That's all. . . . Nothing was happening like it is happening right now. So for that time, for ten years, families were thinking: this is a nice place to live; this is a safe place to work. With the hope of getting a legal permit in the future, let's buy a house, let's buy a car, things like that. A lot of families were with that idea. Just be here and live here and be productive here. But everything is—I mean, the sad part is, why did they give us opportunity from the beginning and once they build something nice, they just come and destroy everything. To deport a person means to destroy the complete family. They lose their homes, they lose everything basically, and they go back to their country and start over.

In his opinion, these laws and their repercussions for families and communities seem not to conform to the image that the United States promotes of itself: "I don't think this is a law for a country that believes in God. That is not God's rules at all, that's not what the Bible says. But humans, though, in this case they have their own opinions. It's interesting to ask these people if they go to church on Sundays, and I think they'd say, 'Yes.' But probably, they just go . . . and give the money and [think], 'They are going to be happy with my money,' but nothing changed in [their] heart."

Few native-born citizens of the United States without close relationships to Latino immigrants are aware of the changing climate for immigrants in their communities, nor do they understand the impact on organizations such as churches of laws and agreements that increasingly have shifted immigration enforcement into local control. Yet, remarkably, in some churches the native born have found that something indeed "changed in their heart" as they struggled to find ways to live and worship alongside unauthorized immigrants. As we will see, out of this change have emerged several innovations that merit close attention.

Ray-Thomas Memorial Presbyterian Church: "A Little Picture of Heaven"

There are many ways to tell the story of Ray-Thomas Memorial Presbyterian Church, where we began this chapter. One way would be to start with a largely white congregation in financial crisis. During a period of significant expansion for the church, in the late 1980s and early 1990s, the former pastor of Ray-Thomas took a sort of "build it and they will come" approach, and the church moved out of a relatively small space into a large, light-filled, and expensive sanctuary with seating for six hundred. When the current pastor, Carrie Scott, arrived at Ray-Thomas, she and the lay leaders of the church began what they described as a burden of both living faithful to their mission and finding a way to pay the bills.

From Crisis to Innovation:
The History of a Multicultural Experiment

In the 1980s, the area surrounding Ray-Thomas Memorial Presbyterian Church was growing at an extraordinary rate, but as that growth slowed and a new pastor came to the church, the congregation's rate of growth dwindled, while the mortgage grew. Eileen, a founding member of the church, explained the series of events that eventually brought the congregation to its decision to reach out to immigrant communities:

> When we first started it out, it was a very young church. We had one couple, maybe two couples that were over sixty when it started. . . . We didn't have a gray-haired section. We had a very strong evangelism program. . . . When you're building up new subdivisions and the subdivision is complete, you can cover a lot of ground by just putting flyers in mailboxes. And we did grow then, and there was just a lot of energy around the church. Over the next few years, Carrie [the pastor] was a little too left-wing for some of the groups and there was some discussion about money—"we think you should be doing this with the money instead of doing this with the money."

Crisis hit the congregation in the early 1990s, when Pastor Carrie joined an interfaith group in calling Cobb County to task for the county's refusal to rescind an antigay ordinance related to the 1996 Olympic venues in Cobb County. Many members of the congregation, angered by their pastor's public stand on this issue, left the church. Eileen explained, "But I think the worst thing that happened was when Carrie showed up at a march of other pastors protesting the resolution that homosexuality is not consistent with the Cobb County lifestyle or Cobb County thinking. And the schism hurt. There is no doubt about it. The schism hurt. And that's one of the things that's been trickling down ever since. . . . You start on a path. You're either going to grow as a church or you're going to shrink, and we are on the shrinking path." From that time forward, the congregation began to decline significantly in size and change in composition, resulting in expansion of the "gray-haired section" and reduction in programming geared toward children and youth. The very small but committed group that remained began to question their continued existence in a space that was much too large for their needs, and they began to feel the call to "be neighbor" to all those living in the area. As Pastor Carrie explained, "Neighbor doesn't just mean those who look like us."

The congregation engaged in a period of intense prayer and reflection about its future, and seeing the growing presence of Latin American immigrants, they decided that their new mission was to reach out to them. Seeking ways to do this, they discovered a small Brazilian Pentecostal congregation of eighty members that was looking for a place to worship. After what members described as prayerful deliberation, Ray-Thomas invited this Brazilian church to come in. Ray-Thomas leaders, eager to ensure that the Brazilian congregation would not feel like a "basement church," not only refused to charge rent but also encouraged the two congregations to integrate. Brazilians were invited to become elders in the church and to sit on the lay governing board, which is called the Session. In so doing, they began an earnest attempt to share finances and decision making with the original members of Ray-Thomas. The Brazilians experienced sometimes patronizing attitudes and unequal distribution of power, particularly in such decisions as when and where they would be able to hold worship services. Many in the original church community left, feeling that, in the words of Pastor Carrie, "the church was no longer theirs."

Meanwhile, down the road, a Korean Presbyterian church was growing exponentially, from one hundred to seven hundred members over the course of a few short years. Not only did the church have a large membership, but it had significant financial resources, thanks to the dedicated tithing of its members. The pastor of that church, whose family history was shaped by Presbyterian missions in Korea, explained that, 120 years ago, "the Presbyterian Church helped my family. It is now time for me to take care of my mother church."[8]

When the shrinking and financially distressed original congregation of Ray-Thomas invited the Korean church, Bethany Presbyterian, to join them, the Koreans brought a thriving, economically well-off, and technologically savvy congregation. Bethany took over the mortgage and began a significant renovation project. They immediately set about renovating the sanctuary in a way that would allow for such high-tech innovations as simultaneously translated sermons. Multicultural worship is logistically challenging, expensive, and time-consuming. Yet, largely because of the Korean church members' commitment, Bethany and Ray-Thomas together had the resources to meet the challenge.

Longtime members of Ray-Thomas, most of whom are white Americans, often describe their excitement when they see the sanctuary filled on a Sunday morning, or when they witness young children and teens gathering for Sunday school or choir. They also express admiration for the degree of commitment immigrant members have to the church. As Eileen explained,

I don't think the American congregation of Ray-Thomas . . . I don't think we are as practicing in our faith—I don't want to say deep in our faith. We've got so many other things going on in our lives, so maybe it's that we are busier than the immigrant community. I know that sounds crazy, because they are busy, too, but they're away from home, or away from their homeland. They take more time to get together and focus on Jesus, or focus on God, or focus on biblical study.

Brazilian participants, many of whom are unauthorized immigrants, see the multicultural church not only as a safe space where they can preserve their language, culture, and religious traditions without having to separate themselves into an ethnic church, but also as a fulfillment of the universal message of Christianity. As one of the Brazilian pastors puts it: "The Gospel does not know national or cultural borders. It has to be taken to all nations, to all cultures. All these nations and cultures could and should congregate under one single roof."

"A New Pentecost": Theologies of Multiculturalism

Ray-Thomas and Bethany's leadership, the pastors of its four congregations and key lay leaders, explicitly articulate that the mission of their church is to do multicultural ministry. What it means to do multicultural ministry is being worked out by this congregation in a deliberate and sometimes tense process. What distinguishes this model from other models is that it aims to bring together congregants from a range of distinct cultural settings (Brazilian, Korean, white American) in a way that celebrates and preserves difference. In other words, the church aims not to "melt" differences in a melting pot but to learn about them, engage them, worship with them. This church's leaders understand the project to be rooted in the call to live toward the Kingdom of God, to be an example of how people of very different backgrounds and cultural traditions can become one body in the church.

Pastor Peter describes himself as a "1.5-generation" Korean American. He was born in Korea but moved to the United States as a young child. He leads the Korean English Ministry at Ray Thomas, and is thoughtful and articulate about what it means to do multicultural ministry. He explained:

My understanding of a multicultural ministry, though, is that it's not an acultural ministry. I think oftentimes people when they talk about multicultural church, you are letting go of your heritage and culture and adapting into an aculture. I don't see it as that. I see it as you're bringing your culture and somehow in the great salad bowl of the church, somehow all the cultures are accentuated and you have a great multicultural feel to it. And I think when you experience that you really see the power of God. You can really see just what the church, what the Kingdom of God is all supposed to look like. And there is an amazing sense of joy and brotherhood that is very hard to describe when you see a setting like that.

Members of these congregations often describe this "power of God" as akin to the Pentecost, the event described in the Acts of the Apostles of the Christian Bible (Acts 2:1–6). The text explains that when the Holy Spirit descended upon the disciples of Jesus after his resurrection, people of all nations were gathered together. Miraculously, they were able to communicate because they spoke in a language that all could understand as their native language. Eileen explained that when the various congregations gather under one roof, "We are having our own Pentecost."

Others explain the experience of, and motivation for, multicultural ministry as a foretaste of the Kingdom of Heaven on earth. Thomas, a white American who works extensively with the Brazilian congregation, explained:

You know, the whole idea, from a theological basis, is we're going to be worshipping together in heaven with people from all over the globe, from all kinds of ethnic backgrounds. So the theological basis for a multicultural church is that we are doing here what we will ultimately do. . . . And so we do have to break down those cultural barriers because we are called to be one church. And the benefits of it are that when you overcome those obstacles—and they are difficult for any of us—when you overcome those obstacles, then you really begin to experience what Christ told us that the church is supposed to be. And there are obvious benefits in terms of, you gain cultural sensitivity and cultural understanding that, you know, largely don't exist in the world.

The process of developing this understanding at Ray-Thomas and Bethany has been slow and challenging. Pastor Peter explained of the obstacles they have faced: "You're going against culture. You're going against everything in you that tells you that this is not normal. . . . Oftentimes people talk about multicultural ministry but when it really happens there's a second take: I'm not sure this is exactly what I want." In the years since Ray-Thomas began this experiment, there is no doubt that some members have wavered, and the church continually struggles to overcome misunderstandings brought about by cultural and theological differences and by the imbalances of power inside the church. Yet church leaders remain committed to the effort. As Thomas explained, "We have to build the bridge for those who are willing to cross. And some will and some won't."

"You Have to Walk a While in Their Shoes":
Relationships Changing Perceptions

It is clear that one of the most significant things happening at Ray-Thomas, and at churches like it, is the simple opportunity to create relationships with unauthorized immigrants.

This is particularly important in places where, as we saw in Chapter 3, a great deal of racial distancing occurs. Churches, quite simply, are among very few spaces in which opportunities to overcome such distances are available, and they often offer theological and ethical arguments to undergird the need for closing the distance.

Don has been a member of Ray-Thomas for more than twenty-five years and also is a native of Cobb County. Following in the path of his father, he works in manufacturing for a large military contractor in Cobb County. Several of the members of his family work in local law enforcement. He expressed sympathy for people in his community who are disturbed by the growth of unauthorized immigrant population. He said, "Those who are against immigration, at least the level of illegal immigration in this area, I think they are worried about the cost for their lives. They feel an impact." He continued, though, "I don't think that the bulk of the population understand how difficult it is for the immigrant family." When asked how he gained such understanding, he replied simply, "Well, I have many friends in this church who are immigrants." As he explained why his own perspective on immigration policy diverged significantly from that of his friends and colleagues who are not a part of Ray-Thomas, he said simply, "Well, you just have to walk a while in their shoes."

In churches such as Ray-Thomas, it is through these relationships that native-born citizens begin to reexamine their own perceptions and to challenge the perceptions of those around them. As places of human encounter, churches can offer an important resource to overcome the negative myths about unauthorized immigration, serving as the leading edge for raising awareness from the ground up. In discussing this transformation, Eileen returned to the issues that initially plagued her own congregation: "And I think it's like, sort of like the homosexual issue. When you are just thinking in your mind about homosexuals, 'Oh, it's gross,' or something like that, but after you get to know one person, well, you know, he's okay . . . And then you meet another person, and they're okay, too. And they're okay, and they're okay. And so it's going to gradually have to happen."

Danielle, who works with the Brazilian community extensively, described creating opportunities for this gradual change as one of the key endeavors of the church: "So that's, I think, the thing that the church needs to do—to seize on and create opportunities . . . to at first kind of force people to get to know each other. Because, when you get to know each other, you feel differently about people when you really sit down to get to know them." Her husband, Thomas, continued, "And that's where the challenge really comes, to say, 'I can fully retain being an American, but I can walk in the shoes of a Brazilian.' "

St. Thomas the Apostle: "Picking up the Cross"

In a small, dingy room on the sprawling cancer wing of a local university hospital, P.J. Edwards, a forty-year-old native-born U.S. citizen, stood and walked away from the bedside of Emmanuel, a twenty-year-old leukemia patient and unauthorized immigrant from the state of Quintana Roo, Mexico. P.J. approached the whiteboard where nurses generally scribbled their notes, uncapped a dry-erase marker, and wrote "P.J. was *aquí.*" He turned to grin at Emmanuel, and the two began to chuckle, laughing at P.J.'s Spanglish and perhaps also laughing at the improbability of the two of them having spent so much time together in hospital rooms over the past weeks.

These two men faced many difficulties communicating with one another, and their differences were profound:

P.J. was a college-educated professional, a husband and father of two; Emmanuel, before being diagnosed with a life-threatening illness, had been a dishwasher in a restaurant, recently broken up with his girlfriend. P.J. was a citizen of the United States with health insurance; Emmanuel was an unauthorized immigrant and, for this reason, was among the uninsured. P.J. spoke very little Spanish; Emmanuel spoke very little English. P.J. was healthy and vivacious; Emmanuel was sick and nearly despondent. Yet P.J. had emerged as the unofficial leader of a small group of people, most of them members of St. Thomas the Apostle Catholic Church, in Cobb County, Georgia, who took as their mission to accompany Emmanuel. When Emmanuel was receiving outpatient chemotherapy, they drove him from his Cobb County apartment to the university hospital, waited with him all day as he received treatments, and then returned him home. During his long inpatient stays, they visited, brought DVDs and magazines, carried into the hospital his favorite foods from McDonald's, and asked many questions of his doctors, struggling to keep up with the complex details of Emmanuel's treatment process. Because Emmanuel was extremely ill and unable to work, they pooled their own resources and the resources of their church and denomination to help him pay his rent, purchase medication, and keep his cell phone activated. As their friendship with Emmanuel grew, they visited him at his apartment and took him out for meals and even on outings to local professional sporting events.

Emmanuel was diagnosed with leukemia one year after arriving alone in the United States. The university hospital admitted Emmanuel, still a teenager, into its children's hospital and began to treat him through the hospital's mercy care program. After several months, Emmanuel began to show improvement. He was sent back to his apartment in

Cobb County and was instructed to return regularly for chemotherapy. Upon his return to Cobb County, Emmanuel found that the members of his already limited network of friends were struggling with the increasingly difficult environment of the county that had resulted from the implementation of a 287(g) agreement. Emmanuel was afraid to drive, since he did not have a license, and he could not find any friends who were willing to risk making the long drive through Cobb County and into Atlanta. They also were unauthorized, and fears of roadblocks, detention, and deportation weighed heavily on them.

He began to miss appointments at the hospital, and his case was brought to the attention of a social worker. By coincidence, a woman who worked as a therapist in the hospital had met P.J. and knew that his church was in Cobb County, near Emmanuel's apartment. She reached out to him and asked if the church would be willing to help. Within days, a small but committed group of volunteers had assumed responsibility for virtually every aspect of Emmanuel's care.

Members of this group later learned that they would need to accompany Emmanuel to traffic court in Cobb County. Before they knew him, he had been issued a ticket for driving without a license. They were well aware that this simple citation would, in Cobb County, result in an order of deportation, and that their days with Emmanuel were limited. Yet they made a commitment to accompany him to court and through his uncertain future.

All of their work on Emmanuel's behalf is, in one sense, a traditional act of mercy, well known in the Christian tradition. Yet their work together has several nontraditional components that link both to the challenges of "living illegal" in Cobb County and to the remarkable story of one Catholic parish in that county. P.J. often takes pains to remind himself and others that the name Emmanuel means "God with us." As he reflected toward the end of one of his frequent e-mails to the group that explained Emmanuel's needs for the week:

> Some people have asked me why I don't find an agency to drop Emmanuel off at his appointments and pick him up. I believe Emmanuel is giving us the chance to be compassionate by not pawning him off to others. The word *compassion* means "to suffer with." Taken this way, compassion is quite unnatural. We generally take great strides to avoid pain in our own lives; so, it seems almost inconceivable that we would voluntarily enter into someone else's pain—particularly someone we don't really know. . . . The point is that if we want to come closer to God, we are called to be compassionate with one another. If we want to take living a Christian life seriously, we have to stay with those who are suffering, marginalized, or exploited. Our glimpse of the world through his eyes makes our vision more clear. For Emmanuel, I hope our presence gives him the feeling God is with him through us. I really believe that in helping Emmanuel and being there with him, both of us come a little closer to knowing Jesus.

Reflecting later on the challenges of their work with Emmanuel, P.J. explained, "I see Emmanuel's situation giving us, as a community, a chance to put our faith into action." Explaining the commitment to work with Emmanuel as emerging from desire to follow Jesus, he said, "I've also learned that Jesus said following him would be *good.* He did not say it would be easy or safe. So far, with the baby steps I've taken down the way, it really has been *good.*"

At St. Thomas the Apostle Catholic Church, a growing

contingent of lay leaders and clergy have begun to take baby steps toward understanding the ways in which their lives are intertwined, and to meet the needs that arise among the members of their church and community. The process has been far from easy or safe. Members of the church have had to learn to deal with issues that they never expected to confront, issues that require them to understand local and federal law and to have close contacts with attorneys. They have experienced shock and dismay as, increasingly, active leaders in their own parish face detention and deportation for reasons that they have difficulty comprehending. Father Jaime, the priest in charge of Spanish masses, explained one such instance:

> There was an instance in which a family that was very involved here, immigration went to their house looking for a person they had ordered deported and had given their address . . . That person had given an address that wasn't his, [immigration] went to look for him there, and they grabbed the husband, but the husband was home alone with a child and the child started crying so they left him. They didn't take him but getting out of there they did get like eight people, all of them known here in our parish. . . . And they took them because in those apartments there was a lady that made lunch for them and they came to pick it up from her. So since [immigration] was in those apartments—they went to look for that lady—they started just grabbing everyone who was there, everyone who was there to get their lunch.

P.J. reflected on the way that cases in which they have found their church's members involved have shaped their own consciousness and actions:

At the church, ourselves, we are getting educated, un-fortunately, about how the system *really* works. This thing with posting bond—it's not that posting bond in Cobb County, for a parishioner who got arrested in Cobb County for driving without a license—it's not that it's going to get him out of [jail]. He doesn't want to fight deportation. He probably doesn't have a chance of an argument to stay. He just wants to speed up the process. So all we're doing is posting bond so that then ICE will pick him up so that he will go to [the] Stewart [Detention Center], so that he will get home to Mexico, we hope, before Christmas. So definitely, we have had to learn these things. We have had to make friends with attorneys and we have to know, is an attorney what we need? So, in many cases, someone doesn't have a chance, but they're desperate and they want an attor-ney, but are they going to get taken advantage of? So, definitely, we have had to learn a lot, when friends get caught in traffic court and detained, their families need help, and they need rent money. So, it's really forced us to do things we hadn't planned on doing. . . . We talk about, maybe we need to have a fund for bonds, maybe we need to be able to loan people money for bonds as a parish, so that they don't have to pay outrageous interest. . . . The day-to-day, we're kind of still learning to do it—when there's a problem.

These tasks of working outside the church to address the needs of unauthorized immigrants and their families are daunting, and they have profound implications for individu-als and families associated with the church. But when mem-bers of St. Thomas the Apostle reflect on the most difficult hurdles they have overcome as a parish, those hurdles have been the ones faced *inside* the church.

Unlike the members of Ray-Thomas Memorial Presbyterian Church, the members of St. Thomas the Apostle did not *choose* to share a church, and their leadership made no explicit efforts to develop a multicultural ministry. The distinctions in these churches' experience links to broader differences between Catholic and mainline Protestant churches in the United States. Many Catholic parishes throughout the United States, and particularly in new immigrant destinations, are organically growing and diversifying at extraordinary rates, as Catholics from around the world relocate to the neighborhoods surrounding existing Catholic parishes and seek church homes near where they live. This organic change has surprised and, in some cases, angered long-term members of such parishes, who see the identity of their own church home radically shifting under their own feet. The story of how St. Thomas the Apostle grappled with such growth and diversification, and eventually found a way to unite around common projects, merits close attention, since in many ways it reflects the changes happening in local communities—changes that tend to fuel anti-immigrant sentiment.

"The Beginning of the End":
The Journey of a Majority-Minority Church

In 1999, the nascent Latino ministry at St. Thomas welcomed Father Jaime Molina, a Mexican priest who traveled to Atlanta to study English. Longtime members of the church understood the development of a small Spanish-language ministry as fitting well into their existing mode of parish life. As the community surrounding the parish had slowly changed, so also had the church, seeing Vietnamese, South Asian, and Nigerian Catholics increasingly fill their pews. But the case of the Latino Catholics who would soon join them was different. As one staff member explained, "Somehow they found Father Jaime and . . . then it exploded. It was like, that was the beginning of the end."

The parish always had prided itself on being multiethnic, and for at least a decade it had included several small minority groups, but the overwhelming majority of parishioners had been white. When Padre Jaime came to the parish, this began to change extraordinarily fast. The Latino population of the parish grew exponentially between 2000 and 2007. By 2007, the parish had increased to two and a half times its 2000 size. The parish had almost six thousand registered families, 43 percent of whom were Latino. Whites, comprising 39 percent of the parish population, were no longer in the majority. The proportion of Africans and African Americans held steady at 13 percent, and the Asian proportion declined to 5 percent. Over the course of a few short years, St. Thomas the Apostle had transitioned from being a majority white American parish to being a majority-minority parish. Ninety-five percent of the Latinos worshipping in the parish were of Mexican origin, and a significant majority of those were unauthorized immigrants.

The growth of the Latino immigrant membership at St. Thomas can be attributed to what everyone who is paying attention describes as a spiritual awakening among these immigrants and their children, who participate in a unique program that Padre Jaime brought with him from Mexico.[9] The program, called SINE (Sistema Integral de la Nueva Evangelización, or Integral New Evangelization System), entails intensive retreat experiences, followed by integration into the life of the parish by way of small Christian communities of eight to twelve people. These communities gather weekly to pray and offer spiritual, emotional, and material support. At St. Thomas, retreats regularly attract 350 to 400 participants, and more than a hundred small Christian communities currently exist at the parish.

Nestor arrived in Cobb County in the mid-1990s as an unauthorized immigrant from El Salvador. Over the years, he developed a successful small business as a painter and became settled in his community. He explained that before becoming involved in the SINE program, "My life was just working and drinking weekends and worrying about buying things. I didn't worry about the poor or anything else, just myself and my family." He explained that for years he had no interest in attending church, but he did go occasionally at the urging of his wife. Now, by contrast, Nestor—like many of the active members of the parish who are involved in the SINE program—exhibits a remarkable level of commitment to the church. He can be found at the parish several days a week, training catechists, serving on committees, and attending mass. Reflecting on the reasons for this change, he explained:

> The reason is these retreats, these encounters with Jesus. There were a lot of questions in my mind about being in this church. I didn't like it. I didn't like to be in a Catholic church. I didn't see any reason to be there every Sunday. I always was thinking, "I don't learn anything here." I just come and sit and see what they're doing. To me at that time it was always the same. Whatever happened last Sunday it happened again and again. I didn't feel in my heart—nothing. It was just routine to go to church. I was just coming and it was always the same. But these people invited me to this retreat. It was [the] Latinos invited me to this retreat. It was just part of the people who have received this. It's the mission, you have to invite more people to have this encounter with Jesus. And I decided to do this, and it

really changed my life. It really opened my eyes and I learned, I mean I started to understand being a Catholic, and church, it is great . . . And since I received that retreat, like six years ago, I haven't missed any masses and I'm involved as much as I can, as far as my time and the ministries and everything.

Nestor was not alone in experiencing profound change in his life as a result of the program. He explained,

One surprise of the SINE program that Father Jaime brought from Mexico is that this program has reached a lot of people. It is an invitation for people who don't know about Jesus. It is a program for people who would just come to mass but didn't know about anything. That is why St. Thomas grows the way it does. If people just come to attend the mass, there wouldn't be such a big growth. If there's somebody who doesn't attend any church, and I say, "Hey, you need to try this out. It's going to change your life." And they ask, "Where is it?" "It's in St. Thomas." "But I live in Roswell." "It's okay." They come to St. Thomas to live the experience, and then they register in St. Thomas.

The extraordinary success of the SINE program has attracted the attention of several other parishes in the area, and Nestor and other leaders in the program have helped them to bring the program into their churches. In fact, Nestor recently was asked to "pre-evangelize," or prepare for the first retreat, the director of Latino Ministries for the Catholic Archdiocese of Atlanta. In Nestor's words, he felt that "other churches are all talking about St. Thomas, and he wants to know what it is." He intends to bring several other members of his own parish with him, so that they can return to their church and start a small Christian community upon completion of the retreat. St. Thomas the Apostle has brought, from outside the United States, a program that is rejuvenating religious life in the United States to such a degree that it has gained the attention of the Catholic hierarchy in Atlanta. This rejuvenation has happened largely through the work and commitment of unauthorized immigrants.

For his part, Nestor believes that although the program has the capacity to create a life-changing "encounter with Jesus" for any person, the hunger for this encounter, and for involvement in the church, is even greater for unauthorized immigrants. An unauthorized immigrant himself, Nestor explained:

> I need to be in church. I need to pray every day because I don't have documents and . . . I don't have a driver's license and I need to pray because, you know, maybe the police are going to arrest me. I have to pray to get a job because I have to send money to my mom and my brother and my sister and to all my relatives because they're poor. And so we feel differently our faith, and are really touched in different ways. So, I can understand, it's going to be very hard for *americanos* to feel the way we feel, to live faith the way that we live our faith.

Referring to the *americanos*, Nestor was very aware that, although the program has been extraordinarily successful, it has not been well received by most of the native-born members of the parish. As a result, St. Thomas the Apostle, a parish that long prided itself on its inclusive, multiethnic qualities, found itself struggling with several developments that, according to longtime members, challenged the church's fundamental identity.

Fire Trucks on Ash Wednesday:
Overcoming Tensions and Misunderstandings

When members of St. Thomas tell the story of their parish's recent history, they often begin on Ash Wednesday 2007. On the Christian liturgical calendar, Ash Wednesday is the first day of Lent, the forty-day period of fasting and repentance that leads to Easter. The Ash Wednesday service in February 2007 was a bilingual mass. It offered a rare opportunity at this parish for Spanish-speaking and English-speaking members of the church to worship together, and the sanctuary was filled far beyond capacity. A disgruntled member of the English-speaking congregation, fed up with the overcrowding of his own church, called the local fire marshal to report the problem, and very soon fire trucks had arrived outside the sanctuary to disperse the crowds. The parish was put under strict orders not to exceed the capacity of church facilities for any event, and the staff began the delicate process of rearranging the church's very busy schedule to comply with the regulations imposed upon them.

The process entailed working out a balance of power inside the parish that often seemed less than fair. For instance, there was a Spanish mass each Sunday at 7:00 a.m. in the parish hall, across from the large sanctuary. The mass consistently filled the hall beyond capacity, and something needed to change. At 7:30 on Sundays, a sparsely attended English mass occurred in the large sanctuary, and the 150 or so attendees comfortably could have fit into the parish hall for their mass. The solution that emerged, though, rather than switching the location of the masses, was to move the Spanish mass to 6:00 a.m. on Sundays, so that the English mass time and place would not be disturbed. Remarkably, more than four hundred people attend this mass, one of four Spanish masses (and nine total masses) offered at the parish each weekend. As Nestor explained, this was perceived by Spanish-speaking immigrant parishioners as just another opportunity to express their deep faith: "If you attend a 6:00 a.m. mass, it means that you are in love with Jesus!"

This enthusiasm, perhaps strangely, is one of the sources of tension between the Latino immigrants and native-born members of the parish. As Amy, a member of the parish in her late thirties, explained, the Latinos involved in SINE spend at least four days a week participating in church-related activities. She continued, "So it's a pretty monster commitment, and pretty involved. They're asked to do a lot of things, and the general feeling is that the English-speaking parish is not ready for that kind of commitment. Or, being truly evangelistic, literally going out and knocking on doors and recruiting people to come to the church, isn't something that the traditional English-speaking native church has done a lot, from a parishioner's standpoint—at least not here. So that's a big change." In addition to their discomfort with door-to-door evangelization, which another parishioner described as "very foreign to the American Catholic experience," and the huge time commitment required by the form of Catholicism being practiced by Latinos in their church, native-born members sometimes feel as if their pastoral leadership holds up immigrant Latinos in the church as exemplary. As Amy articulated, "I think some people feel like 'The Hispanics are doing it right and you guys aren't doing it right' is what they hear from our priests sometimes—is what the feeling is."

During this period of extraordinary growth, three members of the staff of St. Thomas, all white American women who had been a part of the church for decades, expressed their concerns. As they sat in folding chairs around a metal table in one of the Sunday school classrooms, they engaged in a frank and open dialogue. Striving to put words to her discomfort with the changes in the parish, one of the women explained of Padre Jaime's work, "It's hard not to see what he is doing as good. I mean, what he's doing, it's obviously very good. It's so radically different than who we are so that the challenge is, how do you become one St. Thomas the Apostle Catholic church when within the walls are two faith communities that don't just not speak the same language, but we almost have a different understanding of our faith life?" Another member of the staff continued, "And our walls just aren't big enough to hold them anymore. They're bursting, just bursting." A third member of the staff reluctantly explained: "It's like, when you have a family, a large family, you just sometimes have to realize that you've outgrown it. But then at the same time people look at you as, you're being prejudiced. Because you can't admit to say, 'It's not working anymore.' " Staff members and other longtime members of the parish consistently expressed concern that they would be perceived as prejudiced. They challenged the assumption that their concerns were based in prejudice, and instead highlighted several specific issues that had emerged in the church: different understandings of culture, ecclesiology, and priestly authority within Catholicism, issues around use of space in the church, slow rates of English-language acquisition among Latino immigrants, different levels of education, and cultural concerns such as control of children in public. Each of these emerged as key sources of tension, and staff at the parish had reached a point at which they were prepared to throw up their hands and say, in the words of one of the women around the table, "it's just not working anymore."

In January 2008, P.J. and Amy Edwards began—without knowing it at the time—a process that would reverse the course of this tension-filled parish. The couple had joined the parish thirteen years prior, as recent college graduates. P.J. explained of his participation in the church, "I wasn't getting anything out of it, and as a Eucharistic minister, I was participating in some way, but . . . I was like, 'Okay, I've done my sacraments and there's really not a lot else here for me' . . . I was really focused—I was a businessperson, a business executive at the time, and more focused on myself and my family than anything else." He explained what happened next:

Also about that time, presidential elections were coming up and Amy and I . . . decided that we needed to learn more about the issues, immigration being one of them. We knew we didn't know, and we knew there was a lot that was probably not clear, maybe even myths going around. We wanted to learn a little bit more, so we went to this event at [a local college] that was supposed to be a faith-based presentation about immigration. . . . It was very contentious—there were Minutemen there and various groups. So every time they asked a question, it would be a five-minute statement followed by maybe a two-word question. It was very contentious, and we decided that it is very difficult to have dialogue around this issue, but we wanted to bring it back to our church because our church—it had always been diverse, but the Latino population was growing very rapidly at the church, and so we thought that it was important to bring some of this thought-provoking educational material back.

The event was transformative for them, and they realized that their own parish needed to begin a dialogue on immigration. Around the same time, all members of the parish staff attended an event held by the Catholic Archdiocese of Atlanta, which aimed to educate them about Catholic social teachings on immigration and about the economic and legal issues that unauthorized immigrants face.

These lay leaders, along with the director of adult faith formation, approached the pastor and asked for the opportunity to begin a dialogue about immigration in the parish. The pastor enthusiastically embraced the idea, explaining that members of the church were being called to a "conversion," "called to change our hearts." The group began to work with the director of parish social ministries for the archdiocese, and to explore materials provided by the United States Conference of Catholic Bishops' Justice for Immigrants program. A small group of parishioners also began an intensive thirty-week spiritual formation program called Just Faith. The program delved deeply into the social teachings of the Catholic Church, particularly those linked to peace and social justice. The group decided to focus their sustained attention on the issue of unauthorized immigration.

Initially, they considered having the pastor address immigration policy in his homily on Sunday mornings, or offering a session for all attendees of the morning mass. Concerned that many in the parish would be hostile toward such an approach, they eventually decided to begin the campaign by inviting all lay leaders in the parish—members of the parish council, the finance committee, and other key organizations—to attend an education session. The first session, in the spring of 2008, included a film, discussion with the Mexican consul in Georgia, and discussion of information about immigration myths and realities. Leaders were invited by the pastor and strongly encouraged to attend. Those who did not attend were sent a follow-up letter inviting them to a second session. To date approximately two hundred native-born U.S. citizens who are lay leaders in the church have attended these events.

As the pastor of the church explained, the goal of the events was "first to help us to respond as a gospel people, to be who we call ourselves to be. But I think it's also . . .

introducing a venue or opportunity to . . . change some of their thinking. You know, the thing that scares me sometimes is the politicization of the whole [immigration] question, which again comes back to some of the problems that you have in this area, Cobb County." Perhaps the most effective strategy for doing this at the parish has been the most simple. P.J. explained,

We decided the way to get people together is to get them to spend time together. Just like if America is about to go to war, we have to make the enemy less than human. We have to see them as separate and different and it's that distance that causes the challenge. So we know we have to get people to become friends, but even before that . . . I think on the American side, education is very important because people have all this misinformation and all these reasons to hate the other, all this information that dehumanizes immigrants— that doesn't consider the root causes of immigration, poverty, the effects that America has had on these other countries. So the education part is the first part. The other thing we need to do is . . . we knew friendship is important, and we wanted to work together. To get people in small groups to sit down and get the perspectives of the Americans on their piece of the truth, and get the perspectives of the immigrants on their piece of the truth. . . . So, you know, you have to widen your view by looking through other people's eyes. . . . That was really, kind of the first seed that started.

"Am I My Brother's Keeper?"
Learning to Love New Neighbors

The fundamental principle that guides the work of this parish group is the commandment to love God and neighbor. Members of the community struggle to articulate a broad vision of who constitutes their neighbor. As P.J. explained,

> And it's easy to love the people that are like you, but we are called to love the people that are different, that are quote-unquote "enemies." I'm thinking about St. Francis and his conversion. He was overly paranoid about leprosy and he hugged the leper and that changed him. There were people within the community that wanted to reach out to the other, and luckily, by divine intervention or what have you, we connected in that way. I felt like there was still a lot of mistrust. I had a hard time getting Latinos from our community—and still do, to some extent—to come to these sessions. . . . It wasn't like the whole community started loving the whole other community overnight, and we're still not there. But . . . I think that all of the priests are doing a pretty good job of kind of pushing us to make that connection, to make that meaningful connection, because it's almost impossible not to recognize that somebody is a whole lot like you once you spend some time together, and those days when we got together and had dinner together, and we spent time together and just heard each other's stories, and you see that they're not that different, after all. Culturally, we have some different practices, but deep down, we're the same.

The process of learning to love new neighbors, according to P.J., is much more profound than developing friendships across cultural or class divides. P.J. stated simply, "I think that our salvation is intertwined with one another." This process of profound interdependence links to another guiding principle for the journey members of this parish are undertaking, a principle of living in community. P.J. explained,

> The first book of the Bible asks, "Am I my brother's keeper?" And the joke is that the whole rest of the Bible says, "Well, yes. Yes, you really are." Society taught me that the goal was to be self-dependent, to be individual, not to need others. And I was pretty proud of that: I don't need my parents' money; we are fully functional. But, when you start to read the Gospel, it's not that. It's about living in community. It's to be dependent on others, to recognize each other's gifts and to combine them to do the work of God. . . . The saying is, we judge our society by how it treats the least among us. And when we start looking at America through that lens, it looks very, very different than it looked . . . when you were just taking care of your family, climbing the ladder, buying a new TV. That's the fundamental base of the theology.

Through their efforts to get the Travelers Together program off the ground at their parish, P.J., Nestor, and their families have become intimate friends. Although Nestor experienced a spiritual conversion through the SINE program and P.J. was transformed by his participation in Just Faith, they articulated a shared understanding of the theological foundations for their work together. Their growing interdependence constituted not just a friendship but a relationship characterized by a radical sense of community.

They sat one afternoon around P.J.'s kitchen table and shared their reflections on the course of events that brought them together. Nestor recalled the first time P.J. asked him to participate in the group, "One of the first things that got my attention was he was talking to a friend of mine and somehow we got to talking and then he gave me a hug. And I was telling my wife: 'That *americano*, he gave me a hug! . . . He gave me a big lesson. He's teaching me I have to love, too. I have to love the others. It doesn't matter who they are or what their skin color is.' " P.J. built upon these reflections, explaining, "I remember doing the education sessions, and Nestor's wife, one time she came to the session and she was crying, and she said that she was crying—I'm paraphrasing—but she just couldn't believe that Americans even care at all. Where, I felt like I was getting so much from spending time with Nestor and his family. It was really filling me up inside and opened me up to new things, and so uplifting."

P.J. left the table, walked into his living room, and returned holding a photograph of four families from the church— three immigrant families (some of them unauthorized) and his own family—who recently had vacationed together. He explained,

> And you can see, I mean, this [photograph] is on the TV. I look at this every day and just smile. To be together, like that, to come as we have come together as a family has been so fulfilling. The lonely, American, individualistic life—realizing that it's dry. I will be hungry again. It's like in *Pirates of the Caribbean.* I eat something and it turns to sand. I get a new car, I get another new car, I get a new phone. Am I any happier? I'm not any happier. I'm still outside of community.

P.J. continued, gesturing toward Nestor, who sat across the table from him,

I need *him.* He brought me into a community. It's totally different. Now I depend on other people, and it's a beautiful feeling. . . . If I continued down my path, I would probably die a grumpy old man who was mad at immigrants for causing all of our problems, or something. But together—I think for the Latino community, they feel some sense of hope that someone like me cares, and it energizes them. And for me, it's that sense of community and belonging that I didn't know before—of love. It energizes me.

Conclusion: "Pray with Your Feet"

On Holy Thursday, in the spring of 2009, more than five hundred members of St. Thomas the Apostle gathered in a march to transform the streetscapes of Cobb County. Latino and white lay leaders, many of whom had participated in the Travelers Together campaign, came together with staff and priests from both the English- and Spanish-speaking congregations to plan and implement one leg of a Holy Week pilgrimage for immigrants. The pilgrimage, described in flyers distributed around the church, was billed as an "act of faith, solidarity, and hospitality." The flyer explained, "Recalling on the central tenets of every major religion practiced in the United States, communities of faith hope this pilgrimage reminds us that the hardest walls to destroy are the walls of fear built into our hearts. To hold this pilgrimage during Holy Week offers a transformative connection to the teachings of Jesus who said that whenever we fail to welcome the stranger, we fail to welcome him." Pilgrims traveled through the areas of metro Atlanta most hostile to new immigrants, stopping at such destinations as county jails and federal detention centers, and ending, on Good Friday, at the gravesite of Dr. Martin Luther King Jr.

The St. Thomas group volunteered to host and organize the leg of the pilgrimage that would travel through Cobb County, which drew more participants than any other leg of the event. St. Thomas lay leaders described the event not as a political protest but as an opportunity to "pray with your feet." The walk began at St. Thomas, where approximately eighty African American and white church members joined more than four hundred Latinos, predominantly Mexican immigrants, for a prayer service in the church. The group then walked eight miles, while singing and praying the rosary, to the town square of Marietta—the county seat of Cobb County. When hecklers rolled down car windows and yelled such phrases as "Go home!" participants did as instructed by event organizers: they simply continued to walk and pray. Midway through the event, pilgrims stopped at a social hall owned by a Mexican immigrant family that attends St. Thomas, where African American and white members of the Knights of Columbus (a Catholic fraternal organization) and the ladies' auxiliary served lunch to pilgrims. Leaving the social hall, the pilgrims crossed out of the city of Smyrna and into unincorporated Cobb County, meaning that the very sheriffs who had detained and placed in deportation proceedings undocumented immigrants from their own congregation were now escorting the pilgrims. Acknowledging the tensions surrounding this shift, one white participant quietly exclaimed, "We're not in Kansas anymore."

Upon arrival in the town square, participants gathered around a stage, while the pastor of the church read scripture and led the group in prayer. Then the group enacted the typical Holy Thursday foot-washing ritual with a twist: six unauthorized immigrants were invited to come onto the stage and sit in folding chairs. Then six native-born citizens of the United States were invited to come and wash their feet. Five whites and one African American washed the feet of the immigrants, while the crowd cheered loudly. All the while, four members of the Dustin Inman Society, a radical and profoundly influential anti-immigrant organization based in Cobb County, circulated among the crowd, taking photos, filming the event, and reporting on what was happening by cell phone. (The society later posted photos from the event on their website under the caption "Photos from the illegal alien march for amnesty.") Not noticing, or at least not acknowledging, the presence of key anti-immigrant activists, the pilgrims completed their journey with a song, repeated several times. With each repetition, participants took the hands of a nearby person, gazed into the face of that person, and sang (in Spanish): "I love you with the love of Jesus. I see in you the face of God."

Reflecting later on the pilgrimage, P.J. explained,

> It wasn't a protest. It wasn't anything but a walking prayer that said: "If we believe that we are all equal under God's eyes, that God doesn't see borders, then let's have a walking prayer during Holy Thursday." And I thought when we were organizing it—and we did organize it together, [the] Latino and the English-speaking community—I thought that if we got 50 people to walk together on a Thursday, that would be pretty cool, and we had 525 people that year, walking together. And at the end, when we had the ceremonial feet washing for Holy Thursday, we had recent immigrants, undocumented, and we had the American-born wash the feet of the immigrants. It was really powerful in ways that I didn't anticipate. The impact, I can't even describe. It was a high. We really felt like Jesus was there. We experienced something together.

Such an event as this, in such a place as Cobb County, Georgia, was remarkable for many reasons. It signaled the distance that one parish had traveled, from profound tension to intimate relationships across divides that had seemed unbridgeable. Yet it also demonstrated something much more fundamental: in these transformed relationships of mutual love and support, unauthorized immigrants and the native born stand poised to move forward together. One by one, they build connections, guided by principles and values that diverge significantly from those found in their surrounding communities, in newspapers, and on television. Looking across these connections, their perceptions of each other change, and they "pick up the cross" together to do work that is difficult, disheartening, and often overwhelming.

It is no coincidence that such transformative work is happening in churches. As they strive to sketch out "a little picture of heaven," some churches become social incubators, where tension and misunderstanding are replaced with love and interdependence. The stories unfolding in these churches are not complete, and they face many obstacles ahead. Yet they bear telling, since they offer compelling alternatives to today's polarized debates about unauthorized immigration. We frequently hear of the ways in which immigrants, and particularly unauthorized immigrants, drain the resources of local organizations and lead to decline in local communities. But from the perspective of churches—some of the most significant civic organizations in the United States—immigrants are offering much-needed vitality, youth, energy, and resources to organizations in decline. In these newly energized American churches, we catch a glimpse of a real and meaningful alternative emerging, which challenges the harsh sterotypes and racial distancing that have characterized so much of our national conversation on immigration. Yes, native-born members of these declining churches have offered much-needed services and assistance to new immigrants, easing the pain of "living illegal." But we cannot forget that, in these churches, immigrants—both authorized and unauthorized—are offering the native born something very important in return. We turn now to address the question of whether their energy and vitality can be harnessed, and whether transformed relationships can serve as the foundation for broad social, economic, and political change.

5

Migrants Mobilize

Finding a Voice in Local and National Debates

It was Monday, March 29, the second day of the 2010 Holy Week Pilgrimage for Immigrants in Atlanta, and a small group of pilgrims walked silently along a busy highway in Gwinnett County. They were traveling on foot to the Gwinnett County Sheriff's Department, where they would offer prayers for immigration reform. A middle-aged Euro-American man leapt out of his vehicle and began to take photographs of the participants. Anton Flores, the primary organizer of the pilgrimage, was walking at the rear of the procession. Initially, he had difficulty understanding the content of the man's angry shouts. Eventually, as Anton approached, the words became clear: "How's it feel to be marching with felons?" Anton went to the angry man and initiated a conversation on the side of the road. He patiently explained that the laws regulating immigration are civil laws, and that the unauthorized immigrants that the man photographed were not felons. When Anton learned that the man, whom he called Matt, had graduated from seminary, he pointed to a Church of God that stood next to a Catholic Church across the street from where they spoke. Anton asked Matt, "While their theological differences abound, I bet they can find common ground. Can we search for where we find agreement?" As the pilgrims traveled on, Anton stayed behind and continued their roadside conversation. Eventually Matt and Anton agreed that "most immigrants have a deep faith, work hard, and share many of the same socially conservative values that Matt espouses."

Reflecting later on the conversation that ensued, Anton described it as "a wonderful exercise in nonviolent communication." He explained, "As Matt continued to tell me his fears of immigrants, about how 'amnesty' would unravel democracy, change our language, flood our jails and hospitals, I felt compassion and the need for a reconciling common ground. . . . Change brings fear, and I sensed Matt was afraid." Anton understood well the change that Matt and his community had experienced. At the time, Anton lived in the small west-central Georgia town of LaGrange, but he had moved to Gwinnett County as a child in 1980, and had lived there for most of his childhood. He recalled that in the 1980s, as a boy of Puerto Rican descent, he had been in a very small minority of nonwhites. "Now," he explained, "immigrants from all corners of the world—Latin America, Asia, Eastern Europe, and elsewhere—are lining up the streets with new businesses that seem strange, and even threatening, to home-grown Gwinnettians like Matt." His encounter with Matt ended peacefully, though: "In the end, we exchanged a handshake and, surprisingly, Matt offered me a ride to rejoin the pilgrimage—the one he initially protested." [1]

Indeed, in Gwinnett County, the Hispanic population increased from 2 percent to 18 percent of the total county population between 1990 and 2008, and the county is recognized as having the largest Latino population in Georgia and one of the fastest-growing Latino populations in the United States.[2] The county participates in both the 287(g) program and the Secure Communities program of Immigration and Customs Enforcement. This county's high-profile sheriff, R.L. "Butch" Conway, has garnered national attention for his active enforcement efforts, which have made Gwinnett County a place in which fear pervades not only the lives of native-born Gwinnettians but also those of unauthorized immigrants. These two-pronged fears drive many of the decisions that local communities and the nation face as they consider how to address issues surrounding unauthorized immigration.

Throughout the nation, though, small movements are taking shape to challenge directly the politics of fear, address the consequences of a broken immigration system, and encourage immigrants and the native born to seek a common path forward. In this chapter, we examine three such movements, each of which has emerged in the context of the U.S. Southeast. While each movement is unique, and each responds to the specific context in which it emerged, all of these movements offer profound exemplars to the nation. They offer concrete strategies to reform immigration policy and, perhaps more important, model a society in which all humans are treated with dignity, and the contributions of all to the economy, polity, and culture of America are celebrated.

The first approach, exhibited by the El Sol Community Center in Jupiter, Florida, develops a collaborative model in which local government, local institutions, and local activists work together to develop solutions to the problems resulting from a broken immigration system—in this case, the vulnerability of day laborers. The case of El Sol offers a compelling alternative to the approach of many other local and municipal governments. Rather than working to deflect immigration, the center aims to create more favorable conditions for immigrants, which will benefit the entire community.

The second approach, exhibited by the Alterna Community in west-central Georgia, develops a small intentional Christian community that aims to live a radical alternative to the broader society. Alterna demonstrates, to the local

community and to the region, intense expressions of interethnic solidarity and love. Emerging from this alternative
community are several initiatives, many of which are directed at a specific consequence of the broken immigration
system: the detention and deportation of unauthorized immigrants. Alterna's initiatives aim both to provide comfort
and solace to unauthorized immigrants and their families
and to transform systems that Alterna members identify as
unjust. Alterna's approach is particularly compelling in local
communities that exhibit significant levels of hostility and
in which possibilities for collaboration between immigrants
and local governments are significantly limited.

The final case we explore is that of the Trail of Dreams,
an initiative undertaken in 2010 by a small group of young
adults, who drew upon a range of resources to organize direct political action against the federal government. Their
work addresses the consequences of a broken immigration
system by bringing attention to the plight of unauthorized
young adults who were brought to the United States as children. These young adults have been educated in U.S. schools
and reared as Americans. Yet as they complete high school,
they find that they have profoundly limited opportunities
for higher education and no means to adjust their status to
legal residency. These Dream Walkers exhibit remarkable
promise, as they appropriate substantive citizenship in the
absence of formal citizenship. Their courageous action builds
on a range of social movements to call for specific federal
legislation and to confront the politics of fear.

El Sol Neighborhood Resource Center

It is a typical weekday morning at El Sol, a neighborhood
resource center in the south Florida town of Jupiter, and
the building is bustling with activity. On the first floor,

approximately fifty workers gather around tables for "table-top training" as they await employers. The training operations include learning about town ordinances, developing job skills, and accessing educational opportunities. Upstairs, another thirty workers are divided into three English classes taught by volunteers. A dozen volunteers shuttle between the welcome desk and the kitchen, where a daily meal is prepared and then offered on a pay-as-you-can basis to the workers. Behind a partition, twenty monitors glow on the faces of a group of young men. These men are learning computer skills on used machines donated by the local school system and university.

Just six years ago this former church building sat empty on the town's property, immediately adjacent to the police station. The town was in turmoil, as residents and the town council debated what to do about the growing population of primarily immigrant day laborers. Yet today El Sol fills this space as it works to live out the mission of improving the quality of life for all residents of the town of Jupiter. El Sol strives to achieve this goal by organizing and supervising Jupiter's day labor hiring in a controlled and sanitary atmosphere; educating Jupiter's day laborers and contractors about their rights and responsibilities; assisting Jupiter's immigrant population to become an active and integrated part of the larger Jupiter community; building bridges and communication among a range of ethnic, cultural, and religious groups in Jupiter; and providing occupational training, language and literacy instruction, counseling, health education, legal services, and other services to individuals in need. The center's mission is based on the assumption that true integration occurs when immigrants and the native born work together to achieve common goals and resolve local issues. El Sol's primary function is as a day labor center that replaces the previous informal labor market on Center Street.

But beyond its functions as a labor center or hiring hall, El Sol has become the locus for a more expansive process of immigrant integration in Jupiter.

A Local Community Grapples with a National Issue

El Sol formally opened in 2006, but the process of planning and organizing for the center began many years earlier. The context of the center's founding, and the controversies that its founders worked to resolve, offer several important insights into the process of mobilizing local communities to address issues that emerge around a growing unauthorized workforce. As in many communities around the United States, the most visible manifestation of the growing immigrant community in Jupiter in 2000 was the group of day laborers who gathered along Center Street each morning seeking work. The apartments and duplexes along Center Street and the surrounding neighborhoods had long served as affordable housing, but as the construction industry boomed in the late 1990s and early 2000s, the number of day laborers on the street swelled to between 150 and 200 per day. While some lived in the apartments on the street, other migrants walked from nearby neighborhoods to seek work. Hiring began as early as 6:00 a.m., but groups of job seekers frequently remained on the street through the early afternoon. As it has in communities from Virginia to California, the visible presence of immigrant day laborers in a public location quickly became a flashpoint for a number of interrelated issues and concerns.[5]

As part of an initiative aimed at improving the quality of life in some of the older neighborhoods (called Charter Neighborhoods), the town encouraged local residents to form groups that would discuss neighborhood improvements and other issues. It quickly became evident to town authorities that immigration was the primary issue on the minds of residents living close to Center Street. Many longtime residents complained bitterly that homes in their single-family neighborhoods were changing to rental units, now filled primarily by migrant laborers. Complaints about the day laborers on Center Street ranged from public urination to harassment of women by workers. Large construction and landscaping vehicles were pulling into residential neighborhoods early in the morning to pick up workers, leading to further grumbling. Although the housing bubble was still rapidly inflating during this period, residents also complained about lowered property values resulting from the immigrant influx in their neighborhoods.

Concerned residents regularly attended town council meetings to voice their opinions about the immigrant population in Jupiter, frequently mixing complaints about local quality-of-life issues with general concerns about immigration. A 2004 article from the *Jupiter Courier* exemplifies the sort of rhetoric that characterized the complaints: "Longtime residents complain of noise, trash, public urination and drunkenness and an environment that threatens their safety. 'We've had fights and stabbings and the problems are getting worse,' said [a concerned resident]. . . . 'You hardly ever see residents walking or jogging anymore . . . and what really irks me is that they are working illegally.' "[4]

Approximately twenty residents began to attend council meetings wearing red shirts, to protest that the town was not taking action on their complaints. During the public comment period, residents would address the council to voice their concerns and implore the town council to call immigration authorities. One resident claimed that twenty-seven men were living in a single three-bedroom home on her street. Others made statements linking Jupiter's immigrants to everything from local litter problems to crime, drug use, and gangs.[5]

Representatives of the town of Jupiter did, indeed, attempt to contact immigration authorities, and ICE conducted limited operations in Jupiter. Yet, as town authorities would soon discover, the impact was minimal, and immigration authorities seemed unconcerned. In an interview with CNN, Jupiter police chief Richard Westgate explained, "We have called INS in the past. The illegal immigrant situation with the Guatemalans is not a high-priority item with INS, but it is a local problem."[6]

Native-born residents of the town were not the only concerned parties, though. For the workers, the informal process of being hired was very dangerous. Because those who hired them had relative anonymity, workers were exposed to physical danger and in some cases were assaulted and robbed by those who ostensibly hired them. Furthermore, abusive employers could, and often did, deny day laborers pay after the work had been completed. People hiring the immigrant workers knew that there was a very small chance, if any, that workers would report them for wage theft, and this made immigrant workers extremely vulnerable. A string of robberies targeting migrants in Jupiter highlighted the vulnerability of the migrant population:

> Five [migrant workers] were robbed at gunpoint and left in a cemetery along County Line Road in Martin County, the latest of what investigators believe are dozens of Hispanic victims. . . . "They were targeting Guatemalans, and Guatemalans don't believe in banks," said Martin County Sheriff's Detective Leo Ferreira. . . . Jupiter police and sheriff's detectives are still trying to track down victims, but believe that there

could be 50 or more, many of whom never reported the holdups. . . . The Jupiter location was hit repeatedly.[7]

The immigrant community also felt these simmering tensions. Workers on Center Street were frequently the targets of insults and trash thrown from passing cars. Many immigrants reported acts of discrimination and outright intimidation in neighborhoods and local businesses. In one particularly egregious incident, someone painted over a "Slow Children Crossing" sign in front of the Jupiter elementary school, so it read: "Slow Illegal Immigrant Children Crossing."

Many communities across the United States find themselves facing similar issues to those that plagued Jupiter during this period. A brief overview of the history of the process offers insight into how—in Jupiter and other similar communities throughout the United States—immigrants can, indeed, mobilize effectively, and communities can be proactive in addressing issues related to unauthorized immigration. In Jupiter, the process of moving from identifying the problems to gaining a coalition in support of a reasonable solution did not happen overnight. The Jupiter story thus also reveals which forms of alliance are likely to be most influential in the process.

Building Bonds and Bridges: From Fiesta to Mobilization

The immigrant community in Jupiter first began to organize itself around cultural and religious concerns. In 2001, representatives of the Jacaltec Association in Jupiter solicited meetings with representatives from the local university in order to discuss a cultural exchange event on campus. In the process of talking about potential events, the possibility of having some marimba music, traditional dancing, a parade, and a soccer match between students and the migrants emerged. The leaders of the Jacaltec community soon began planning the celebration of the fiesta for the Virgin of Candelaria, the patroness of the town of Jacaltenango. They organized committees to be in charge of various aspects of the fiesta—the flowers, the deer dancers, the music, the food. Soon the Jacaltec community was meeting weekly to organize the fiesta. Later that year, more than seven hundred people attended the first celebration in the newly minted Abacoa community, an upscale and predominantly white planned community that houses the campus of Florida Atlantic University. The large event illustrated the success of the Jacaltec community's mobilization.

The process of organizing the first fiesta revitalized the Jacaltec organization in Jupiter, and they set out to reestablish Corn Maya, a nonprofit organization formed by Mesoamerican refugees and advocates in south Florida in the early 1980s. The organization had been founded initially to represent and assist the thousands of refugees, mostly Mayan, who were fleeing civil wars in Central America. Though Corn Maya was still active in the community, its nonprofit status had lapsed in the late 1990s. In 2002, the organization renewed itself in the process of planning Jupiter's Fiesta Maya, and it regained nonprofit status. The Jacaltec community forged strong bonds of solidarity while planning the fiesta. As this community worked with the local university and some town authorities to organize events, important alliances began to develop as well. Soon after the reestablishment of Corn Maya, the organization secured enough funding to rent a small office space in Jupiter, from which they ran a small-scale pilot program featuring many of the services that later would be offered at El Sol. Demonstrating the importance of new alliances, students from the local university began teaching ESL courses to members of the immigrant community.

These initial contacts between immigrants (now organized under Corn Maya) and the local university facilitated the further mobilization of the immigrant community. Faculty members from the local university worked to persuade town authorities of the need for a labor center, as they undertook research and presented the findings to town authorities. Meanwhile, the student group of ESL teachers evolved into an official student organization aiming to support local migrants in a range of ways. Another key partner organization for the migrant community was the local Catholic church. Prompted by activists from an organization called People Engaged in Active Community Efforts (PEACE), a congregation-based community organization, leaders of Jupiter's migrant community held a series of meetings at the local Catholic parish in Jupiter, St. Peter's.

To build a coalition of support for a labor center, representatives of Corn Maya also made themselves available to any local groups interested in learning about the immigrant community, the problems related to day labor, and potential solutions. Working contacts already made with the local university, representatives of the group spoke to the Jupiter Democratic Club and met individually with town council members and the town manager. In 2005, the bonds between Jupiter and Jacaltenango were further strengthened through the signing of a sister city agreement between the two towns. Although the event was primarily symbolic, it offered representatives of the Florida town (the mayor in particular) the opportunity to interact with representatives of the immigrant community for an extended period of time. As she would later recount, this interaction shaped her perspective on the labor center and on other issues related to the immigrant community.

Over time, this nascent coalition of immigrants, representatives of the Catholic Church, university students and faculty, and community residents coalesced around the need to open a labor center, which would address concerns about immigration and day labor in Jupiter. The coalition members, however, faced steep opposition from local groups at town council meetings. Residents who opposed the idea of a labor center organized as Jupiter Neighbors Against Illegal Labor (JNAIL). Members of JNAIL attended town council meetings wearing red shirts and voicing their opposition to the possibility of a labor center. At one meeting, a member of the opposition held up an enlarged photograph of Mohamed Atta's Florida driver's license to imply that by supporting a labor center, the town of Jupiter would be inviting terrorists to move in. Members of JNAIL also expressed concerns about the alleged "illegal activity" surrounding Jupiter's immigrant population. An attendee at a town council meeting explained that he "did not understand how a hiring hall would address the problems of drugs, crime, prostitution, overcrowding and gangs," while another attendee stated that "the Town needed to stop enabling illegal activities and did not feel there was a need for a hiring center."[8]

The idea of the labor center also attracted national attention. The Federation for American Immigration Reform (FAIR) sent a letter to the town of Jupiter opposing the center. Mark Foley, a member of the United States House of Representatives at the time, also sent a letter to the town of Jupiter expressing his opposition. *Lou Dobbs Tonight* even featured Jupiter's initiative in a segment depicting groups of Hispanic men climbing onto pickup trucks, as well as overcrowded streets and angry Jupiter residents.

In this tense environment, the town council scheduled a roundtable discussion on the "labor issue" for their February 2005 meeting. At this discussion, Mayor Karen Golonka "provided a table delineating the issues that seemed most important to residents and Council." These included "neighborhood deterioration, Center Street as a nuisance, Day Labor Center, cultural assistance and illegal immigration."[9] A major turning point in the process came when the possibility of a labor center was listed as a formal discussion item at a public town council meeting. As occurred during many of the town meetings in that period, twenty or so members of the JNAIL group were present to express their opposition to the center. Yet this time more than one hundred immigrants, students from the local university, and other neighborhood supporters mobilized to offset the opponents' presence. Members of this group attended the meeting wearing blue T-shirts with a logo for the resource center. As many spoke out in support of the center, the tide began to turn in El Sol's favor.

The visible mobilization of the immigrant community and other supporters profoundly influenced the town council. Councilor Jim Kuretski, who had been attending the coalition meetings, threw his support behind El Sol. Both he and the mayor had been challenged in the 2004 election by candidates who opposed the creation of a center, yet both won handily. In the 2005 elections, council member Kathleen Kozinksi, one of the most vocal opponents of the center, lost her seat to Robert Friedman, a local architect who supported the creation of a center. The ground was now set for a move forward. After much debate and the consideration of many alternative options, the town council voted to lease a recently purchased church building to Corn Maya, a group called the Friends of El Sol, and representatives of Catholic Charities so that these three organizations could collaborate to run the center.

The key to this process and the center's success was that immigrants themselves were at the heart of the movement. They put the center at the top of their agenda and chose a path of collaboration and coalition building rather than continuing to live their lives in the shadows. While some local activists had promoted a confrontational strategy to demand that town authorities open a center, immigrant members of the coalition sought instead to move forward by working within the structure of the town's procedures.

"I Wanted to Give Something Back": The Impact of El Sol

Since opening its doors in 2006, El Sol has provided both a critical set of services for immigrant integration and a pathway for some longtime Jupiter residents to conceive of immigration in more human terms. El Sol hosts a community service program through which immigrants give back to the community by participating in monthly volunteer projects. A legal clinic at El Sol helps workers to address wage theft, immigration issues, and other legal concerns. The Health Committee at El Sol organizes a yearly health fair where basic services, such as immunizations and health screenings, are provided. The food program at El Sol serves two meals a day, seven days a week. Among the most important programs provided at El Sol is the educational program, which hosts daytime and nighttime English classes, computer literacy classes, financial literacy courses, vocational training, family literacy classes, and civics courses. The immigrant community of Jupiter takes full advantage of the programs offered at El Sol, entering an avenue for integration and community participation that otherwise would be unavailable to them.

El Sol's success can be measured both by the center's impact on the daily lives of the immigrants who use it and by the center's resolution of a range of problems for immigrant and nonimmigrant residents of the town of Jupiter. El Sol's programs and outreach have established links between a remarkable range of local institutions and the immigrant community. Shortly after the opening of El Sol, Jupiter's elementary school opened a dual-language program. The same school allows the immigrant community to utilize its soccer field for a Sunday league. The Jupiter Public Library accepts identification cards issued by El Sol as appropriate documentation to obtain a library card. In addition, the town now has a place to inform and connect with the immigrant community. Prior to the opening of El Sol, the migrant community held a strong distrust of the police, but levels of trust have increased since police officers began coming to the center to report on issues of local concern (ranging from bike theft to gangs), and immigrants now report crimes to the police with more frequency.

Since the center opened, help from unexpected places has also broadened the scope of services El Sol provides. For example, several banks have given workshops about the U.S. banking system and opened checking and savings accounts for El Sol clients, who were previously targeted by criminals because they were known to carry their savings and wages in their pockets. El Sol also receives local support from grocery stores, coffee shops, restaurants, and other businesses that donate to the lunch and breakfast programs, and the Chamber of Commerce and local and regional newspapers have endorsed the El Sol Center.

Many towns around the United States have witnessed ugly confrontations and even violence in the face of similar issues. By contrast, this town has mediated community tensions by successfully moving the informal labor market and associated problems to a clean and organized structure, which also builds a critical bridge between the immigrant and native-born populations of Jupiter. The El Sol Center has evolved into an innovative community-building initiative that successfully resolves local tensions by bringing a range of ethnic, racial, and religious groups together to collaborate in problem solving and network building.

An event that transpired on Christmas Eve 2009 clearly illustrates the success of the center. A worker entered and approached the director as the center was about to close. When she asked how she could help him, he held out $40 and said, "When I lost my job I came to the center and I was able to improve my English and find steady work . . . I know it is not much, but I wanted to give something back to El Sol." There could hardly be a better measurable outcome of positive integration than this young man's gesture.

"Restoring Order to the Streets of Jupiter":
Challenges and Opportunities

While El Sol has been successful, it has had to face several challenges in its short history. Perhaps the most visible challenge that El Sol has faced to date comes from protesters. El Sol's success has made it a magnet for anti-immigrant groups and a rallying point for Jupiter residents who are upset by the lack of immigration reform or enforcement from the federal government. The group that most opposed the opening of El Sol before the Jupiter town council was JNAIL, but that group did not last long after the opening of the center. Beginning in late 2007, a new group calling itself Floridians for Immigration Enforcement (FLIMEN) began protesting outside El Sol on Saturday mornings. FLIMEN is not from Jupiter, but they picked El Sol as part of their Florida-wide campaign in December 2007 "to protest the distribution of Guatemalan Consular ID cards by the Mobile Guatemalan Consulate," as stated on the group's website. The group continued to protest at El Sol on a weekly basis, brandishing signs asking the mayor and the town to shut down El Sol and making such broad and generalizing statements about immigration as "Immigrants Depress Wages" and "Stop the Invasion." Protesters photographed employers who went to El Sol looking to hire day laborers. In an interview with the South Florida *Sun Sentinel*, David Caulkett, the vice president of FLIMEN, said: "The town of Jupiter is a symbol of what is wrong with this country. Jupiter is blatantly complicit in felonious hiring transactions." [10] El Sol detractors also made their voices heard through the local newspapers. A December 2007 opinion letter sent to the *Palm Beach Post* read: "[The mayor] should be supportive of federal laws that were enacted to protect her and the citizens of Jupiter. Instead she chose to support the interests of foreign nationals who have no legal status to be in this country, yet work here, over the interest of American citizens." [11]

For groups like FLIMEN, El Sol represents a magnet for immigrants and demonstrates the lack of enforcement of immigration laws. Ironically, the presence of these protesters has served as a recruiting tool for El Sol. Many Jupiter residents who drive by on Saturday mornings are outraged by the nativist slant of the protesters' complaints and are motivated to volunteer their time or make donations to El Sol. El Sol has welcomed many of its most involved and vital volunteers as a result of the Saturday protesters. With the reelection of three of the strongest supporters of El Sol to the town council in March 2010, the protesters gave up their vigil, and they have yet to return to El Sol.

Despite its many ongoing challenges, the story of El Sol is the story of successful immigrant mobilization in a small community that has opted to address issues related to immigration positively at the local level. In taking this approach, Jupiter offers a profound alternative to the approaches developed in many surrounding local communities. Rather than developing laws and relationships with local governing bodies that aim to deflect immigration by making the local community inhospitable to new immigrants, Jupiter's residents developed initiatives and relationships with local government and organizations that aimed to build trust and to develop common solutions to shared problems on the basis of this trust. In the process, El Sol has improved the quality of life for both immigrants and the native born. As Dan Moffet, a member of the *Palm Beach Post* editorial board, explained:

> The practical value of the El Sol experiment is self-evident. Dozens of workers aren't flagging down vehicles on street corners looking for jobs each morning. El Sol brought structure and safety to what was messy business. Congress has failed to solve the immigration problem, but the center has succeeded in restoring order to the streets of Jupiter.[12]

Moffet's opinion has been echoed by local residents in Jupiter. In the documentary *Brother Towns*, one young Jupiter resident explains his opinion to the interviewer:

> I live [very close to the immigrants] . . . they always ride their bike by my house and everything . . . they always throw trash by my yard and everything . . . I'm not even joking about that . . . it had become a big problem, but they opened the El Sol Resource Center and that's helped out a lot.[13]

Perhaps most notably, the sense of restored order and security is shared by longtime residents and newcomers as well. Members of the immigrant community have come to embrace the center and see it as a place where they feel welcome and safe. In an interview with the *Palm Beach Post*, one young worker expressed an often repeated theme within

Jupiter's immigrant community: "Before El Sol, I found work standing on Center Street. I was robbed once. Here, I feel safe."

Lessons from the El Sol Case: Solidarity, Bridge Building, and Local Action

A number of key elements of the Jupiter model merit attention. First, prior to the opening of El Sol, the ethnic, linguistic, and religious homogeneity of the initial mobilizing group was crucial to the initiation of the project. This homogeneity created in-group solidarity. The initial group of Jacaltecos used cultural and religious ties to organize the first fiesta and mobilize a base of support. Jupiter's Jacaltecos generated solidarity by organizing people around a common goal and a common identity. From there, they mobilized to reestablish the nonprofit Corn Maya Inc.

Second, the immigrant community did not mobilize itself alone; it sought connections with nonimmigrant Jupiter residents by establishing networks with local government and nongovernmental organizations, including the local university, local churches, and political groups. Educational and religious institutions served as crucial bridges to the community, providing resources and garnering community support from students, residents, and parishioners.

Third, religious institutions played a particularly significant role in this process. Religious organizations have been among the only social organizations open to Jupiter's new immigrants. Churches provided spaces, resources, lay leaders, and clergy who helped to mobilize both the immigrants and those who share the pews with them. As we emphasized in Chapter 4, churches and other religious organizations are key actors on the front lines in places like Jupiter and in other new destinations for immigration from Latin America.

Fourth and finally, the process of founding El Sol required a range of educational initiatives. Representatives of the town of Jupiter went through a long process of education about the immigrant community and how other cities had dealt with the issue of day labor. It was particularly important to create nonconfrontational opportunities for interaction between the town council members and representatives of the immigrant community, in such venues as the sister city event. The immigrants also had to be educated about the benefits of using El Sol and leaving Center Street. This required a process of trust building between leaders of the immigrant community and the town. The El Sol center is located on the same campus as the police station, and it took time to convince immigrant leaders that the local police were not planning to report them to the immigration authorities.

Perhaps most important, the El Sol solution was framed as a local response to local issues. El Sol is not capable of addressing issues of national immigration policy. National and international forces are far beyond the control of local authorities, but these have tangible and deleterious effects in specific communities. Although El Sol has not avoided protesters who seek to utilize the center as a lightning rod for national immigration debates, the center's mission has always been to serve as a local institution with a focus on improving the quality of life for everyone in the local community. The center has drawn upon both the remarkable solidarity and organization of immigrants from a particular region of Guatemala living in Jupiter and the openness and accessibility of local government and local institutions. In other local communities, however, both in-group solidarity and opportunities for building bridges between immigrants and local organizations are profoundly limited by the tenuous conditions in which new immigrants live and by a climate of hostility that influences local government and other institutions. We travel now to LaGrange, a small city in west-central Georgia, seeking to understand how mobilizations have formed in this very different local context.

The Alterna Community

A modest brick bungalow with a deep front porch, the home of Anton and Charlotte Flores looks, from the exterior, no different from the homes of other working- and middle-class families in this ethnically diverse neighborhood in the small town of LaGrange, Georgia. Visitors are welcomed to this home with a small sign, drawn by a child, that is posted adjacent to the screen door. Entering this home on a typical Monday or Tuesday evening, though, a visitor encounters a scene that is both simple and remarkable: Latino immigrant and American families crossing boundaries of citizenship status, class, and ethnicity to gather for a shared meal. As tables are pushed together and couches pushed aside, and as families crowd into the kitchen to pile food onto their plates, the participants begin not only a meal that sustains their bodies but also a set of spiritual practices that sustain their community. These include dining together, praying together, singing together, and reflecting together on biblical texts.

The families that gather under this roof constitute Alterna, an intentional Christian community built from what its co-founder, Anton Flores, describes as a "fearless love" that "crosses borders." Anton makes clear that a culture of fear pervades the lives of both immigrants and nonimmigrants:

> The immigrant knows fear. She knows fear the moment she turns her back to her home and takes her first legally unauthorized step to "El Norte." He knows fear the very moment he steps into the Arizona desert braving the brutal elements and trusting the potentially

unscrupulous coyote. They all know fear every time
they drive (unable to obtain a license) down a Cobb
or Gwinnett county road on their way to work or worship or Wal-Mart. Then there are the irrational fears of
some U.S. citizens. At times, I rail against the absurdity
of these fears that are so easily manipulated by certain
politicians and their hate-group affiliates, all for some
narrow self-interest like amassing political power or
personal prestige. Ultimately however, the power and
prestige these individuals have are illusory. Real power
can only be found in selfless love, and the good news is
everyone can be powerful because everyone can love.[14]

The members of the Alterna community firmly believe that
"fearless love" makes *all* cross borders, and that it releases
not only the poor and marginalized but also the privileged
and wealthy, who often descend into a "pit of selfish ambi-
tion," "impoverished and possessed by possessions."[15] Anton
explains: "Charlotte and I now live in a cooperative housing agreement with two families from Guatemala, two from
Mexico, and three from the United States. Across all imag-
inable barriers we pray for one another, serve one another,
and love one another. We are families from three different
countries united in love, demonstrating an *alternative* to this
culture of fear. That is why we are called *Alterna*."[16]

Alterna describes itself as "a Christian missional community comprised of U.S. citizens and Latin American immigrants committed to faithful acts of accompaniment,
advocacy, and hospitality."[17] Their work in Georgia includes
assisting immigrants, and particularly the unauthorized, as
they confront the daily challenges of consumer, employment, legal, medical, and housing-related negotiations; engaging in advocacy on local, state, and federal policy issues,
with the aim of bringing about laws and policies that "better

reflect the Values of the Reign of God"; offering workshops and training to churches, schools, and other local organizations that assist them in better understanding the issues surrounding immigration in their local community; monitoring courts to ensure that immigrants receive fair treatment and adequate representation; facilitating Spanish-language Bible study in the county jail; and hosting visitors and overnight guests, including immigrants in acute crisis. Alterna also promotes local food consumption by maintaining a community garden as a food source and learning plot and by gifting chicken coops to local immigrant families.

Alterna organizes a range of advocacy efforts as well. The most significant of these are the annual Holy Week Pilgrimage for Immigrants, which began in 2009 as an effort to "pray with your feet" for unauthorized immigrants, and the Georgia Detention Watch, a coalition that monitors conditions at a nearby federal immigrant detention center and actively challenges practices at the center that they deem inhumane and unjust. Alterna's work, and particularly the leadership of Anton Flores, has been increasingly influential, not only in this west-central Georgia community but also in metro Atlanta. In 2010, Anton Flores was named by *Atlanta Latino* newspaper, the largest independent Hispanic newspaper in Atlanta, as "*Atlanta Latino*'s Person of the Year." [18]

The "Smallest of All Seeds": The History of Alterna

Members of Alterna make clear that their project emerged not as a political movement to challenge immigration policy but as a set of concrete relationships. In the words of Anton, "My introduction to the issue of immigration and illegal immigration was through relationships, and I think that has been one of the keystones of Alterna, that we are always trying to humanize and also trying to help people see the importance of relationships preceding ministry."[19] Ramona, an immigrant from Mexico City and a co-founder of the Alterna Community, explained, "When we founded Alterna, we didn't know what Alterna would be, but our work has been a blessing from God." She described Alterna as akin to the "mustard seed" described by Jesus in a parable.[20] She explained that it began as the "smallest of all seeds," but, with faith, it has grown to become a tree in which birds can come to make nests and rest.

The seeds of Alterna were planted in 2000. In that year, Ramona and her son arrived in LaGrange to reunite with her husband, Eduardo, who had come to work several years prior. Eduardo had work, with members of his family already in LaGrange, but the challenges facing the family were significant. They encountered extremely difficult living conditions, and both Ramona and her son were beset with illnesses. Partly because of the need to care for and accompany his mother, and partly as a result of his own illnesses, her son missed thirty days of school during his first year in LaGrange.

During that year, Anton and Charlotte Flores also were undergoing significant life change. They adopted a son, Jairo, from Guatemala. Anton, a Puerto Rican born in New York but raised in Atlanta, and Charlotte, a white American from Spartanburg, South Carolina, sought a way for their young son to stay in contact with Guatemalans and to learn the languages and cultures of his country of origin. They decided to attend a small Baptist church, Primera Iglesia Hispana. It had been founded two years prior as the first Spanish-language congregation in LaGrange, as a mission of Rosemont Baptist Church, a Southern Baptist congregation.

Although not reared Southern Baptist, Ramona and Eduardo also had begun to attend the church, and it was there that they met Anton and Charlotte. Ramona explained,

"We met Anton and Charlotte through the Iglesia Hispana and the English classes that they offered. So, there, we began a friendship, and we didn't know what this friendship would become." In December 2001, Ramona was pregnant with a second son and experiencing significant complications with the pregnancy. She had been hospitalized, and the Flores family visited her several times. When she was released from the hospital, she and Eduardo invited the Flores family to a New Year's Eve dinner at their home. They lived in a trailer park, a large complex of dilapidated trailers that could each be rented by the week and which served as a first destination for the majority of new Latino immigrants in LaGrange. Ramona explained, "At that time, the trailers in which we were living weren't very healthy or safe. They were filled with cockroaches and rats, and there were many problems there." Anton described his reaction to visiting them in their home for the first time:

> When we went to their trailer for the first time I was shocked by its deplorable condition. Not because I wasn't used to poverty housing; I had once worked as a school social worker in this community and had spent much time in many of our community's substandard dwellings. But this trailer park was different. It was comprised almost entirely of Latino immigrants, mostly single men who for various reasons—depression, estrangement, or culture—had strewn the trailer park with empty beer cans. I saw the roaches, Eduardo and Ramona told me about the rats and about the man from Atlanta who would bring prostitutes who would knock on the trailer doors soliciting their services. All this and the family was paying $100 per week for them and their eight-year-old son to live in this unhealthy environment. So I was left with a question. Not "What's my

political position on immigration?" but "How do I let my friends live this way?" That was the question I had to answer.

Anton and Charlotte had taken out a home equity loan on their home as a way to finance their son's adoption. When a house near their own home became available for purchase, they decided that the equity could be used for what Anton described as a "redemptive purpose." They offered to purchase the neighbor's home and provide it to Ramona and Eduardo for a rental rate that would bring them no profit. They asked for a three-year commitment from Ramona and Eduardo and explained that if at any time Ramona and Eduardo wanted to leave the home, they would split equally the equity that they had built in the home. Ramona and Eduardo agreed. Eight years later, the community has grown to include five free-standing homes, one apartment, a community garden, and three chicken coops. This cooperative housing agreement between friends developed into an intentional Christian community.

"Generous Simplicity": The Work of Alterna

The Alterna community strives to build solidarity between immigrants and nonimmigrants as a radical alternative to the culture that surrounds the community, and as an example that there is another way for immigrants and nonimmigrants to live, a path that diverges sharply from the path guided by fear. Alterna is a very small, inward-looking alternative Christian community that—shaped by the Anabaptist tradition of Christianity—seeks to live by the example of Jesus and his early followers, which compels the members of the community to reject many of the values of the world around them. Yet, because Alterna aims to accompany Latino immigrants living in their midst, the members of this small Christian community have found themselves engaging in a range of endeavors beyond the community, endeavors that work to make lasting and significant change in the local area, the nation, and the region of the Americas.

Alterna describes its intent as "to follow the *kenosis* example of Christ, who emptied himself, took on the form of a servant, and made his home among us, a community in need of redemption."[21] Alterna describes this commitment as based on a principle of "relocation: living a life of simplicity in solidarity with migrants."[22] The Alterna community also draws on the example of Jesus and his early followers to develop an attitude toward money described as "generous simplicity":

> There is no topic that Jesus focuses on more than that of our relationship to money. Our culture has convinced us that acquiring wealth is the means to being generous. We marvel at what mega-wealthy philanthropists do and say, "when I'm rich I'll . . ." But the truth is the average American is possessed by possessions, imprisoned by interest, and living such a fast-paced life that autodrafting a donation to our favorite charity is a twenty-first-century illustration of how we have redefined living simply and generously. Richard Foster states, "simplicity is freedom . . . brings joy and balance . . . is an inward reality that results in an outward life-style." We commit to waging war on the evil of materialism by offering all of our services pro-bono, living below our means, and being more generous with our time, talents, and treasure.[23]

This simple generosity serves as the foundation for the community's commitment to hospitality, particularly to people deemed "strangers." Alterna strives to live the biblical theme of "hospitality to strangers" as "the greatest antidote to our society's epidemic of fear." [24]

Early in the life of the Alterna community, the members undertook "an experiment to live within one mile of our home." Anton explained, "And that also meant, literally, love our neighbor. So we said, let's make all of our social interactions within a mile of our home." Ramona explained that from the day that she and Eduardo and their young children moved into the home, they began to have gatherings for members of the neighborhood: African American, Latino, and white families. They offered block parties and cookouts, outdoor concerts, and celebrations of such holidays as Three Kings Day, a traditional holiday celebrated throughout Latin America. Ramona explained, "And that was the beginning of Alterna. We were starting it without even knowing it. We started to realize how beautiful it was, to start something that we didn't even recognize, but the Lord knew. It began that way, and after that, we began to see the needs—the needs of the people in the community."

The members of Alterna quickly came to understand that hospitality and "love of neighbor" also would mean service to those around them. With the Latino families in Alterna as bridge builders and translators, Alterna's members simply began to offer help to Latino immigrants wherever it was needed: they began to monitor courts and visit prisons, to accompany Latino immigrants on visits to doctors, and to serve as intermediaries when immigrants faced difficult circumstances in their daily lives. Ramona explained that this path of accompaniment was one that her fellow Latino and Latina immigrants found difficult to comprehend: "Many people don't understand why we would leave behind the things that are for fun and also for our families, to work for the things of Alterna. Sometimes they think it is our work, and some even think that we work for the government. To the contrary! To the contrary!" Indeed, anyone familiar with Alterna's expanding work in the region would find it difficult to believe that the members of this intentional community work for the government. On a range of issues impacting the lives of unauthorized immigrants, Alterna has undertaken a series of endeavors that are in radical opposition to the work of the United States government, but that also engage government officials and policies in the spirit of reconciliation and with a commitment to "pursue peace through active nonviolence." As with Alterna's commitment to living in community, these values emerge, in their understanding, as a direct modeling of the actions of Jesus and his earliest followers, and they draw from New Testament texts, as well as a range of relationships and inspirations, to build the foundation for these commitments.

The Holy Week Pilgrimage for Immigrants, which we discuss in Chapter 4, is only one among several initiatives born out of the Alterna community's accompaniment of unauthorized immigrants. In early 2009, Anton began to consider the idea of a pilgrimage, a prayerful walk through north Georgia in solidarity with unauthorized immigrants. Reflecting later on the seeds of this idea, Anton explained that he was influenced by the civil rights movement, in which "walking was a way to draw attention to suffering and needs," and by several friends of his who were Buddhist monks and "whose order walks for peace." He explained that year after year, these monks would come to LaGrange, and the members of Alterna would walk with them. He continued, "The more I saw them, the more I realized that a lot of the transformation was inner: a conversation with others on the walk and internal dialogue and reflection." He developed the idea of the pilgrimage for immigrants and established contact, through a friend in Atlanta, with the director of Parish and Social

Justice Ministries for the Catholic Archdiocese of Atlanta. Engaging the networks of this ministry, Alterna quickly was able to build a five-day pilgrimage in which approximately 1,300 walkers participated. Most of them were Latino and Latina immigrants. Reflecting on the pilgrimage, Anton explained: "It is one of the few expressions I know that allows the political and the spiritual to intersect and that offers liberation to all: the people shouting us down and, most important, the immigrant. I know of another Holy Week pilgrimage, but it's mostly Anglo progressives. I like that this is owned and done by immigrants." When Anton discusses the first two years of the Holy Week Pilgrimage for Immigrants, he seems genuinely surprised by the groundswell of popular support and participation. Yet he also seeks actively to expand the pilgrimage by including a broad range of ethnicities and creating a more ecumenical event in which immigrants of a range of religious traditions can participate.

One of the most significant and controversial of Alterna's endeavors has been the group's work in and protest of the Stewart Detention Center, which opened in a very small, rural community in southwest Georgia in 2006. Alterna co-founded the Georgia Detention Watch, a coalition that catalogs human rights violations occurring inside the Stewart Detention Center, and that calls these to the attention of government and the media. As a member of Georgia Detention Watch, Alterna leads humanitarian visitations to the detention center. Volunteers visit with detainees as an act of love and solidarity, but they also ask detainees a series of questions about the conditions in which they live inside the center. Alterna shares this information with Georgia Detention Watch, which compiles the information into reports for distribution. Alterna's members, and particularly Anton Flores, have managed to develop a cordial working relationship with the warden of this detention center, which he hopes will facilitate his continued access to detainees.

The Stewart Detention Center was built in the economically depressed town of Lumpkin, Georgia, by the Corrections Corporation of America (CCA). In late 2006, after having its new prison lie dormant for a few years, CCA, the largest privately owned prison corporation in the United States, entered into an agreement with Stewart County and Immigration and Customs Enforcement to fill the medium-security facility with male detainees awaiting deportation. Currently, it is the largest immigrant detention center in the United States, with approximately 1,900 beds. Anton Flores described CCA's strategy in prison building as sort of a "field of dreams" approach: they found a remote, economically depressed area in need of jobs and built a large prison. Then they sought bodies to fill the prison—in this case, the bodies of unauthorized immigrants who had been detained by ICE. When the center opened in 2006, not all of these beds were filled, but largely as a result of surrounding counties' entry into 287(g) agreements with ICE and the expansion of the Secure Communities program, the center currently finds itself filled beyond capacity. The center exemplifies the complex relationship that private prison corporations, such as the Corrections Corporation of America, have with local communities seeking economic opportunity and with a growing prison industry that operates according to the principles of profitability. As National Public Radio recently reported, this industry, and CCA in particular, helped draft and secure passage of SB 1070 in Arizona, demonstrating how the emphasis on enforcement not only has profound effects on immigrants and their families but also on the health of U.S. democracy.[25] In this case, rather than a transparent public conversation informed by historical realities and the values of a representative democracy, the interests of powerful and lightly regulated corporations frame immigration policy.[26]

In a 2007 rally organized outside the Stewart Detention Center by Alterna, Anton Flores described this relationship: "We see here the building of detention centers that only serve to entice small communities in need of an economic infusion, so as to have them not realize their complicity in this whole structure that leads folks into an Exodus." In a stirring and impassioned speech, Anton made clear that the unauthorized immigrants who have been detained inside the facility are not the only victims of this system:

> So I say that when we can recognize that we are U.S. citizens who have gained from the exploitation of these individuals who have worked in our fields, who build our buildings—even government buildings, even barracks at Fort Benning [a military base in nearby Columbus]—when we can recognize that we are complicit in this benefit, in this economic exploitation, but when we also can recognize that we are the ones who are imprisoned with them, that our freedom and our justice is intertwined with theirs, then and only then can we say with clarity: "Let my people—my people who work here, who make their paychecks off of this— let them go! Let them live in a more just world." And to the twelve hundred who are in here who are not criminals, who are trapped in a political game, we can say, "Let my people go!"

Every year since 2007 Alterna has hosted a vigil outside the Stewart Detention Center in late November, and every year the message is the same: a call to solidarity across presumed boundaries of difference. The vigil calls for the working-class African Americans and whites who work in the prison to recognize what they share in common with the detainees whom they monitor, and it calls for citizens of the United States to recognize their own interconnectedness with unauthorized immigrants. For Alterna, border-crossing justice is the outcome of border-crossing love.

"A Bath of Cold Water": Challenges Faced by Alterna

By contrast to the case of El Sol, the Alterna community has confronted a range of challenges stemming from the lack of opportunity to build broad-based coalitions with local government and institutions. While Alterna's recognition has grown, its ability to build a coalition of supporters and co-laborers in their home region of LaGrange remains limited. Members of Alterna describe some local institutions as outright hostile to the immigrant community, and to Alterna by association.

The institutions that Alterna members most want to build alliances with are the local churches, but progress has been minimal. The church where the Flores family worships makes financial contributions and assists with cultural events, but Alterna feels the local church can and should do much more to exert their moral and spiritual influence. They seek for churches to address issues of injustice that impair immigrants' development and shape their experience in the community. For example, Anton explained,

> I always found it interesting that in LaGrange, the first Spanish-language congregation was actually Southern Baptist—not Catholic, not Pentecostal. And I think the reason that [the English-language] congregation [that founded Iglesia Primera Hispana] has—they still support the ministry of that congregation—I think that it was for very evangelistic ideals. They were a very

mission-oriented church, and they thought, "God is bringing people here, and they can go back and take the faith to their home countries." That was the goal: missions. I definitely wouldn't say that they had any understanding of solidarity or broader issues.

Ramona described the reaction of this church, where she first met Anton and Charlotte, when Alterna began to promote advocacy around immigration reform:

> Our church is a church of immigrants—we are almost all undocumented. The pastor, he is one of the exceptions. He has papers. So we began to inform the people and to share information about meetings and marches. Many were willing to participate, but others were not because the church limited them. The church limited them to such a degree that the pastor, one Sunday, saw one of our flyers about a march, and he came up to us and said that we shouldn't get confused. We shouldn't confuse the church with the things that are not of the church—that are outside of the church. So, for me personally, this was like a bath of cold water. Many of us in the church were illegals, and we needed immigration reform, and if we don't organize and march, we can't get that. So when the pastor told us that, it really bothered me. I thought that it was unjust, since he was one of the very few among us who had papers. But many people agreed with him. So this was something that made me decide that I would continue in the fight, but not from inside the church. I left the church. They always told me that we should just pray—that prayer was the response we should offer. And I said, yes, we should pray, but prayer without action doesn't have any outcome. Yes, I am one of those people—like Anton—

yes, I confide in God. Yes, I pray, but I also act. I won't
be passive in the things of the Lord.

With some sadness, Ramona continued to describe her current relationship to the church:

> So I decided to leave the church and to focus more on
> Alterna. Alterna fills me, and I also am able to give in-
> formation to the people, try to tell them about the laws,
> tell them to be careful, to tell them what's going on. . . .
> Many people think that I have strayed from the path
> because of the simple fact that I no longer go to the
> church, but I say that if the churches limit us in our
> work outside of the church, I say no—the Lord gave me
> freedom, I can't leave behind the love of freedom that
> the Lord gave me. I believe that my faith is strong—I
> pray, I try to communicate with the Lord in my wak-
> ing and in my going to bed, I try to give comfort to
> others, and if there is any necessity, I try to help. And
> now, what fills me is the Bible studies and the work of
> Alterna.

The radical alternative that Alterna embodies has not been
an easy path, and all members have experienced discourage-
ment and disillusionment. Anton recalled the beginnings
of his work at Alterna, and his desire at one point to leave
LaGrange for a city where his efforts on behalf of the unauthorized would be more appreciated: "It was very hard for
me to be in a small conservative town in the South with very
conservative values. At my church, there was never a cross.
But you've heard the question, 'Which would you take out of
your church first, the cross or the flag?' Well, in my church,
after September 11, they put a flag in! If there ever was a
time for a cross rather than a flag in the church, that would

be the time!" Before founding Alterna, Anton had struggled
to find a way to work inside powerful local institutions. Having built relationships with unauthorized immigrants, he
and his family saw a clear need for change, but they struggled to find a way to promote change. He ran for public office, hoping to work within the municipal government to
create lasting change. Ramona explained, "When he did not
win the position, he became very demoralized. He said that
he was going to move away from LaGrange. He kept saying
all the time that he was going to leave LaGrange." Ramona
recalled this period, when the two families had begun to live
in a cooperative housing agreement but had not yet formed
the Alterna community: "So, in one of our Bible studies,
he began to pray about this, saying that he wanted to leave
the town because he wanted to help the people. And I said
to him, 'Okay, Anton, you want to leave this town, but the
needs are here. Perhaps this is where the Lord is telling you
that you should be.' So these words stayed with Anton and
he decided, 'Okay, we will stay here.' And this was when we
began to see what Alterna would be."

Anton began to work full-time building this intentional
Christian community. He and Charlotte stayed a part of their
church, a nondenominational evangelical church, and they
stayed in LaGrange. Now, members of the church that Anton and Charlotte belong to often can be found visiting Alterna for a meal or special event, and some even support the
community financially. As Alterna's reputation grows within
the local immigrant community and within the state and national immigrants' rights community, Anton still holds the
transformation in the lives of the co-founders, Eduardo and
Ramona, as central:

> And to be honest, I think sometimes it's still like that,
> like, "Anton, what are you getting us into now?" But at

least now, eight years later, we have this deep, abiding trust and increasingly interdependent lives. Eduardo and Ramona's family has been transformed—they're earning equity and living in a safe, decent home; their children and ours are growing up like cousins. In fact, the most ironic part of this is that their oldest son, who missed over thirty days of school the year he lived in the trailer park, every subsequent year of his elementary education when he lived here with us in a healthier neighborhood, with parents who are very active in his education and with my wife, Charlotte, tutoring him during those formative years, every year of elementary school their eldest son was named, get this, "Citizen of the Year" at his school. And now, in high school, he's in Junior Beta.

Anton continued, a deep sadness entering his voice, "He's a junior in high school and we don't know what we are going to do to help him further his education."

A New "Demonstration Plot": The Impact of Alterna

One of the most important inspirations for Alterna is Koinonia Farm, a renowned intentional Christian community and pecan farm in Americus, Georgia. This community, with which Alterna maintains a relationship, was founded in 1942 as a "demonstration plot for the Kingdom of God."[27] Koinonia, whose ancient Greek name means "loving fellowship or community," developed as an interracial community where white and African American families could live and work in solidarity, surrounded by the poverty and racism of the Deep South. Koinonia played a crucial role in the civil rights movement, as a witness to simplicity, nonviolence, and racial solidarity, even as the community was targeted by firebombs, bullets, KKK rallies, threats, and excommunication from churches. The community suffered greatly during the civil rights era, but it survived and thrived, later birthing several other important movements, including Habitat for Humanity, and also initiating other intentional communities, such as Jubilee Partners, in Comer, Georgia, where refugees and the native born live in solidarity. Drawing on the inspiration of Koinonia, Alterna already has begun to initiate a movement of nonviolent activists for our day, who challenge the climate of injustice faced by unauthorized immigrants in America and the culture of materialism with which it is linked, while also demonstrating a profoundly compelling alternative.

The Alterna community models a radical alternative to "the world," with members attempting together to draw upon the example of Jesus and the early Christian church to offer a foretaste of the Kingdom of Heaven on Earth.[28] In contexts such as that of LaGrange and other relatively hostile new immigrant-receiving destinations throughout the Southeast, an alternative community such as this one may be among the only viable strategies for seeking a way forward and for seeking an antidote to the fear and misunderstanding that pervade local society. In the absence of opportunities to build broad coalitions with local and regional institutions, Alterna developed a model of collaboration that would stand apart from these institutions, offering both an exemplar and a challenge, and—perhaps most important—reminding those who took the opportunity to observe the community that there is indeed an alternative way to live in this world.

Although the members of Alterna may not be completely *of* this world, they still exist *in* this world, and the obstacles faced by all unauthorized immigrants also must be confronted by the community's members. Perhaps the most formidable and distressing of these obstacles is the dead end faced by the young adults in the community. They are among nearly two million young people in a generation who have come of age in the United States, but have a future neither here nor in their place of origin. It is to these young people that we turn now.

The Trail of Dreams

A few weeks before Anton Flores encountered Matt along the route of the Holy Week Pilgrimage for Immigrants, a much smaller group of pilgrims also had made their way to the Gwinnett County Sheriff's department. On Wednesday, March 3, day sixty-two of a five-month walk from Miami, Florida, to Washington, D.C., four young adults arrived at the office of Sheriff R.L. "Butch" Conway, seeking to meet with him. Juan Rodriguez, Gaby Pacheco, Felipe Matos, and Carlos Roa were walking what they called the Trail of Dreams, a form of nonviolent civil protest that aimed to call attention to the challenges faced by unauthorized students who have graduated from high schools in the United States and face significant barriers as they seek to continue their schooling. Along their journey through the Southeast, these four students became increasingly aware of the effects of 287(g) agreements in local communities, and they began to speak forcefully against such agreements as they traveled toward Washington, D.C. It was for this reason that they planned a stop in Gwinnett County, which had developed a national reputation as one of the least hospitable counties in the United States for Latino immigrants, and which recently had entered into a 287(g) agreement.

Before they began their walk on that March morning, the students wrote the telephone numbers of important contact people on their legs in permanent black marker. Three of the four were unauthorized immigrants, and, by publicly stating their status in Gwinnett County, they would risk detention and deportation. They needed to be prepared. With a small group of protesters and media representatives gathered around them, the four young walkers then left their trailer and traveled on foot to the Sheriff's Department. Sheriff Conway denied their request for a meeting, but they stood at a podium outside the Sheriff's Department and shared their stories. Gaby Pacheco explained, "Our message to Sheriff Conway—whether or not he meets with us—is that the law may say we shouldn't be here, but that doesn't mean the law is just. It's time to change the laws that are destructive to our communities. We immigrants must come out of the shadows of fear." [29] The young pilgrims were not detained on that day, and they continued on to Washington, D.C., drawing increasing attention to their movement and to the need for immigration reform as they slowly traveled north. After arriving in Washington, the Dream Walkers continued their journey. They traveled to Arizona to protest the passage of the state's controversial SB 1070 and met with Sheriff Joe Arpaio in Maricopa County, Arizona. After repeated attempts to meet with President Barack Obama, one of the "dream walkers," Juan Rodriguez, eventually succeeded. As the only one of the walkers with legal status in the United States, he was invited to meet with the president, while the others were denied access. Although he expressed deep disappointment in the president's decision not to meet with the entire group, he nevertheless took the opportunity to speak with the president about the urgent need for passage of the DREAM Act.

The Development, Relief, and Education for Alien Minors (DREAM) Act is proposed bipartisan legislation that would offer conditional permanent resident status to unauthorized young adults who were brought to the United States before the age of fifteen, had no criminal record, and graduated from high school. After six years and successful completion of two years of college or military service, they would be eligible to adjust their status to permanent residency. Since 2001, several forms of this bill have been introduced in both the House of Representatives and the Senate, and support for the act has continued to expand, but as of Juan's meeting with President Obama in the summer of 2010, the DREAM Act had not been passed into law. Juan and his fellow walkers not only aim to call attention to the need for this legislation through their commitment to nonviolent protest but also work to expand networks of unauthorized student activists and their supporters throughout the United States, who increasingly are organizing, marching, and engaging in acts of civil disobedience to promote the passage of this legislation and to draw more attention to the issues facing unauthorized immigrants.

The Problem of the DREAMers

Today, approximately 1.8 million undocumented children under the age of eighteen live and attend school in the United States. Undocumented minors account for around one-sixth of the total unauthorized population of the United States.[30] Hundreds of thousands of these children were brought to the United States by their parents, who worked in the segmented labor market to provide opportunities for their children. Felipe Matos, one of the Dream Walkers, is a young man whose childhood was split between Brazil and Florida. Felipe explained his own journey to the United States:

> My mother, like so many others in this world, went from the countryside to a big city seeking better opportunities. Her desire to better herself led her to work three jobs at a time for pennies, and in horrible conditions. Having to face abuse and poor living conditions,

she never found a way to get an education and like so many others got stuck in cycle of perpetual poverty. She saw in us, her children, hope to break the curse of scarcity that had followed her through her whole life. So she gave us her best, even if it meant that she wouldn't eat until her body couldn't take it anymore. I am in this country as a result of her reaching her physical limits and needing to send me away to be taken care of by other family members when she simply couldn't provide for me any longer. She dreamed again, with my departure, that an education in the United States could keep me forever out of poverty.[31]

The equal protection clause of the fourteenth amendment mandates that states provide K–12 education for unauthorized minors.[32] Because of the 1982 *Plyer v. Doe* Supreme Court ruling, unauthorized children such as Felipe have access to public education. Benefiting from the *Plyer* ruling, almost two million undocumented children are currently being educated in American public schools, joining clubs and student associations, acquiring leadership and organizational skills that help them participate in civil society, yet knowing that they soon will be excluded from full civic, political, and economic participation in the life of the nation.[33]

Approximately 65,000 unauthorized students graduate from U.S. high schools each year.[34] The *Plyer* ruling only addressed the issue of K–12 education, not higher education. This means that upon graduation from high school, unauthorized students have very limited options. If they want to enroll in a university in the state where they reside, they find themselves subject to out-of-state tuition because they are not legal residents of their states. Out-of-state tuition costs are more than 140 percent of in-state tuition costs, a prohibitive amount for many unauthorized students of modest means.[35] Public scholarships, federal loans, and other forms of financial aid are further out of reach, since neither the students themselves nor their parents can provide the documentation required for such benefits (social security cards, alien registration cards, or even driver's licenses).

Absent federal or state law to the contrary, the decision to admit and enroll unauthorized students belongs to the specific college or university. Federal law does not bar admission, but increasingly state laws are restricting admission. In 2003, only two states, Arkansas and Virginia, had introduced bills to restrict immigrant access to higher education, but by 2008, that number had increased to five, with the addition of Alabama, South Carolina, and North Carolina.[36] Legislators in several other states, particularly in the U.S. Southeast, have placed such restriction measures on their agendas for upcoming legislative sessions, while state boards of regents have prohibited colleges and universities in state systems from offering in-state tuition waivers to unauthorized students.

By contrast, several other states have passed legislation that allows unauthorized students to attend state universities and pay in-state tuition. Between 2001 and 2006, ten states, concentrated in the western and northeastern regions of the country, enacted laws permitting unauthorized students to pay in-state tuition. However, some of those states have, since 2006, considered rescinding such laws and have faced legal challenges to the laws. One state, Oklahoma, did indeed rescind the law in 2008.[37] California's AB 540 in-state tuition policy allows unauthorized students to pay in-state tuition if they meet several criteria: students must have attended California high schools for three or more years, must have graduated from a California high school, and must sign an affidavit promising to file an application to legalize their status. Although the law was challenged successfully in the lower courts of California in 2008, in November 2010 the California State Supreme Court decided unanimously to uphold the law.[38]

Those who advocate in support of the DREAM Act argue that states already have invested in unauthorized students, preparing them to continue their education and enter the highly skilled workforce. This would allow such students to contribute to the economy of their states in much more significant ways than they are able to at this point, when most—even those who have been able to earn a college degree—have no option in the United States but to work in the informal economy.

Betsy, a young woman who came to California from Mexico, explains how AB 540 allowed her to continue her education:

> I came to this country from Mexico when I was three years old. As a child, I never knew what being undocumented was until I started my senior year in High School. While everyone was applying to college and financial aid, I was told that I couldn't attend college because of my status. As the daughter of college-educated parents, I was however encouraged by my parents and peers to attend college through the AB 540 Bill. This bill has given me the ability to attend community college and now UCLA.[39]

While, for now, AB 540 provides some measure of relief, it is far from perfect: though students qualify for in-state tuition, they are not eligible for financial aid. Even if an unauthorized student is able to register for classes and complete the required credits for her degree, she cannot use the skills and education she acquired after graduation. Lu, a young woman from Peru, explains her experience after graduation:

"I received a bachelor's degree in anthropology in June 2008. Unfortunately, due to my immigration status I have had to decline job offers and unpaid internships as some of them require long-distance travel. It is hard to live knowing that what I would like to contribute to my adoptive country is restricted by the lack of a piece of paper. I hope that congress will decide to allow us to help move this country, our home, forward. Do not let our talents go to waste."[40] These unauthorized young adults make clear that the United States is their only home. For most, increased enforcement of immigration law and surveillance of the United States–Mexico border have meant that they have few, if any, ties to their country of origin—indeed, many have never traveled there. Isabel Castillo, a DREAM Act activist who graduated from a private college in Virginia with a degree in social work but is unable to practice her profession, explained in an interview, "I haven't been to [Mexico]. . . . For many DREAMers, sending us back to our 'home countries' is sending us to a foreign country. We are used to this culture. . . . Yes, I was born there, but I think my home is here."[41]

When "Your Dreams Are Shattered":
Embarking on the Trail

Student organizations have emerged across the country to call attention to the precarious situation of unauthorized young people. In Florida, for example, unauthorized students founded the Students Working for Equal Rights (SWER) group to "create possibilities and raise awareness in our communities about social justice and equal access to education, satisfying the needs of all individuals with a passion to further their knowledge, by means of grassroots organizing, political education, alliance building, nonviolent direct action and civic engagement." SWER makes extensive use of blogs and other social media to tell the personal stories of unauthorized immigrants, raising awareness and building a sense of community among unauthorized students. All four of the Dream Walkers were involved with SWER, and also with the Florida Immigrant Coalition (FLIC), a loose affiliation of grassroots immigrant organizations in south Florida.

In 2009, Felipe Matos, Gaby Pacheco, Carlos Roa, and Juan Rodriguez all were students at Miami Dade Community College, participating in a range of advocacy efforts developed by SWER and FLIC, as well as with student organizers around the country. When asked to explain their decision to embark on the trail at the dawn of 2010, they expressed frustration with the slow pace of change and with the structures and methods of traditional immigrant advocacy organizations. Challenging the methods of the groups with which he had been involved in Miami, Juan described to a group of students he met in Atlanta, Georgia, that he believed advocacy was about sacrifice and commitment, not about writing grant applications and organizing meetings. While in Atlanta, Felipe explained, "We felt that we already had protested in so many other ways and found no other option than to do something that required a big sacrifice, that showed the world that we were serious about what we were doing, and also because we were so trapped and . . . a little bit desperate because the situation wasn't getting any better." [42] Striving to escape their desperation and to exhibit the extent of their commitment to nonviolent civic action, the students began a walk, called the Trail of Dreams, from the Freedom Tower in Miami to Washington, D.C. These four young people walked 1,500 miles in an effort to "promote awareness about the need for just and humane immigration reform based on four core principles: (1) Equal access to education for immigrants, (2) An end to the separation of families, (3) Comprehensive worker's rights, (4) A pathway to citizenship." [43]

Carlos Roa, one of the Dream Walkers, explained his motivation for the journey in an interview with CNN's Kyra Phillips in May 2010:

> We did it because as undocumented individuals we wanted to share our stories with our own voices. For too long people have told our stories incorrectly. We have been demonized as "undocumented immigrants" when in reality all we want to do is contribute to this nation, give back to society and provide for our families. . . . I was brought here at the age of two, and all I know is this country, and yet I have limited access to higher education, I can't legally work, I can't legally drive, I can't join the military, which I tried after high school. It's really difficult to live your life and your dreams are shattered. There are hundreds of thousands of undocumented students like myself who want to give back to society and can't because of their circumstances, because the DREAM Act hasn't passed. . . . We did the walk because we wanted to end the nightmare of racial profiling programs, such as 287(g), and we wanted the DREAM Act to pass.

Juan Rodriguez's journey on the Trail of Dreams began a long time before he took the first steps from the Freedom Tower in Miami toward Washington, D.C. Juan recalled a personal episode in 2009 that solidified his commitment to the walk:

> I look back to early November when I came home one day utterly frustrated and depressed about the current state of the life of immigrants . . . and how compelled

I felt to just put on my shoes and begin walking on a journey for liberation. "I'm leaving," I told Felipe. "I can't keep waiting for them to give me an answer, hoping that maybe *someday*, someone will actually listen to my question. I can't just stay here in my daily cycles acting like this way of life is manageable or bearable. It isn't. It can *never* be bearable to lose the people that we love. It can *never* be bearable to wake up each morning and know that people in our communities have disappeared—taken in the darkness of the night by those that claim to be keeping our communities 'secure.'" Will you come with me? We have been working together for several years and we swore to see this battle through to the end, so can I count on you to come with me?"

Juan, Felipe, Gaby, and Carlos actively identify with a range of movements among marginalized groups throughout the history of the United States. They describe their trail's convergence with the Trail of Tears—the forced migration of Creek and Cherokee Indians from the U.S. Southeast in 1839. They also describe their walk as akin to the Underground Railroad. As Juan explained, "They would leave from one town and walk to another, where they would be welcomed by another group of dreamers who would understand their struggle and would help them carry their message into the next city as you go father and father north." [44] Along the trail, walkers visited key civil rights monuments and reflected on the resonance of their own movement with the black student activists of the Student Non-violent Coordinating Committee (SNCC). They were joined, south of Atlanta, by the local chapter of the NAACP as they counterprotested at a Ku Klux Klan rally focused on immigration. Furthermore, they explicitly engage the language and tactics of the LGBT movement in the United States, quoting such gay rights leaders as Harvey Milk and calling for unauthorized students to "come out" of the shadows and publicly announce their status.

Their deep and broad knowledge of the history of marginalized peoples in the United States (and in particular in the U.S. Southeast) is combined with a remarkable global sensibility. The students explain the influence of liberationist and indigenous rights movements in the region of Latin America, and they described in a discussion with Atlanta college students the ways in which eastern European student movements had influenced their strategies and motivation. They engage in civic action in ways that demonstrate a profound awareness of their historical location and a deep knowledge of the role of civic action and civic participation in shaping the democracy of the United States and movements for social change around the world.

"Out of the Shadows": The Dream Walkers Mobilize

As the Dream Walkers slowly made their way north, they were able to deepen and broaden networks with other local immigrant advocacy organizations they met along the trail, and also to inspire and support other local actions. As the four walkers left on the Trail of Dreams, the Fast for Families initiative was launched in Florida. Six people, including some facing deportation, fasted in a Miami church to ask "that the Administration acts in its Executive Authority to SUSPEND raids, detentions, and deportations against families with US citizen family members until there is a legislative resolution to our broken immigration system, and that the Administration sends the Secretary of Homeland Security, Janet Napolitano, down to South Dade to meet with the fasters to discuss what is happening in our community—the daily, violent separation of families."[45] Eventually several fasters had to be hospitalized, and the fast ended on January 17, but their efforts spurred several solidarity campaigns and additional fasts across the country.

The Dream Walkers spoke in many cities along their path, meeting community groups, law enforcement officials, the press, and other interested parties. The walkers also inspired a group of students from New York to embark on a similar walk. On April 10, 2010, Marisol Ramos, Martin Lopez, Daniela Hidalgo, Jose Luis Zacatelco, and Gabriel Martinez began a 250-mile walk to meet the Florida walkers at their final destination. Both groups arrived in Washington, D.C., where the walkers and their supporters staged a protest and a week of action calling for the passage of the DREAM Act and condemning Arizona's SB 1070 initiative.

Developing broad networks through the use of such social media as Facebook, Twitter, and texting, the Dream Walkers promoted several nationwide initiatives, such as the national Coming Out of the Shadows Week (March 15–21, 2010), during which unauthorized youth were encouraged to proclaim their status publicly and call for passage of the DREAM Act. Since they completed their walk, they have used the network of supporters they built to call attention to several specific advocacy opportunities, such as urging baseball commissioner Bud Selig to move the 2011 All-Star game from Phoenix, Arizona, and supporting the reintroduction of the DREAM Act in the U.S. Senate. The Dream Walkers also continued to participate in and attend a range of local advocacy events, consistently reminding those present not only of the need for passage of the DREAM Act but also of the need for immediate repeal of 287(g) agreements.

These young DREAMers exhibit remarkable energy and courage in the face of profoundly discouraging circumstances. An increasing number of unauthorized youth who would be eligible for adjustment of status under the DREAM Act are being detained and deported in counties that have 287(g) agreements with Immigration and Customs Enforcement, while several state governments, in the wake of Arizona's SB 1070, have signaled their intention to pass similar statewide enforcement measures and to develop statewide laws to further restrict access to higher education for unauthorized students.

"We Do Give Back to This Country":
The Impact of the Trail of Dreams

The year 2010 was a remarkable year of mobilization for the Dream Walkers and other DREAM Act activists. Largely as a result of their tireless work, more than nine years after its initial introduction in the U.S. Congress, and after several failed attempts at passage, the DREAM Act was reintroduced in the Senate on September 21, 2010, by the Senate Majority Leader, Harry Reid. It was incorporated into the National Defense Authorization Act for Fiscal Year 2011 (along with the controversial repeal of the military's "don't ask, don't tell" policy toward gay service members). The bill was filibustered in the Senate by all Republicans and one Democrat, including Republican senators who had been co-authors of previous incarnations of the bill.

In December 2010, undeterred immigrant youth converged on Washington, D.C., lobbying senators and making calls to promote passage of the DREAM Act. The Dream Walkers worked tirelessly at the forefront of this movement: visiting senators, making public statements for the media and for advocacy organizations, blogging, tweeting, and organizing callers. On December 8, 2010, their work seemed, finally, to be paying off. A revised version of the DREAM Act passed in the House of Representatives by a vote of 216–198.

Although prospects for passage in the Senate looked grim, they continued to press ahead.

The Dream Walkers emerged as among the most publicly recognized DREAMers. They took pains to remind elected officials of their untapped potential. In the words of Felipe, written in a December 10 press release, "Yesterday alone, we made 77,000 calls to urge senators to vote yes on DREAM; imagine what we can do on election day." [46] Indeed, callers shut down congressional switchboards in mid-December, with tens of thousands of phone calls each day. Gathered in Washington, D.C., from across the country to await a vote in the Senate, these DREAMers even organized a street-corner blood drive. In the words of one young woman from Texas named Lucy Martinez, "We're doing this to show that we have contributed to this society, and we do give back to this country." She also explained that the blood drive would serve as a reminder that "we're all human. We all have the same blood." [47]

Unfortunately, the DREAM Act has been framed by opponents in Congress and in the media as a veiled "amnesty" bill that would further open pathways for "chain migration." Continuing to trade in the currency of fear, Rep. Dana Rohrabacher (R-Calif.) spoke from the floor of the House of Representatives with these words: "Let's wake up, America. Your country is being taken from you and given to somebody else." [48] And, as Rep. Steve King (R-Iowa) simply stated, "If you support this nightmare DREAM Act, you are actually supporting an 'affirmative action amnesty act' that rewards people for breaking the law and punishes those who defend America." Congressional debate on the DREAM Act revealed the deep divisions and profound misconceptions that continue to guide the nation.

On December 18, 2010, as young DREAMers watched from a crowded gallery, wearing graduation caps and gowns, the DREAM Act fell five votes short of the sixty needed to bring it to the Senate floor for debate. The failure of the DREAM Act not only brought many young and idealistic DREAMers to the brink of despair but also signaled much broader trends in American immigration policy. Julia Preston of the *New York Times* reported, "The vote by the Senate on Saturday to block a bill to grant legal status to hundreds of thousands of illegal immigrant students was a painful setback to an emerging movement of immigrants and also appeared to leave the immigration policy of the Obama administration, which has supported the bill and the movement, in disarray." [49] The current administration's strategy for promoting comprehensive immigration reform, which has been to "ramp up border and workplace enforcement to attract Republican votes for the overhaul," [50] clearly has not proven effective, and the leaders of the newly elected Congress, particularly those taking control of the House Judiciary Committee, are "especially keen on tough enforcement." [51] In the context of profound anti-immigrant sentiment and increasing vitriol toward unauthorized immigrants, and in the midst of an economic recession, immigration reform faces steep obstacles. As young activists struggle mightily to gain the attention of the nation and to build upon common humanity and shared values, opponents make clear that misunderstanding and prejudice may win the day.

Despite the overwhelming obstacles they face, this new generation of American activists has come of age. In the words of Gaby, "We are part of the solution, and we are not going anywhere!" [52] These young activists are shaping a new generation of public leaders. They have mobilized thousands of people around their cause, built strong and durable networks with other key organizations, and organized hundreds of peaceful civil disobedience actions throughout the United States. The members of this growing movement of

DREAMers are remarkable in many respects. They are outstanding students and civic leaders who bravely have "come out" to proclaim their unauthorized status, at the risk of their own detention and deportation. They reject assertions that they are unworthy to participate in the polity of the nation-state because of their lack of formal citizenship. Revealing a profound irony, the actions of these "illegal aliens" clearly are those of good citizens of a republic, and they indicate that civic education may indeed still be a viable element of the American public education system. They already have injected vivacity and hope into American civic life, but whether they will be able to contribute fully toward the political and economic flourishing of America remains to be seen.

Conclusion: Laying Claim to Their Own Futures

Each of the movements we examine in this chapter is unique, and each takes a distinctive approach to addressing the issues that emerge for those who are "living illegal" in the United States. All of them, however, seek to overcome the politics of fear and to promote change in an immigration system that trades in the currency of fear. In the words of Felipe, one of the Dream Walkers, such movements call upon unauthorized immigrants to "finally come out of the shadows and lay claim to their own futures," and they call upon the native born to recognize the full humanity of unauthorized immigrants, seek common ground, and work toward an alternative to the current reality of a broken immigration system.[53]

These movements also directly address specific consequences of a broken system: the vulnerability of unauthorized day laborers, the local impact of 287(g) agreements, the impact of the private prison industry on detention and deportation strategies, and the precarious status of unauthorized immigrants who were brought to the United States as children. Each seeks to implement immediate and specific changes that will ameliorate some of the most corrosive effects of the system, working to relieve some of the pressures that emerge out of the broken system, and also pressing toward the greater goal of comprehensive immigration reform. Perhaps most important, these movements strive to push America beyond the polarizing and often poisonous discourse on unauthorized immigration, opening those involved to the human dramas and moral dilemmas behind the labels. As such, they are beacons of hope, pointing toward the possibility of a conversation on immigration that would, in the famous words of Abraham Lincoln, "be touched . . . by the better angels of our nature."

Conclusion

These are difficult times. Millions of Americans have lost their jobs and homes as the country struggles through the most acute economic crisis since the Great Depression. Unauthorized immigrants, who played a pivotal role in the dramatic expansion of the U.S. economy during the 1990s, have also suffered the impact of the crisis. Key sectors of the economy, such as construction, employed a large percentage of unauthorized immigrants. With these in sharp decline, the situation for immigrants is dire. In addition, the United States currently finds itself in the midst of what historian Daniel Kanstroom describes as "a large-scale, decade-long deportation experiment" that is testing America's core founding principles as a nation of immigrants that has lifted the "lamp beside the golden door" for "the huddled masses yearning to breathe free."[1]

The enforcement experiment now under way is predicated on the rapidly escalating policing, incarceration, and deportation of noncitizens, as part of the unprecedented growth of the prison-industrial complex.[2] The growth of this vast and minimally regulated complex is accompanied by some of the sharpest anti-immigrant rhetoric since the days of the Know-Nothing movement in 1840s and 1850s and the xenophobic fears of the Yellow Peril in the 1900s. All of these factors have made the daily lives of millions of immigrants extremely precarious, with little hope for improvement.

Nothing crystallizes the stark reality of living "illegal" in America more than the recent failure of Congress to pass the DREAM Act. Despite the hunger strikes, the pilgrimage across the country, the protests in front of Capitol Hill, and the 77,000 calls to Congress in one day, the DREAM Act failed to garner enough votes to avoid a filibuster in the Senate. Votes fell mostly along party lines. Only three Republicans joined the majority of Democrats in favoring the bill. Republican senators, such as John McCain (R-Arizona) and Orrin Hatch (R-Utah), who had supported the act in the past, voted against it, joining five Democrats from the new immigrant-destination states of North Carolina, Arkansas, Nebraska, and Montana to defeat it. The DREAM Act had already been approved, albeit narrowly, by the House of Representatives (216 in favor to 198 against) and had received support from fifty-six senators, both clear signs that the legislation was making some headway. Its ultimate failure was a bitter disappointment for the DREAMers and their supporters.

The unsuccessful effort to pass the DREAM Act also frustrated the Obama administration. During a press conference following the Senate vote and assessing his performance in 2010, President Obama declared,

[M]y biggest disappointment was this DREAM Act vote. You know, I get letters from kids all across the country—came here when they were five, came here when they were eight; their parents were undocumented; the kids didn't know—kids are going to school like any other American kid, they're growing up, they're playing football, they're going to class, they're dreaming about college. And suddenly they come to

eighteen, nineteen years old, and they realize even
though I feel American, I am an American, the law
doesn't recognize me as an American. I'm willing to
serve my country, I'm willing to fight for this country,
I want to go to college and better myself—and I'm at
risk of deportation. And it is heartbreaking. That can't
be who we are, to have kids—our kids, classmates of
our children—who are suddenly under this shadow of
fear through no fault of their own. They didn't break a
law—they were kids.[3]

A large part of the Obama administration's frustration
emerges from its failed long-term strategy to achieve immigration reform. Taking note of the fierce opposition that
scuttled the Secure Borders, Economic Opportunity and Immigration Reform Act of 2007 (S. 1348), the administration
devised an essentially reactive strategy, hoping that increased
enforcement would eventually persuade the public that the
federal government has control of the border and control
over "illegal" immigration. In turn, this shift in public opinion would provide Congress sufficient encouragement to vote
in favor of comprehensive immigration reform that would
provide a path to citizenship for some unauthorized immigrants. Despite the significant ramping up of enforcement,
however, Congress has failed to come up with more votes in
favor of immigration reform. As President Obama himself
put it:

[M]y administration has done more on border security than any administration in recent years. We have
more of everything—ICE, Border Patrol, surveillance,
you name it. So we take border security seriously. And
we take going after employers who are exploiting and
using undocumented workers, we take that seriously.

But we need to reform this immigration system so we are a nation of laws and we are a nation of immigrants. And at minimum, we should be able to get the DREAM Act done.[4]

Why would our elected representatives fail to support a piece of legislation that, in Obama's words, they know "in their heart of hearts . . . [is] the right thing to do"?[5] The DREAM Act was understood to be the easiest immigration reform bill to pass. According to Wayne Cornelius, a prominent scholar of immigration at the University of California, San Diego, the underlying problem "is that the entire Obama immigration policy strategy was based on a high-risk gamble that winning credibility on border and interior enforcement among members of Congress would buy the political space needed to enact comprehensive immigration reform."[6] As Cornelius made clear, the strategy failed to account for how effectively a tough stance on immigration would mobilize the Republican voting base, particularly in a period of economic recession.

But there is an even deeper problem with the current administration's strategy. The notion that the United States must have enforcement before and above anything else, even before the nation can have a rational and productive conversation about what kind of immigration policy would work for the country, gives the false impression that unauthorized immigration can be addressed simply by enforcing existing laws more strictly. The more elected federal officials try to show that they are tough on immigration, the more they reinforce the fears, prejudices, and the arguments of those who oppose any "amnesty" for "illegal" aliens. There is no end to the logic of "tougher than thou." As the failure to pass the DREAM Act shows, without a fundamental shift in the rhetoric surrounding the issue of unauthorized immigration,

Congress is unlikely to vote in favor of wider immigration reform, despite the administration's clear demonstration of greater success in border and interior enforcement.

What will be the next step for the United States? Studies have shown that the mass deportation of unauthorized immigrants advocated by some is not only logistically unrealistic but also prohibitively expensive. For example, a recent study by the Center for American Progress put the price tag for a five-year strategy of mass deportation of 10.8 million unauthorized immigrants at $285 billion.[7] In 2007, the head of Immigration and Customs Enforcement offered a lower estimate of $94 billion, but this figure is still considerable at a time of large budget deficits.[8] In response to these high estimates, groups supporting tighter immigration control, such as the Center for Immigration Studies (CIS), have proposed a strategy of "attrition through enforcement" to supplement efforts to secure the border. Such a strategy relies on a combination of "mandatory workplace verification of immigration status; measures to curb misuse of Social Security and IRS identification numbers; partnerships with state and local law enforcement officials; expanded entry-exit recording under US-VISIT; increased non-criminal removals; and state and local laws to discourage illegal settlement."[9]

It could be argued that the Obama administration has followed a version of the attrition-through-enforcement strategy with the vigorous implementation of 287(g) agreements and the rapid expansion of the Secure Communities Program. Thus far, the long-term effectiveness of this strategy as a way to solve the problem of unauthorized immigration is highly debatable. A recent study by the Pew Hispanic Center did find that the number of unauthorized immigrants has gone down from 12 million in March 2007 to 11.1 million in March 2009.[10] However, this reduction stems primarily from a drop in the inflow of unauthorized immigrants, not from the massive repatriation of unauthorized residents. Moreover, the sharpest decline in the population of unauthorized immigrants during 2007–2009 took place among those who came from the Caribbean and Central and South America (a 22 percent decline). The Mexican unauthorized population (which accounts for about 60 percent of all unauthorized immigrants) has leveled off since 2007 but has not declined.[11] In other words, the attrition-through-enforcement strategy does not significantly change migration patterns for the largest group of unauthorized immigrants. Indeed, among the immigrants we have encountered in Atlanta and South Florida, there is a generalized, if grim, resolve to hunker down, since it is preferable to live in the shadows and in constant fear than to lose all the investments they have made in this country: the houses and cars they have bought, the businesses they have built, and the local communities and churches to which they have contributed. They also express understandable reluctance to break up their families, which—more often than not—include members with legal status and citizenship.

The figures in the Pew Hispanic Center study are consistent with another, more plausible explanation for the drop in unauthorized immigration. According to Wayne Cornelius, nine in ten people who attempt to cross into the United States without authorization eventually succeed, despite the heavy militarization of the U.S.-Mexico border. Thus, Cornelius attributes the drop in unauthorized immigration less to enforcement than to the economic downturn: "what has changed drastically is the demand for Mexican labor in the U.S. economy."[12] If that is the case, what we are witnessing is nothing more than another predictable turn in the cyclical ups and downs that have characterized Mexican immigration to the United States. As we saw in Chapter 1, despite the fluctuations, Mexican unauthorized immigration has been a long-standing, structural feature of Mexico–U.S. relations. This historical dynamic may explain why the population of unauthorized Mexican immigrants holds steady despite the economic downturn and increased enforcement. This also suggests that unauthorized immigration from Mexico will likely pick up once again as the U.S. economy recovers.

Any examination of the strategy of attrition through enforcement must account for the heavy human toll that accompanies this approach. Profound damage is done to the fabric of American communities as they deport the neighbors and classmates of American children, break up the families of citizens, and fail to tap into the human potential of young people such as Jessica Colotl and Pedro Ramirez, the two college students with whom we began this book. The exclusive focus on enforcement and the criminalization of unauthorized immigrants leaves no spaces to generate alternative, productive conversations that might advance comprehensive immigration reform. In the wake of the failure of the DREAM Act, President Obama seems to have understood this difficult reality. When asked about what to do next, he responded:

> I'm going to go back at it, and I'm going to engage in Republicans who, I think, some of them, in their heart of hearts, know it's the right thing to do, but they think the politics is tough for them. Well, that may mean that we've got to change the politics. And I've got to spend some time talking to the American people, and others have to spend time talking to the American people, because I think that if the American people knew any of these kids—they probably do, they just may not know their status—they'd say, of course we want you. That's who we are. That's the better angels of our nature.[13]

Beyond the Myths about Unauthorized Immigration

The voices that we have heard here show, if nothing else, that the reality on the ground is far more complex than the stereotypes and myths that pervade public discourse on immigration reform.

First, unauthorized immigrants are a very diverse group, encompassing a variety of migration histories. This group includes Mexican farmworkers who have been crossing the border back and forth for generations, following the agricultural seasons; Brazilian middle-class professionals who have overstayed their visas; and young children brought from Guatemala by parents fleeing political persecution. Thus, it is simply wrong to characterize unauthorized immigrants as part of a homogeneous multitude storming the borders of the United States.

Second, unauthorized immigrants are more likely to be victims of violence in their quest for a piece of the American dream than to be perpetrators of violent crime and threats to the safety of communities. The misleading association between unauthorized immigrants and violent crime was crucial to the passage of SB 1070 in Arizona, with Governor Jan Brewer claiming that she had to sign the bill to avoid "murder, terror, and mayhem" in her state.[14] According to FBI reports, though, violent crime is down along the Southwest border region of the United States. For example, between 2008 and 2009, the number of violent crimes dropped by 14 percent in Arizona.[15] Certainly the United States has the right and the responsibility to secure borders as protection against those who would do harm to the nation. Yet there is a clear disconnect between policies such as SB 1070 and the demand for protection along these lines. This disconnect prompted Doris Meissner, the former head of INS, to affirm that it is primarily "antipathy" toward immigrants that is driving the public rhetoric about an out-of-control southern border where criminal aliens invade the country. According to her, "underneath it all [are] the kind of cultural issues of how much immigration is changing us: What it means to the identities of communities, how different groups of people are being incorporated."[16]

Third, unauthorized immigrants "make an overall net contribution to the U.S. economy" not only by paying sales, excise, and property taxes, but also by subsidizing services like social security, Medicare, and food stamps that they are barred from using.[17] In addition, they keep down the cost of goods and services and pump capital back into the economy by spending a good portion of their earnings in the United States. We saw in Chapters 2 and 3 that unauthorized immigrants are incorporated into a segmented occupational market, not necessarily displacing U.S. workers but frequently replacing them in less "desirable" jobs at the bottom of the labor market. This is not to say that unauthorized migration comes without economic costs. In fact, costs are distributed in such a way that they frequently fuel conflicts and frustrations at the local level while the broader benefits of immigration accrue at the national level. There is no question that rapidly changing demographics in new immigrant destinations put significant pressure on schools, hospitals, and other local services. Local and state governments, frustrated by these pressures, have enacted a range of ordinances that aim to deflect unauthorized immigrants from their communities, but these fail to address the problems at the core of unauthorized immigration, and they tend to exacerbate tension and misunderstanding. In these local communities, a patchwork of public institutions, private nonprofit organizations, and religious groups struggle to fill the needs created by such a broken system. In the long term, however, repair of the system can only be ensured through creative and collaborative policy making at the federal, state, and local levels.

Fourth, the decision to migrate to the United States is often a profoundly difficult one, involving high costs for the immigrants, their families, and their communities. These costs sometimes include having to sell all belongings or incurring heavy debts in order to finance the journey. They also often include leaving loved ones—wives, husbands, children, and elderly parents—behind and thus exposing the family to potential breakup. The journey itself is perilous: the increasing militarization of the border has deflected immigration flows toward isolated and inhospitable areas along the border where the risk of death is real. Furthermore, at various stages in the journey, immigrants are vulnerable to exploitation and violent abuse by smugglers, organized crime syndicates, common thieves, and even the state. The recent mass slaughter of seventy-two immigrants from El Salvador, Brazil, Honduras, and Ecuador in the northern Mexican state of Tamaulipas poignantly illustrates this vulnerability.[18]

Given the costs and risks involved in entering the country without authorization, it is not surprising that many of the immigrants with whom we talked would rather stay in their home countries if they had a choice. However, many of these immigrants believed they had no other option but to migrate to the United States as a means to ensure the survival of their families and communities. Because migration is an issue of life and death for many unauthorized immigrants, enforcement, no matter how strong, is unlikely to serve as effective deterrence. Quite the contrary, at least in the case of Mexican immigration, enforcement has had the unintended effect of encouraging unauthorized immigrants to settle in the United States, since it has disrupted the back-and-forth flows across the border that have characterized the history of Mexican labor migrations. We made clear that, because it is increasingly difficult, dangerous, and costly to get into the United States, many unauthorized immigrants are choosing to stay put, settling in the United States even as they live in constant fear of being apprehended and deported.

Fifth, while decisions to migrate are ultimately made at the personal and family levels, they are strongly shaped by larger economic and political processes over which unauthorized immigrants have little control. As the case of Guatemala shows, these processes include actions taken by the U.S. government that contribute to political turmoil in the home country and trigger migration flows. Moreover, the implementation of trade agreements such as NAFTA and CAFTA, which are part of U.S.-driven economic globalization, have produced significant dislocation in sending countries, compelling families and communities to migrate as a survival strategy. Understanding these historical and structural factors makes it impossible to distill the problems associated with unauthorized immigration down to individual choices made by unlawful invaders, and it compels U.S. citizens to take responsibility for this nation's part in creating and sustaining patterns of unauthorized immigration.

Sixth, if given a choice, the vast majority of unauthorized immigrants would come into the United States legally, and those already here would welcome the opportunity to adjust their status and be able to live as full and productive members of U.S. society. Many of the immigrants with whom we spoke were eager to regularize their status by paying fines, demonstrating that they have paid their taxes and not violated the law while they have been in the country, doing community service, or showing their loyalty by serving in the armed forces. However, for the overwhelming majority, this simply is not possible. There are very few work visas available. For example, there are currently only thirty thousand H2A visas available for temporary agricultural workers.

Once in the United States, unauthorized immigrants have no legal process available for them to regularize their status. Those opposed to comprehensive immigration reform regularly portray creating such an opportunity as amnesty. This language makes reform less palatable to the American public and overlooks the fact that, if included in comprehensive immigration reform, legalization would be earned through a rigorous process.

Finally, and most important, the strong desire of unauthorized immigrants to regularize their status reflects the fact that many are deeply embedded in American communities. As we have shown, unauthorized immigrants most often share core American values, particularly the hope for a better future built on hard work. Like most Americans, their foremost concern is the well-being of their families and communities. In their pursuit of the American dream, unauthorized immigrants have revitalized towns that were in decline, buying houses, starting new businesses, and bringing new vigor into churches and community organizations. This has been the case particularly in new destinations for unauthorized immigrants, such as cities and towns throughout the U.S. Southeast.

Our intention in making these claims is not to romanticize unauthorized immigrants. Like any group of human beings, these immigrants are capable of both good and bad actions. Yet there has been a strong and pervasive tendency to demonize them and to equate their decision to come into the United States without authorization with a general and pervasive attitude of lawlessness. To counteract this tendency, we have aimed to recognize and showcase the real contributions that unauthorized immigrants have made and continue to make to American communities. More important, we have tried to emphasize the simple humanity of unauthorized immigrants, characterizing the difficult choices they face as complex and often morally ambiguous. We believe that our public discussion of immigration must engage with the complex stories and ambiguous motivations that shape not only the lives of immigrants but also the lives of citizens. As we saw in Chapters 4 and 5, when citizens take the risk to know the unauthorized immigrants living, working, and worshipping alongside them, they face difficult questions, but they also find surprising and creative new ways to move forward together.

As has been the case for immigrant groups throughout the history of the United States from Plymouth Rock to Ellis Island, religious organizations play a central role for contemporary unauthorized immigrants and for the communities that receive them. In fact, as we saw in Chapter 4, churches frequently stand on the front line of the changing demographics in America, struggling with the challenges of being inclusive. By participating in churches, immigrants develop and practice the civic skills necessary to participate in U.S. democracy. Churches also can serve as spaces of encounter where immigrants and native born meet each other face-to-face; learn about each other's histories, cultures, needs, and aspirations; and move beyond stereotypes and prejudices. These human encounters may lead to new ways of framing the debate on immigration, introducing moral and ethical dimensions that have been missing in so much of the national discourse on immigration. Given the centrality of religious organizations for native born and immigrants, and given churches' historic role in struggles for social and racial justice, we believe that churches and other religious organizations are an indispensable resource to transform public opinion on the urgent need for immigration reform from the pews up.

Religious organizations also play an important role in helping immigrants maintain connections with their places of origin, connections that sustain them during the arduous journey and the increasingly difficult process of settlement. In this sense, the transnationalism of today's unauthorized immigrants bears striking affinities to the one practiced by Jewish immigrants from eastern Europe at the close of the nineteenth century, when they created a rich array of *landsmanschaftn*, mutual aid societies, that kept them connected with their shtetls in Russia, Poland, and the Ukraine.[19] Above all, transnationalism is a defensive grassroots strategy born of the need to navigate the challenges of an increasingly globalized reality. As immigration scholar Peggy Levitt puts it, "undocumented immigrants need the safety net provided by strong homeland connections," particularly at a time of great hostility toward immigrants.[20] As we have made clear, reliance on transnational connections by unauthorized immigrants does not signify an unwillingness to integrate into U.S. society. Rather, it signifies U.S. society's continued unwillingness to integrate these immigrants. As Douglas Massey and Magaly Sánchez explain, "the greatest threat to the creation of a strong, vibrant, forward-looking American identity among immigrants comes not from immigrants but from American citizens themselves, who by embracing nativist ideas and promoting anti-immigrant policies harden the categorical boundaries that define immigrants and make integration more difficult and assimilation less likely."[21]

Transnationalism indeed has its costs: unauthorized immigrants are responsible for the survival of families and communities in their countries of origin, a duty that compels them to remain in the United States despite the hardships. Yet transnationalism also has the potential to enrich American society. As Levitt explains, in a globalized world, "people who know how to function across borders, who are bicultural and bilingual, have the best résumé."[22] We need to acknowledge honestly such costs and benefits as we think about humane and effective ways to address the issue of unauthorized immigration. However, because the dominant public discourse on illegality relies heavily on simplistic and dehumanizing stereotypes and myths, it thwarts productive and detailed discussion. Moving beyond the myths and stereotypes allows us to explore the potential foundations and general outlines of an alternative immigration policy.

Beyond Myths and Stereotypes: Intelligently and Humanely Regulated Immigration

What would immigration policy look like if we were to acknowledge the full humanity of unauthorized immigrants, while keeping in mind the values that have guided the United States and the challenges that the nation faces in the new century? To answer this question, we offer a foundation of ethical and moral principles that should guide specific policies, principles that emerge from the United States' historic identity as an immigrant nation.

1. *The rule of law.* The United States is a nation of laws, and enforcement of the rule of law is essential to guarantee equal justice for all. As we saw in Chapter 2, this is something that many unauthorized immigrants, in fact, deeply appreciate. However, as slavery and Jim Crow demonstrate, laws are not necessarily just and are certainly not immutable. A truly participatory democracy is always a work in progress, requiring its members to ask constantly if the law as it stands corresponds to the values and ideals of the nation. It is the responsibility of citizens to be vigilant and to evaluate whether laws indeed correspond to the nation's core values and evolving realities.

2. *A nation of immigrants.* We need to be wary of anti-immigrant arguments that suggest cultural homogeneity as a core value of this nation. Unfortunately, racism and xenophobia are maladies that this nation has struggled with mightily at various points in history, particularly during periods of economic distress and political turmoil. In light of the current situation, we must take special care not repeat the mistakes of the past and succumb to the temptation of scapegoating immigrants. Political leaders and elected officials have a particular responsibility in this regard. They need to set an example, tackling the challenges and promises of immigration in a temperate and constructive fashion. Despite the shadows in America's history, this nation has experienced and been fed by profound heterogeneity and cultural and religious complexity since its inception. The First Amendment clearly exemplifies this: the founding fathers guaranteed freedom of religion at the nation's beginning, thereby placing a significant form of heterogeneity at the core of U.S. identity.

3. *Strangers and neighbors.* In contrast to many other advanced nations, America prides itself on being a country with strong religious traditions that have contributed to the vitality of the nation's civil society. Most of these—certainly Judaism and Christianity—are clear about the duty of welcoming the stranger with hospitality. We must reflect on how dehumanizing attitudes toward unauthorized immigrants square with broadly shared principles. In the case of unauthorized immigrants, the moral challenge is even more acute, since they are not strangers but in fact neighbors. As we have shown, the daily lives, actions, and decisions of citizens are often profoundly intertwined with theirs.

4. *A common humanity.* As we saw in the case of Ray-
   Thomas Presbyterian Church, St. Thomas the Apostle
   Catholic Church, and the Alterna Community, the encounter with the radical other—the other who is ut-
   terly vulnerable, who is perceived as a nonbeing—can
   be enormously transformative and enriching. Such an
   encounter almost inevitably entails a deep and profound recognition of shared humanity. Encounters of
   this sort require hard work; it is not enough to put people together and hope that the differences will be automatically bridged. As political scientist Robert Putnam
   tells us, increasing racial and cultural diversity initially
   makes people hunker down. However, if the different
   groups are willing to step out of their comfort zones,
   to learn from each other's history, values, needs, and
   talents, the end result of the encounter will be a more
   robust and "capacious We." [23] It is essential that this nation seek ways to hear the voices of unauthorized immigrants as fully human voices, and to understand their
   lived experiences as human experiences. This openness
   to a simple shared humanity will lead to humane policies that place respect for the dignity of all people at
   their core.

What would these policies look like? There is no single sil-
ver bullet that will resolve the issues surrounding unauthorized immigration once and for all, but the United States can
take a series of carefully thought measures to address these
issues directly while also holding fast to the nation's deeply
held values and principles.

In the short term, the U.S. government should expand the
number of temporary work visas, calibrating this number
with the various needs of the economy as it begins to grow

again. This task might be complicated, but if the Federal Reserve can set interest rates to respond to the delicate dynamics of the U.S. economy, why can't the government attempt to have such a rational and flexible approach to changing labor markets? The United States would also do well to attend to environmental variables, taking into account the kind of demographic growth and consumption patterns that will make U.S. society sustainable in the long run.

Increasing the number of work permits would bring unauthorized immigrants out of the shadows and afford them both the protections and the regulations that apply to native-born workers and legal residents. One of the problems with the current guest-worker program is that it ties workers to a specific employer or job. If they intend to leave the contract, they also must return to their countries of origin. This arrangement has created a system in which employers often can exploit workers, refusing to pay the wages agreed upon or subtracting money from their paychecks to cover housing and other essentials. In such a system, workers are viewed as a commodity—either an asset or a burden with respect to the bottom line—rather than as fully human individuals. Any future expanded program should issue visas directly to migrants, allowing guest workers to work anywhere in the United States for a specific period of time.

An expanded and reconceptualized work-permit program would help control the race to the bottom in terms of salaries and also the abuses involved in the informal hiring of day laborers. Sociologist Richard Alba argues persuasively that, as the U.S. economy emerges from recession, we have "an unusual opportunity . . . to advance the racial integration of American society. The exodus of baby boomers from the labor market will provide the opening."[24] As the baby boomers, who are disproportionately white and highly educated and who occupy the best jobs, retire en masse in the coming years, we will have "non-zero-sum" mobility: "a period when minorities can advance economically without threatening the life chances that whites take for granted for themselves and their children." [25] However, in order for non-zero-sum mobility to yield a well-prepared multiracial labor force that can sustain the United States' competitive edge in the global economy, the nation needs to adopt policies that will enhance and take full advantage of the resources and potential that African Americans, Latinos, and Asian Americans bring. The move to bring unauthorized immigrants out of the margins of society would represent a step in this direction. Indeed, the DREAM Act pointed precisely in this direction.

The issuance of work permits, if carefully monitored, would be constructive for all members of the working class, not just immigrants. As Douglas Massey, Jorge Durand, and Nolan J. Malone have suggested, those requesting permits could pay a fee that would allow the U.S. government to administer the program, which could include issuing tamperproof and machine-readable identification cards that the worker must present to the employer.[26] The fees also could be used to mitigate the effects on local communities of sudden demographic shifts. Schools and hospitals in these communities need resources; a good deal of anti-immigrant sentiment emerges from local communities' sense that they have been left alone, abandoned by the federal government, as they undertake the difficult task of incorporating new immigrants and addressing the needs brought by growing and diversifying populations. Effective and humane immigration policy must find a way to address these real concerns.

Once the number of work permits has been determined and issued, the United States would be more able to strictly enforce the law against hiring any undocumented worker. While the nation has a right and responsibility to protect borders, relying on enforcement at the border to control un-authorized immigration is neither effective nor humane.[27] The number of undocumented immigrants entering the country has continued to grow despite the ballooning budget allocated to the Border Patrol (since the early 1980s, the agency's annual budget has risen from $200 million to $1.6 billion). A sole focus on building walls and further militarizing the border might play well as symbolic politics, but it is ultimately inhumane and a waste of taxpayers' money. Simply put: enforcement should target the employers. When the job is not there, the incentive to come to the United States will be greatly reduced. Furthermore, the shift to local enforcement may give local populations the satisfaction of dealing with a problem that the federal government has not been able to tackle. However, the local enforcement strategy is counterproductive and corrodes many of the core values of U.S. society. Many immigrants withdraw into the shadows, not trusting the police, health care providers, or teachers, which in turn raises a range of issues from public health and safety to collective well-being. Over-policing creates a culture of fear and mistrust. Indeed, some localities, such as Arlington, Virginia; Framingham, Massachusetts; Santa Clara County, California; and San Francisco, have found this out the hard way and are now seeking to withdraw from 287(g) and Secure Communities agreements because of their negative impact on local communities.[28]

In the medium term, the United States should set up a multitiered system of legalization. Simply increasing the number of temporary work permits ultimately does not encourage immigrants to become truly integrated into society, nor does it give them the possibility of full participation in the life of the polity. Without these differential paths to legal residence and citizenship, the United States could create a transient population not invested in the institutions and future of the nation. Having a significant group of people who are fully integrated into the U.S. economy but permanently barred from participation in the political system is potentially harmful to democracy and also clearly is not in keeping with the core values of the nation.

Beyond the work permits, the United States could set up differential benchmarks that some unauthorized immigrants have to fulfill in order to become, first, legal residents, and then, under more stringent conditions, eventual citizens. These differential benchmarks signal that the country has the right to determine who can be a member of the polity in accordance with the nation's vision of community. More important than the payment of reparations and penalties for the misdemeanor of having entered the country or remained in it without following proper procedures is the need to generate criteria to ensure that those we choose to legalize will be productive and creative members of society. Among the criteria would be their length of time in the United States and how invested they have become in the system. For instance, such a process might consider whether they have started legitimate businesses that hired legal residents or native-born workers, paid their taxes, learned English, participated in community initiatives as part of their civic education, and maintained a clean record before the law.[29]

In setting up a multitiered system of legalization, the United States should give priority to legal immigrants as they work toward their citizenship. The backlog at USCIS is quite daunting, as unauthorized immigrants are well aware. As is the case among any group of human beings, there are unauthorized immigrants currently living in the United States who seek to take advantage of the broken system. Yet the overwhelming majority of those we have encountered are more than willing to wait their turn in the back of the line and to fulfill rigorous but rational requirements during an extended probationary period. This willingness signals their respect for the rule of law and their eager desire to participate fully and transparently in the legal structures of this nation.

The short-term and mid-term measures above will manage but not solve the problem of unauthorized immigration. In the long term, the United States must work with other nations to fashion durable, structural approaches that seek to manage the root causes of unauthorized immigration. To do this, we have to acknowledge that immigration is not just a national concern but a worldwide one that requires transnational and multilateral solutions. Given the complex economic and geopolitical roots of unauthorized immigration and the enormous dimensions of U.S. borders, the problems surrounding unauthorized immigration simply cannot be solved without creative binational and multinational collaboration. As they stand, regional integration agreements such as NAFTA and CAFTA do not deal with labor issues adequately, nor are they conducive to holistic and sustainable development. In fact, these treaties are part of the problem, because they have dislocated many Mexicans and Central Americans in the countryside, while providing only some minimal additional employment opportunities in low-skilled *maquilas*. As a result, many displaced Latin Americans migrate to the United States in search of a better life.

A bold idea would be to institute a new phase of investment and integration in the Americas, borrowing from the most successful elements of the European Union's model. Initially, wealthier nations in Europe invested substantially in poorer countries in the Mediterranean region. Despite the current economic crisis, the standard of living in these Mediterranean countries has improved tremendously, so much so that there is little risk of Spanish, Greek, or Portuguese workers becoming a problem in Germany, France, or the United Kingdom, for example. A similar regional approach that works toward closing the gap between wages and life conditions in Latin America and those in the United States would not end unauthorized immigration to the north, but it certainly would go a long way toward encouraging potential emigrants to stay in their countries of origin and contribute toward local and national development.

There is no doubt that for some of those who advocate for more stringent immigration restrictions, the mere mention of the European Union will raise the threat of losing U.S. sovereignty. Yet regional economic cooperation need not lead to political, monetary, or even cultural integration. The Europeans decided to move in the direction of full integration. The Americas may wish to go in a different direction, enhancing some ties while preserving flexible boundaries that allow nations to build on their strengths and coordinate regional solutions to hitherto intractable problems such as unauthorized immigration, environmental degradation, and the drug trade. This coordination and cooperation would have to take place not only at the level of governments, but also at the level of civil society.

"That's What America Taught Me"

In light of the defeat of the DREAM Act, it is difficult to envision the implementation of even the short-term steps that we suggest above. Beginning to take these steps will be possible only if there is a real and open public conversation in the United States about the issues surrounding unauthorized immigration. We believe that such a conversation has begun to happen in religious and civic organizations that work to address specific problems emerging in local communities throughout the nation. We advocate for an expansion of such conversations and for citizens to seek real opportunities to engage in face-to-face encounters, learning from and with the unauthorized immigrants among whom they live both as strangers and as neighbors. Only a sustained effort by political leaders to work closely with various sectors of civil society, especially churches and other religious and civic organizations, will change the terms of the discourse on immigration. The need is dire, and the time is now.

This work from the ground and the pews up will no doubt be difficult and slow. But as we have seen, hope comes from the unlikeliest of places. Witness Jimmy, the white owner of the barbershop in Cobb Shopping Center, who has seen the mall evolve "from deli to tortas":

> JIMMY: It's like my grandson, I asked him, I said, "Son . . . how many blacks are in your classroom?" He said, "I don't know, Papa." I said, "Well, how many Mexicans are in your classroom?" "I don't know, Papa." "They're just all people aren't they, buddy?" and he said, "That's right."
>
> INTERVIEWER: They [the children] don't see it the same way.
>
> JIMMY: They don't see it. I have a little bit of the old and a little bit of the new in me. I know what's what, and we have to try to overcome those things because it was just—when we were coming up, a black man couldn't say anything at a white woman . . . but you try to say the world's gonna be better for my grandchild, for all of this stuff to go away, and that's kind of how I look at it.

Even in a place like Cobb County, which has a deep legacy of racial discrimination and has been at the forefront of implementing some of the most stringent laws against unauthorized immigrants, awareness of our common humanity, one person at a time, is still possible. Such an awareness does not entail erasing the differences that have shaped and will continue to shape our experiences. Instead, it calls upon us to engage those differences in a way that rejects fear and seeks reconciliation and collaboration toward a more hopeful future.

We are moved to agree with Benita Veliz, whose parents brought her to the United States without proper authorization when she was eight years old. Benita graduated from St. Mary's University in San Antonio, and she plans to go to law school. However, her future is now in jeopardy because she faces deportation, after having been stopped two years ago on a traffic violation. Upon hearing that the DREAM Act was voted down by the Senate, Benita simply stated: "I am a strong believer in the philosophy that the last thing you should ever give up on is hope . . . I think that's the result of being in America. That's what America taught me." [30]

EPILOGUE

We ended *Living "Illegal"* not with our own words but with the message of hope shared by Benita Veliz, a young DREAM activist who had narrowly escaped deportation. Almost two years later, on September 5, 2012, we watched with anticipation as Ms. Veliz took the stage to speak at the Democratic National Convention in Charlotte, North Carolina, telling millions of viewers, "I feel just as American as any of my friends or neighbors."[1] Her very presence on that stage signified that unauthorized immigrants have begun to speak boldly for themselves in the nation's public arena, and to transform its political life.

On that night, Benita Veliz made history, becoming the first unauthorized person to address a national political convention. This milestone marked both the extraordinary distance that the DREAM activists have traveled over two years and also the mounting challenges that they and others face. On the one hand, the continued expansion of interior enforcement efforts and the passage and implementation of punitive state laws have made daily life more precarious than ever before for many unauthorized immigrants. On the other hand, the Deferred Action for Childhood Arrivals (DACA) program, which offers temporary reprieve from deportation for as many as 1.7 million unauthorized immigrants[2] and the November 6, 2012, elections have built new incentives for federal legislators to enact comprehensive immigration reform.

On June 15, 2012, President Barack Obama stood in the White House Rose Garden and announced the most important immigration-related federal initiative in nearly two decades: DACA, a program that would allow young unauthorized immigrants who are a low enforcement priority to remain temporarily in the United States and to obtain a two-year work permit. In order to qualify, applicants would be required to have entered the United States before the age of sixteen and to be younger than thirty; to have continually resided in the United States for at least five years; to be enrolled in school; to have a GED or have served in the military; and not to have been convicted of a felony, a major misdemeanor, or multiple minor misdemeanors. Implementation of the program began in mid-August, and within two months almost 180,000 applications had been received and more than 4,500 had already been approved.[3]

At least two significant forces influenced Obama's decision to exercise prosecutorial discretion in this manner. The first was election-year partisan politics. The DACA program was in part an effort to reinvigorate support from the important and increasingly frustrated Latino electorate. The second was the profoundly influential DREAM activist movement. When he announced the program, Obama explained, "I believe that it's the right thing to do because I've been with groups of young people who work so hard and speak with so much heart about what's best in America. . . . I know some have come forward, at great risk to themselves and their futures, in hopes it would spur the rest of us to live up to our own most cherished values."

Over the course of our research in new immigrant destinations, we have followed the stories of many such DREAMers. In 2001, when we first interviewed Norma in their small

Atlanta apartment, Norma's son, Eduardo, had just returned from his fifth-grade safety patrol trip to Washington, D.C. We sat across a table from him as he proudly described photographs of the Lincoln Memorial and the National Mall. Ten years later, we sat across a table once again—not in his family's Atlanta home but in a small house a mile from the Stewart Detention Center, the largest privately run immigrant detention center in the United States. Although a handful of his friends and family members had been detained at Stewart over the past two years, Eduardo was not in the area to visit loved ones. Instead, he was working as a volunteer at a hospitality house, serving families of detainees. Although most of his fellow volunteers also visited detainees at the Stewart Detention Center, Eduardo could not. He feared entering the detention center as a visitor because he was still an unauthorized immigrant.

This was about to change—temporarily. Eduardo was eligible for DACA, and he was using downtime at the hospitality house to finish the required paperwork. We listened as he carefully translated a Spanish-language newspaper article from 2001 that announced his selection as Student of the Year at his local elementary school: "Eduardo, a young man of 10 years old is an example of how students who have recently arrived to the country can succeed with great ease if they are given the correct attention and education."

Ten years later, the article's opening words offered a poignant irony. Eduardo has faced significant obstacles, but he graduated from high school in 2008. His best friend from the wrestling team continued to the University of North Carolina at Chapel Hill with a scholarship, graduated, and returned to Atlanta to work for Teach for America. During the same period of time, Eduardo has completed thirty-two hours toward an associate of arts degree. His grades have been good, but he has been required to attend as an international student, paying triple the amount of tuition that an in-state student would pay. For the first few semesters, his parents helped him to pay for school, but the impact of the economic recession on their income has forced Eduardo to go to work with his mother in her private housekeeping business and earn the money he will need to return to college.

Eduardo found working with his mother to be a good source of income, and he appreciated the work. But he explained that, once his DACA application went through, "my mom said she was going to fire me! She said I need to get a better job or at least have two jobs." When asked how DACA would impact Eduardo's life, he answered simply: "It's a great opportunity that Obama has given the DREAMers. Now I can apply for a job legitimately, so hopefully I can get a better paying job, save up some more money, and go back to school to try to finish the associate's—which is better than nothing. It's halfway there."

"Halfway there" is an excellent description of the precarious status of DACA recipients. Ten U.S. Immigration and Customs Enforcement (ICE) agents already have filed suit against the Department of Homeland Security (DHS), claiming that "the Directive commands ICE officers to violate federal law."[4] The complaint was filed with funding from the anti-immigration organization Numbers USA and with representation from Kris Kobach, who is of counsel to the Immigration Reform Law Institute (the legal arm of FAIR, the Federation for American Immigration Reform) and has been largely responsible for drafting state-level immigration laws promoting the strategy of "self-deportation." In Arizona, Governor Jan Brewer issued an executive order to deny valid drivers' licenses and other public benefits, such as in-state tuition, to DACA recipients. Brewer's announcement points toward the concerns expressed by the many unauthorized students who are eligible for DACA but have chosen not to apply.

Unlike the DREAM Act, Deferred Action is a discretionary program that is temporary and does not confer permanent residency or offer a pathway to permanent residency. The program's early results have been highly successful in terms of participation rates among eligible young people, and ICE has demonstrated fair and efficient adjudication of cases.[5] Yet the long-term status of "halfway there" for the participants raises important questions about the meaning of citizenship, belonging, and access to the American dream. The results of the November 2012 elections make a long-term solution appear more viable for the future, but in the meantime unauthorized immigrants such as Eduardo and his family live with increasing insecurity. The first four years of the Obama administration brought unprecedented enforcement efforts targeting unauthorized immigrants, including federal programs such as 287(g) agreements with local law enforcement and the Secure Communities programs.

The Georgia county where Eduardo and his family live participates in both the 287(g) program and Secure Communities. Eduardo recalled how much life has changed in the three years since his county implemented 287(g): roadblocks have become commonplace on the streets surrounding his neighborhood, and several of Eduardo's friends, family members, and acquaintances have been deported after encountering a roadblock without a valid driver's license. When asked how this has impacted the community of immigrants from his hometown of Santa Ana, Eduardo explained, "A lot of people that I know have moved back because ultimately if one of the parents in a family gets sent back, everything they have worked for to stay here has been diminished. They have to sell their stuff, or sometimes they just leave and lose everything. I know people who have bought houses and just left them, left all of the money they put into them. It's hard because people think their life is set here, but . . . things have changed."

This story is unfolding throughout the nation, because of both the Obama administration's unprecedented interior enforcement efforts and state and local enforcement initiatives. Instead of moving quickly during the president's first term to push through comprehensive immigration reform, the Obama administration pursued a get-tough strategy on unauthorized immigration, with "historic levels" of deportations.[6] As of July 2012, the Obama administration had deported 1.4 million unauthorized immigrants.[7] ICE removals averaged close to 400,000 annually during Obama's first term (compared to approximately 250,000 per year under the two-term George W. Bush administration).[8]

The rate of expansion of the 287(g) program slowed considerably during the Obama administration, as the DHS shifted focus to expanding the Secure Communities Program, which began toward the end of the Bush administration. Since 2008, DHS has expanded Secure Communities from fourteen jurisdictions to more than three thousand as of August 2012, representing 97 percent of all jurisdictions (3,074 out of 3,181) and including all jurisdictions along the southwest border.[9]

The expansion of the Secure Communities program has generated significant controversy. Confusing and contradictory information about the program led many to believe that participation in the program would be optional. The states of Illinois, New York, and Massachusetts either declined signing the agreement with ICE or decided to suspend it. These states argued that the program was not effective at targeting unauthorized immigrants with a serious criminal history, but rather detained and deported minor offenders. They also argued that it was promoting racial profiling and mistrust of local police.[10] In some communities, women who have called 911 to report cases of domestic violence have become victims of the Secure Communities program and now face deportation.[11]

Nevertheless, Secure Communities has continued to expand across the nation, while many state legislatures have crafted and implemented their own laws to address the issue of unauthorized migration. According to the National Conference of State Legislatures, 1,607 immigration-related bills were introduced in 2011, up from 1,400 the year before.[12] Alabama (HB 56), Georgia (HB 87), Indiana (SB 590), South Carolina (S 20), and Utah (HB 497 and SB 288) passed laws that mirror or build upon Arizona's SB 1070, all operating with the premise that making everyday life difficult for unauthorized immigrants will lead them to "self-deport." Arguably, the most draconian of these laws is Alabama's HB 56. Like Arizona's controversial immigration legislation, Alabama's law requires employers to use E-Verify to check employees' immigration status and deputizes the police to check the status of anyone they stop if they suspect that the person is in the country without proper authorization. The Alabama law orders public elementary, middle, and high schools to ascertain the immigration status of students upon enrollment and report the number of unauthorized immigrants to state education officials. Furthermore, it criminalizes the act of harboring, transporting, or assisting undocumented immigrants.

Passage of the new law had a dramatic effect on Alabama's unauthorized immigrant community. According to Reverend Paul Zoghby, pastor at St. Margaret of Scotland Church, which has a large Latino congregation, "This is the saddest thing I have experienced in my 18 years as a priest. . . . We've already lost 20 percent of the congregation in the past few

weeks, and many more will be gone by next week. It is a human tragedy." [13] Churches have been particularly concerned
with the provision of the law that would criminalize transporting or assisting unauthorized immigrants, seeing it as
interference with their core pastoral work. In response, four
bishops—Methodist, Episcopalian, and Catholic—sued the
state of Alabama. Calling the law "the nation's most merci-
less anti-immigration legislation," the suit argued, "If en-
forced, the Law will place Alabama church members in the
untenable position of verifying individuals' immigration
documents before being able to follow God's Word to 'love
thy neighbor as thyself' (Matthew 22:39)." [14]

Following the U.S. Supreme Court ruling striking down
portions of Arizona's law for being preempted by federal law,
HB 56's most intrusive provisions, such as registering the
immigration status of children in public schools, were also
struck down by an appeals court. However, as of this writing,
both the Supreme Court and lower courts have allowed the
controversial "show me your papers" provisions of these laws
to stand.

Other states have taken a different approach, exploring
more integrative policies and attempting to resist or limit
participation in the Secure Communities Program. For example, the Trust Act in California would have created a
"bright line" between local police and ICE by prohibiting
law enforcement officials from complying with an immigration detainer unless the person had been convicted of or was
currently in custody for a serious or violent felony. The bill's
sponsors claimed that the law would "guard against profiling and wrongful detention of citizens and crime victims and
witnesses" by encouraging local law enforcement to develop
plans to prevent racial profiling and wrongful detentions. [15]
The bill was endorsed by several prominent Democrats in

the state; religious leaders, including archbishop emeritus of Los Angeles Cardinal Roger M. Mahony; law enforcement leaders; and immigrant rights advocates. Although the bill passed both the California Assembly and Senate, Governor Jerry Brown, a Democrat, vetoed the bill on September 30, 2012.

Perhaps no other state than Utah more clearly reflects the reigning ambivalence toward unauthorized immigrants. The conversation on immigration there has been framed by "The Utah Compact," a set of five principles endorsed by the Church of Jesus Christ of Latter-Day Saints, which stresses the need to strengthen national borders and "respect the rule of law and support law enforcement's professional judgment and discretion," while also opposing "policies that unnecessarily separate families," recognizing the "economic role immigrants play as workers and taxpayers," and endorsing immigrant integration.[16] The Utah legislature ultimately adopted legislation that continues to emphasize local enforcement while simultaneously offering mechanisms for unauthorized immigrants to normalize their status through a guest-worker program. The program, which requires applicants to clear a criminal background check and pay fines of up to $2,500 in order to qualify, is designed primarily with the interests of employers in mind, raising the possibility of labor abuses.

Although state-level restrictive policies have generated the most media attention, many local and municipal authorities around the country have also quietly pursued more integrative policies. More than sixty cities around the country have issued local "limited cooperation" ordinances between local police and immigration authorities in non-felony crimes.[17] More than a hundred other communities around the country have opened day-labor hiring sites, such as the one in

Jupiter, Florida.[18] As the tide of restrictive state and local legislation begins to ebb, it is possible that more inclusionary
alternatives will find space to grow.[19]

The November 6, 2012, elections have alerted the nation
to the growing significance of the Latino vote, especially in
crucial swing states. With Latinos projected to become 30
percent of the total population by 2050, their electoral weight
will only continue to grow. Eliseo Medina of the Service Employees International Union (SEIU) summed up the Latino
impact on the 2012 election this way: "The sleeping Latino
giant is wide-awake and it's cranky. We expect action and
leadership on immigration reform in 2012. No more excuses.
No more obstruction or gridlock."[20]

The Latino vote as a percentage of the overall electorate
increased from 9 percent in 2008 to 10 percent in 2012. According to the exit polls, President Obama won 71 percent of
the Latino vote nationally, improving upon his 2008 performance of 67 percent. More important, the Latino vote was
a key component of Obama's winning coalition in several
swing states, including Colorado, Florida, Nevada, and even
Virginia. In Florida, where Obama won 60 percent of the
Latino vote, Latinos voters constituted 17 percent of the electorate, up from 14 percent in 2008.[21]

The president's increased support among Latinos was
closely connected to the immigration issue. Although the
economy and jobs were the number-one issue for Latino voters (53 percent), immigration was cited as a top priority by
35 percent.[22] Moreover, the immigration issue is intensely
personal for Latinos, many of whom have family members
or friends who have been directly affected by restrictive immigration policies. During the Republican primaries, Governor Mitt Romney's comments about "self-deportation,"
his support for SB 1070 in Arizona, and his opposition to the
DREAM Act alienated the overwhelming majority of Latino

voters. In contrast, Obama's decision to implement the DACA program had a galvanizing effect in the Latino community and mobilized young DREAM activists to get out the vote. Prior to the decision, Obama was facing growing disaffection in the Latino community because of his enforcement-first policies and the lack of progress on immigration reform. Latino Decisions, the premier Latino political opinion research firm, found that Latino enthusiasm for Obama increased significantly after the announcement of DACA.[23] As Ezra Klein of the *Washington Post* put it: "Changing people's lives is always more effective than another campaign ad. And this policy [DACA] is looking like it's going to change a lot of lives."[24]

Given the record Latino turnout and the broader demographic trends in the country, including the shrinking white vote, it was not surprising that there was much discussion by both parties about the importance of immigration reform in the aftermath of the elections. Exit polls showed that two-thirds of Americans supported a path to legalization for undocumented immigrants working in the United States.[25] During his victory speech, President Obama pointed to immigration reform as one of the top priorities for his second term. Vice President Joe Biden and Senate Majority Leader Harry Reid voiced their determination to push forward with comprehensive immigration reform. On the Republican side, political strategists worried aloud whether Republicans could ever win at the national level without significantly increasing their support among Latino voters. Prominent Republicans including senators Lindsey Graham and Marco Rubio, former New York City mayor Rudy Giuliani, and former Republican National Committee chief Haley Barbour, urged the party to reconsider its position on unauthorized immigration going forward.

As this epilogue goes to press, one thing is clear: America

is becoming more diverse, and our political leaders will find it increasingly difficult to use simplistic and polarizing language to deal with the human dilemmas posed by unauthorized immigration. The rise of the sleeping Latino giant offers a unique opportunity to redirect the conversation on immigration away from derogatory labels and counterproductive piecemeal approaches and toward a coherent immigration system that reflects America's evolving identity and place in the world. For their part, Eduardo and his family, who have watched federal immigration reform fail many times in the past, continue to remain hopeful. When asked what the outcome of the 2012 elections meant to him, Eduardo told us, "That's great that Obama won. Now he really needs to keep up his promise."

November 2012

ACKNOWLEDGMENTS

As a collaborative endeavor, this book project has drawn support from multiple sources. First and foremost, we owe a debt of gratitude to the Ford Foundation for the generous grant that supported the research for this project and a series of outreach activities to benefit the immigrant communities we studied. We are especially thankful to Sheila Davaney, who accompanied us through multiple phases of the project and provided critical guidance and support. At various stages of research and writing, we also received support from the Center for Latin American Studies, the Departments of Religion and Political Science at the University of Florida, the Wilkes Honors College of Florida Atlantic University, the Woodrow Wilson International Center for Scholars, Fulbright, the Social Science Research Council, the Louisville Institute, and the Association for the Sociology of Religion.

We also want to give full recognition to the contributions of Sandra Lazo de la Vega in researching, writing, and editing portions of this manuscript. Although Sandra's work on this project began as a research assistant through Florida Atlantic University, it rapidly expanded during her internship at the Woodrow Wilson Center and ensuing assistantships funded by the University of Florida Center for Latin American Studies. Specifically, Sandra co-authored portions of chapters 1, 2, and 5 and provided critical background research for the appendix and other portions of the manuscript. This book could not have been brought to completion without her invaluable assistance.

Special thanks as well to Marc Favreau of The New Press, whose careful and wise editorial work greatly enhanced this book. In addition, we would like to thank key people who facilitated our fieldwork: Susan Stevenot Sullivan, Anna Peterson, Karol Ramos, Elizabeth Friedmann, Dr. Lúcia Ribeiro of the International Welcome Center in Atlanta, Reverend Carrie Scott, Anton Flores, and P.J. and Amy Edwards.

While some of the interviews, life histories, and individuals stories detailed in this volume were collected directly by the authors, others were collected by our close friends and collaborators from Brazil, Mexico, and Guatemala. In particular, we would like to thank Lúcia Ribeiro, José Claúdio Souza Alves, Carol Girón Solórzano, Silvia Irene Palma, Patricia Fortuny, and Mirian Solís for making our collaboration one of the most fulfilling and engaging academic and personal experiences of our professional lives. Daisy Perez, a graduate student in Latin American studies at the University of Florida, provided excellent research assistance, and Lucia Hulsether, an undergraduate student research associate at Agnes Scott College, also conducted important research in Atlanta and offered extraordinarily valuable insights throughout the writing process. Many thanks also to the A.L. Burruss Institute of Public Service and Research at Kennesaw State University, which conducted a phone survey and focus group interviews for us.

Finally, we would like to offer our deepest gratitude to the many individuals who kindly gave us access to their lives, homes, and congregations in our research in Florida, Georgia, Mexico, Guatemala, and Brazil. Their names are too many to list, but their contributions to this book and to our society are invaluable.

APPENDIX

Time Line of Important Immigration Policy

Naturalization Act of 1790: Set a two-year residency requirement for citizenship.

Naturalization Act of 1795: Set "good moral character" and a five-year residency requirement for citizenship.

Alien and Sedition Acts of 1798: Several acts that severely restricted civil liberties and increased the stringency of citizenship requirements. These set a fourteen-year residency requirement for citizenship, required the registration of all foreign-born people living in the United States, and gave the president of the United States the power to deport any alien who was considered a threat to "the peace and safety of the United States," as well as any aliens whose country of origin was at war with the United States.[1]

Naturalization Act of 1802: Reduced the residency requirement to five years.[2]

Act of 1819: Required passenger manifest lists to be reported to local customs as well as to the secretary of state. Official collection of immigration data for the United States began with this act.[3]

Act of 1862: Banned Asian, primarily Chinese, laborers from being transported in American vessels.

Act of 1875: Marked the beginning of "direct federal regulation on immigration" by prohibiting entry to certain "undesirable" immigrants, namely prostitutes and criminals.[4]

Chinese Exclusion Act of 1882: Suspended immigration from China for ten years and barred the Chinese already living in the United States from citizenship. Another law passed the same year included "lunatics" and those "unable to care for themselves" in the category of undesirable immigrants that had been created by the Act of 1875.[5]

Alien Contract Labor Law of 1885: Made it illegal for any company or person interested in hiring labor to finance the transportation of foreign-born labor.[6]

Act of 1888: Provided for the deportation of people in violation of the Alien Contract Labor Law of 1885.

Immigration Act of 1891: Established the Bureau of Immigration under the Department of Treasury. The "undesirable" category was further expanded to include people who had required financial assistance for their travel.

Ellis Island opens in 1892.

Act of 1893: Expanded reporting requirements for foreigners arriving in the United States to include their literacy, the amount of money in their possession, their mental and physical health, and other characteristics.

Act of 1902: Extended the Chinese Exclusion Act (1882) until a new treaty was reached with China.

Act of 1903: Expanded the "undesirable" category to include anarchists, epileptics, polygamists, and beggars.

Naturalization Act of 1906: Required knowledge of English for naturalization and introduced standard naturalization forms.

Immigration Act of 1907: Expanded the "undesirable" category to include "imbeciles, feebleminded persons, idiots and insane persons."[7] The act also required vessels departing the United States to report data on passengers, thus beginning the official collection of emigration statistics.[8]

Immigration Act of 1917: Required a literacy test and barred illiterate people from entering the country. This act also established the "Asiatic barred zone," which disallowed Asian immigrants from entering the United States.

Quota Law of 1921: Established an immigration quota of no more than "3 percent of the number of natives of the given country enumerated in the 1910 census." Non-quota categories were created for citizens of countries in the Western Hemisphere and wives and children of U.S. citizens.[9]

Immigration Act of 1924: Established a national quota system (2 percent of the 1890 country of origin population living in the United States). Citizens of Western Hemisphere countries and wives and minor unmarried children of U.S. citizens remained non-quota immigrants.[10]

Alien Registration Act of 1940: Required that all resident-aliens over the age of fourteen living in the United States be fingerprinted. It also expanded the list of deportable aliens to include aliens who had knowingly aided other people in entering the United States in violation of the law and aliens who had been convicted of carrying certain weapons, among other offenses.[11]

***Bracero* program officially begins in 1942:** An executive agreement signed by Mexico and the United States allowed Mexican and Central American workers, especially farmworkers, to work temporarily in the United States to cover some of the labor shortages caused by World War II.

Act of December 1943: Ended the Chinese Exclusion Act.[12]

War Brides Act of 1945 and G.I. Fiancée Act of 1946: Waived certain visa requirements for foreign-born wives and fiancées of American soldiers. In the same year, legislation was passed exempting Chinese wives of American soldiers from quota categories.

Displaced Persons Act of 1948: Allowed 205,000 refugees to be admitted into the United States over a period of two years, with preference for agricultural workers, construction workers, and blood relatives of U.S. citizens.[13]

Internal Security Act of 1950: Expanded grounds for exclusion to include Communists, required resident-aliens to report their address annually, and introduced a civics test for citizenship.

Immigration and Nationality Act of 1952 (McCarran-Walter Act): This act "codified and repealed earlier legislation to become the basic immigration and naturalization act."[14] It removed race and gender as barriers or relevant variables for immigration and naturalization but maintained some aspects of the quota system that continued to reflect racial preferences in immigration. Specifically, northern and western European nations received a large majority of the total annual immigration quota, thus preserving the national-origins system of discrimination. This act also declared people suffering from leprosy and users and traffickers of narcotics, as well as other designated groups, to be inadmissible.

Refugee Relief Act of 1953: Expanded the number of visas for refugees allowed by the 1948 act.

Bracero **program officially ends in 1964.**

Immigration and Nationality Act of 1965 (Hart-Celler Act): Abolished the national-origins quota system and replaced it with a hemispheric system. An annual ceiling of 170,000 visas (20,000 per country) was set for the Eastern Hemisphere. Also set a limitation on immigration from the Western Hemisphere for the first time, by setting a quota of 120,000 per year.[15] A priority system was established that favored relatives of U.S. citizens and workers with special skills.[16] The Eastern and Western Hemisphere immigration ceilings were eventually combined in 1978, establishing a worldwide ceiling of 290,000.

Refugee Act of 1980: Established a system for admitting and resettling refugees in the United States; reduced the annual ceiling for migration to 270,000.

Immigration Reform and Control Act of 1986 (IRCA): Granted legal status to immigrants who had unlawfully resided in the United States since January 1, 1982. IRCA also created penalties for employers who knowingly hired undocumented workers and enhanced border enforcement.

Immigration Nursing and Relief Act of 1989: Granted nurses who had been working on an H-1 visa in the United States as of September 1, 1989, the opportunity to apply for permanent residency.[17]

Immigration Act of 1990: Revised grounds for deportation and authorized the granting of temporary protected status to immigrants from designated countries that were subject to armed conflicts.[18] Set the annual number of immigrants at 700,000.

American Baptist Churches (ABC) Settlement 1991: Allowed thousands of Guatemalans whose refugee claims had been dismissed by the INS because the United States did not oppose the strongly anticommunist regime they were escaping to remain in the country. As part of the settlement, the INS agreed to revisit thousands of previously denied asylum cases.

Illegal Immigration Reform and Immigrant Responsibility Act of 1996: Added section 287(g) to the Immigration and Nationality Act (INA), thereby enabling "the secretary of the U.S. Department of Homeland Security (DHS) to enter into agreements with state and local law enforcement agencies, permitting designated officers to perform immigration law enforcement functions . . . provided that the local law enforcement officers receive appropriate training and function under the supervision of sworn U.S. Immigration and Customs Enforcement (ICE) officers." [19] This act also sped up the deportation process for some detained immigrants and barred future entry into the United States for people who had overstayed their visas, entered without inspection, or violated the terms of their status (for example, people on student visas who worked outside the permitted parameters). People who had overstayed their visa or lived in the United States without authorization for less than one year were barred for three years, and those who had overstayed for one year or more were barred for ten years.

Nicaraguan Adjustment and Central American Relief Act (1997): Allowed Central Americans protected under the ABC settlement to apply for permanent residency in the United States.

USA PATRIOT Act of 2001: Revised the INA to expand the scope of deportable and inadmissible aliens to individuals associated with governments or organizations classified as supporting or endorsing terrorism or undermining U.S. anti-terrorism efforts.

REAL ID Act of 2005: Set minimum standards at the federal level for driver's licenses and state ID cards. Anyone seeking to obtain a valid identification must be able to produce proof of a social security number (or eligibility to get one) and evidence of lawful status in the United States, among other requirements.[20]

NOTES

Introduction

1. This television commercial originally aired in 2010 to support the candidacy of Sharron Angle, a Republican candidate opposing Harry Reid, the Democratic senator and majority leader from Nevada. See "Sharron Angle TV ad: 'At Your Expense,' " YouTube, http://www.youtube.com/watch?v=uJC_RmcO7Ts&feature=channel (accessed December 8, 2010). See also "Another Fear Mongering and Anti-Latino Ad from Sharron Angle," YouTube, http://www.youtube.com/watch?v=_wdcxvP4tyE&feature=related (accessed December 8, 2010).

2. Kathryn Dobies, "Traffic Stop Puts KSU Student in Jail as an Illegal Immigrant," *Marietta Daily Journal*, May 1, 2010, http://www.mdjonline.com/view/full_story/7265546/article-Traffic-stop-puts-KSU-student-in-jail-as-an-illegal-immigrant.

3. Ibid.

4. See Diana Marcum, "He's the Cal State Fresno Student Body President—and an Illegal Immigrant," *Los Angeles Times*, http://www.latimes.com/news/local/la-me-1118-illegal-immigrant-presiden20101118,0,5635027.story (accessed December 8, 2010).

5. Mark Davis and Helena Oliviero, "New Face on an Old Debate: Colotl Case Spotlights Illegal Immigration Saga in Cobb County," *Atlanta Journal Constitution*, May 16, 2010.

6. On immigration and the construction of citizenship, see Rainer Bauböck, *Transnational Citizenship: Membership and Rights in International Migration* (Aldershot, Hants, England: E. Elgar, 1994). See also Peggy Levitt, *God Needs No Passport: Immigrants and the Changing American Religious Landscape* (New York: The New Press: 2007). See also Saskia Sassen, *Guests and Aliens* (New York: The New Press, 1999).

7. We focus in this book on unauthorized immigrants from Latin America for two reasons. First, we, the authors of the book, have decades of collective experience working in Latin America and with Latin American immigrants in the United States. Second, and more important, approximately

three-quarters (76 percent) of unauthorized immigrants in the United States are from Latin America, and the majority (59 percent) are from Mexico. See Jeffrey Passel and D'Vera Cohn, *A Portrait of Unauthorized Immigrants in the United States* (Washington, DC: Pew Hispanic Center, 2009).

8. These comments were made by Rep. Curry Todd of Collierville, Tennessee, when told during a hearing that Cover Kid, a state-funded health program, does not require proof of citizenship for a mother to receive prenatal care, since any child born in the United States is a citizen. See Erik Schelzig, "Bredesen Slams Rep. Curry Todd's Immigrant 'Rats' Remark," Associated Press, November 13, 2010, http://www.tennessean.com/article/20101113/NEWS02/11130324/Bredesen-slams-Rep-Curry-Todd-s-immigrant-rats-re mark (accessed December 16, 2010).

9. Peter Slevin, "Deportation of Illegal Immigrants Increases Under Obama Administration," *Washington Post*, July 26, 2010, http://www.washingtonpost.com/wp-dyn/content/article/2010/07/25/AR2010072501790.html.

10. *Terror and Isolation in Cobb: How Unchecked Police Power Under 287(g) Has Torn Families Apart and Threatened Public Safety*, American Civil Liberties Union Foundation of Georgia, October 2009, http://www.acluga.org/287gReport.pdf. A recent article in the *New York Times* focusing on neighboring Gwinnett County reported that 45 percent of those arrested under the 287(g) program were detained for traffic offenses other than driving under the influence. See Julia Preston and Robert Gebeloff, "Some Unlicensed Drivers Risk More than a Fine," *New York Times*, December 9, 2010.

11. The selection of these three groups allowed us to study comparatively a national group that has had a long history of migration to the United States (i.e., Mexicans) and two newer immigrant flows. We studied these groups in nonconventional destinations in Florida, outside the Miami-Dade metro area, and in Atlanta, Georgia, and its suburbs in order to document the misunderstandings, stereotypes, tensions, and the opportunities for cross-cultural encounter that emerge as communities witness a rapid growth of unauthorized Latino immigrants. We have examined these tensions and interethnic exchanges through a variety of methods ranging from participant observation and in-depth interviewing in congregations that have had to deal with rapid changes in their ethnic composition to the gathering of oral histories among Latino immigrant populations. We also conducted focus group interviews with native-born U.S. citizens, both white and African American. In addition, we conducted a random phone survey with seven hundred respondents in the five-county metro Atlanta area, focusing on local attitudes toward immigration and race.

1. Why Migrate? Making Sense of Unauthorized Migration

1. The name of this town has been changed to protect the identity of its residents and emigrants. Between June 2002 and December 2002, we conducted interviews (N = 16) and participant observation with residents of this town and also with emigrants living in metro Atlanta, and we have conducted informal follow-up interviews with emigrants and return migrants between 2007 and 2010.

2. See Jeffrey Passel and D'Vera Cohn, *A Portrait of Unauthorized Immigrants in the United States* (Washington, DC: Pew Hispanic Center, 2009).

3. Per capita GDP on a purchasing power parity basis (PPP), obtained from the CIA World Factbook, World Bank's World Development Indicators database.

4. For detailed explanation of this approach to understanding migration (often referred to as "migration systems theory"), see Stephen Castles and Mark J. Miller, *The Age of Migration: International Population Movements in the Modern World*, 4th ed. (New York: Guilford Press, 2009).

5. The Washington Consensus is a shorthand term that describes a series of policy prescriptions crafted by organizations such as the International Monetary Fund, the World Bank, and the U.S. Treasury Department to rescue developing economies in crisis by opening them up to global capitalist markets. Typically, these prescriptions included currency devaluations, elimination of trade tariffs, privatization of national industries, and the downsizing of the welfare state. See Jean Grugel, Pia Riggirozzi, and Ben Thirkell-White, "Beyond the Washington Consensus? Asia and Latin America in Search of More Autonomous Development," *International Affairs* 84, no. 3 (2008): 499–517.

6. See Douglas S. Massey, Jorge Durand, and Nolan J. Malone, *Beyond Smoke and Mirrors: Mexican Immigration in an Era of Economic Integration* (New York: Russell Sage Foundation, 2002): and Mae M. Ngai, *Impossible Subjects: Illegal Aliens and the Making of Modern America* (Princeton, NJ: Princeton University Press, 2004).

7. For a detailed discussion of this process, see Ngai, *Impossible Subjects*, ch. 4.

8. Massey, Durand, and Malone, *Beyond Smoke and Mirrors.*

9. See Helen Shapiro, *Mexico: Escaping from the Debt Crisis? Teaching Note* (Boston, MA: Harvard Business School, 1991).

10. In short, as Douglas Massey and his colleagues bluntly state, "U.S. policy toward Mexico is inherently self-contradictory, simultaneously promoting integration while insisting on separation" Massey, Durand, and Malone, *Beyond Smoke and Mirrors*, 83.

11. Massey and Espinosa explain, "Immigration is inherent to the structure of postindustrial economic life. . . . Mexico-U.S. migration is not caused by disparities in wage rates, the effects of social capital, or failures in

Mexican capital and insurance markets but is caused by a built-in demand for immigrant labor that is intrinsic to advanced industrial societies. . . . Capitalist development [is] inherently disruptive, bringing about social and economic transformations that displace people from traditional livelihoods and force them onto transnational labor markets." See Douglas Massey and Kristin Espinosa, "What's Driving Mexico-US Migration? A Theoretical, Empirical, and Policy Analysis," *American Journal of Sociology* 102, no. 4 (1997): 939–99.

12. Between 2000 and 2005, we conducted research in Jupiter and Jacaltenango, utilizing quantitative and qualitative methods that included surveys, participant observation, in-depth interviews, focus groups, and oral histories.

13. For a detailed account, see Victor Montejo, *Voices from Exile: Violence and Survival in Modern Maya History* (Norman: University of Oklahoma Press, 1999).

14. For a more detailed explanation of the coffee crisis, see Panos Varangis, Paul Siegel, Daniel Giovanucci, and Brian Lewin, "Dealing with the Coffee Crisis in Central America: Impacts and Strategies," World Bank Policy Research Working Paper 2993, 2003.

15. Alejandro Portes and Ruben Rumbaut explain: "Immigrants do not come to escape perennial unemployment or destitution in their homeland. Most undertake the journey instead to attain the dream of a new lifestyle that has reached their countries but that is impossible to fulfill in them. Not surprisingly, the most determined individuals, those who feel the distance between actual reality and life goals the most poignantly, often choose migration as the path to resolve this contradiction." See *Immigrant America: A Portrait*, 2nd ed. (Berkeley: University of California Press, 1996), 19.

16. Jacoby also added a fourth point—that the native born are simply not pursuing higher degrees in the fields of science and engineering at nearly the rates that immigrants are. This leaves an unfilled demand in the technology and science sectors of our economy as well.

17. See Alejandro Portes, "The New Latin Nation: Immigration and the Hispanic Population in the United States," in Fran Ansley and Jon Shefner, eds., *Global Connections and Local Receptions: New Latino Immigration to the Southeastern United States* (Knoxville, TN: University of Tennessee Press, 2009), 3–34.

18. See Laura Wray-Lake, Amy K. Syvertsen, Laine Briddell, D. Wayne Osgood, and Constance A. Flanagan, "Exploring the Changing Meaning of Work for American High School Seniors from 1976 to 2005," Network on Transitions to Adulthood Research Network Working Paper, Pennsylvania State University, September 2009. They explain, "The value high school seniors placed on status and prestige, respect, advancement and earnings increased from the late 1970s until the late 1980s, when they reached their highest levels (84–85%). After a moderate decline from 1990 to 1992, these

values have remained high and stable at around 80% through the 1990s and early 2000s."

19. Massey and Espinosa, "What's Driving Mexico-US Migration?"

20. See Jeffrey Passel, *Unauthorized Migrants: Numbers and Characteristics* (Washington, DC: Pew Hispanic Center, 2005), http://pewhispanic .org/files/reports/46.pdf, and Randy Capps, Karina Fortuny, and Michael Fix, *Trends in the Low-Wage Immigrant Labor Force, 2000–2005* (Washington, DC: Urban Institute, 2007).

21. See Migration Policy Institute, "Georgia Fact Sheet," http://www .migrationinformation.org/DataHUb/state.cfm?ID=GA (accessed September 18, 2010).

22. In Michael Bess, "Transnational Trends, Regional Reflections: The Emergence of Mexican Immigrant Communities in the State of Georgia," April 2007, http://www.galeo.org/pdfs/mbess_immigration.pdf, 37.

23. Ibid., 38.

24. Teodoro Maus, "Atlanta's Global Future," in *Georgia Leaders Shaping Atlanta's Global Future* (Decatur, GA: Agio Press/International Business Club at Georgia Tech, 2003), 15.

25. See Michael Kirkland Bess, "Across Imagined Boundaries: Understanding Mexican Migration to Georgia in a Transnational and Historical Context," Master's Thesis, Department of History, Georgia Southern University, 2008.

26. See William Perez, *We Are Americans: Undocumented Students Pursuing the American Dream* (Sterling, VA: Stylus, 2009). We discuss further the issues facing unauthorized students in Chapter 5.

27. For a summary of United States immigration legislation, see the Appendix.

28. See Passel and Cohn, *A Portrait of Unauthorized Immigrants in the United States.*

29. U.S. Department of State, "Visa Bulletin for January 2011," http:// travel.state.gov/visa/bulletin_5212.html (accessed December 20, 2010).

30. See Reed Ueda, *Postwar Immigrant America: A Social History* (Boston: Bedford Books/St. Martin's Press, 1994).

31. See Roger Daniels, *Coming to America: A History of Immigration and Ethnicity in American Life* (New York: Harper Perennial, 1991).

32. These arguments are most famously made by Samuel Huntington in his book *Who Are We? The Challenges to America's National Identity* (New York: Simon and Schuster, 2004).

33. See Erika Lee, *At America's Gates: Chinese Immigration During the Exclusion Era, 1882–1943* (Chapel Hill: University of North Carolina Press, 2003).

34. For a more complete history of the Japanese in the United States, see Roger Daniels, *The Politics of Prejudice: The Anti-Japanese Movement in California and the Struggle for Japanese Exclusion*, 2nd ed. (Berkeley: University of California Press, 1977).

35. For a more detailed account of immigration legislation, see Charles Hirschman, "The Impact of Immigration on American Society: Looking Backward to the Future," in *Border Battles: The U.S. Immigration Debate.* (New York: Social Science Research Council, 2006), http://borderbattles .ssrc.org/Hirschman.

36. For instance, Mexico is experiencing an unprecedented demographic transition of its own, with fertility rates falling at unprecedented rates. Within twenty years, Mexico's own aging population may generate the same sort of service sector jobs the U.S. economy does today.

2. People in Motion: Life Crossing and Across Borders

1. See Douglas S. Massey, Jorge Durand, and Nolan J. Malone, *Beyond Smoke and Mirrors: Mexican Immigration in an Era of Economic Integration* (New York: Russell Sage Foundation, 2002), 45.

2. Wayne Cornelius, "Death at the Border: Efficacy and Unintended Consequences of US Immigration Control Policy," *Population and Development Review* 27, no. 4 (2001): 661–85.

3. Ibid., 663–64.

4. Ibid.

5. Wayne Cornelius and Idean Salehyan, "Does Border Enforcement Deter Unauthorized Immigration? The Case of Mexican Migration to the United States of America," *Regulation and Governance* 1 (2007): 139–53.

6. Department of Homeland Security, *FY 2011 Budget in Brief*, 52, http://www.dhs.gov/xlibrary/assets/budget_bib_fy2011.pdf.

7. Department of Homeland Security, *FY 2005 Budget in Brief*, http:// www.dhs.gov/xlibrary/assets/FY_2005_BIB_4.pdf.

8. Department of Homeland Security, *FY 2011 Budget in Brief.*

9. "Testimony of Douglas S. Massey Before the Senate Judiciary Committee," Senate Judiciary Committee, http://judiciary.senate.gov/hearings/testimony.cfm?id=3859&wit_id=7939 (accessed November 30, 2010).

10. Ibid.

11. See Jeffrey Passel, *Unauthorized Migrants: Numbers and Characteristics* (Washington, DC: Pew Hispanic Center, 2005), http://pewhispanic .org/files/reports/46.pdf.

12. Maria Jimenez, *Humanitarian Crisis: Deaths at the U.S.-Mexico Border* (San Diego: ACLU of San Diego and Imperial Counties and Mexico's National Commission on Human Rights, 2009), 8, http://www.aclu.org/ files/pdfs/immigrants/humanitariancrisisreport.pdf.

13. Ibid.

14. "Testimony of Douglas S. Massey Before the Senate Judiciary Committee."

15. "The *Grupo Beta de Protección a Migrantes* is an unarmed humanitarian assistance force set up by the National Migration Service to provide

help to migrants, regardless of their legal status, who are at risk of abuse, dehydration, starvation or exposure. There are 144 agents divided between 16 Grupo Beta units, primarily operating near the northern border, with some on the southern border. Agents also inform migrants about the dangers they face and their rights. They are not authorized to carry out migration status checks." See Amnesty International, *Invisible Victims: Migrants on the Move in Mexico* (London: Amnesty International Publications, 2010), 3.

16. Instituto Nacional de Migracion, *2009 Boletin Estadístico Anual* (México: INAMI, 2009), 80, 84, 91, 94.

17. See Amnesty International, *Invisible Victims*, 15.

18. Ibid.

19. David Stoll, "From Wage Migration to Debt-Migration," *Latin American Perspectives* 37, no. 1 (2010): 123–42.

20. David Stoll does not argue that women are purely victims, as he documents several instances in which women were engaged in predatory lending practices themselves. See Stoll, "From Wage Migration to Debt-Migration."

21. U.S. Census Bureau, Census 2000.

22. For a detailed discussion of the factors contributing to the growth of "new destinations," see Victor Zúñiga and Rubén León, eds., *New Destinations: Mexican Immigration in the United States* (New York: Russell Sage Foundation, 2005).

23. Jorge Durand, Douglas Massey, and Chiara Capoferro, "The New Geography of Mexican Immigration," in Zúñiga and León, eds., *New Destinations*, 2–3.

24. See Manuel Vásquez, Chad E. Seales, and Marie Friedmann Marquardt, "New Latino Destinations," in Havidan Rodriguez, Rogelio Saenz, and Cecilia Menjivar, eds., *Latinas/os in the United States: Changing the Face of America* (New York: Springer Press International, 2008), 19–35.

25. Ibid., 23.

26. Based on data from the 1990 and 2000 U.S. Census and the 2007 American Community Survey.

27. See Jill Taylor and Pamela Perez, "5 Day Laborers Robbed, Dropped off in Martin," *Palm Beach Post*, September 24, 2005.

28. Maxine L. Margolis, *Little Brazil: An Ethnography of Brazilian Immigrants in New York City* (Princeton, NJ: Princeton University Press, 1994).

29. Elizabeth Fussell, "Post-Katrina New Orleans as a New Migrant Destination," *Organization and Environment* 22 (2009): 458–69.

30. See Jeffrey Passel and D'Vera Cohn, *A Portrait of Unauthorized Immigrants in the United States* (Washington, DC: Pew Hispanic Center, 2009).

31. Ibid., 8.

32. Ibid.

33. The circumstances of their migration mean that many unauthorized

migrants take part in the construction of what Pierrette Hondagneu-Sotelo and Ernestine Avila have termed "transnational families." Such families are characterized by long-term separation between spouses, children, and extended families. See Pierrette Hondagneu-Sotelo and Ernestine Avila, " 'I'm Here but I'm There': The Meanings of Latina Transnational Motherhood," in *Gender and U.S. Immigration: Contemporary Trends*, ed. Pierrette Hondagneu-Sotelo, 317–40 (Berkeley, CA: University of California Press, 2003).

34. Peggy Levitt, "Social Remittances: Migration Driven Local-Level Forms of Cultural Diffusion," *International Migration Review* 32, no. 4 (1998): 926–48, 927.

35. Organización Internacional para las Migraciones, *Cuadernos de Trabajo Sobre Migración 27: Encuesta Nacional Sobre Remesas 2009 Niñez y Adolescencia* (Guatemala: IOM, 2009), 58.

36. Immigration and Customs Enforcement, *Fiscal Year 2008 Annual Report* (Washington, DC: 2008), iii.

37. National Immigration Forum, "Secure Communities," Washington, DC, November 23, 2009.

38. Ibid.

39. See Government Accountability Office, *Alien Detention Standards: Telephone Access Problems Were Pervasive at Detention Facilities; Other Deficiencies Did Not Show a Pattern of Noncompliance* (Washington, DC: Government Accountability Office, 2007), 1.

40. See Richard Stana, *Alien Detention Standards: Observations on the Adherence to ICE's Medical Standards in Detention Facilities* (Washington, DC: Government Accountability Office, 2008), 5.

41. See Government Accountability Office, *Alien Detention Standards*, 1.

42. See the Appendix for a brief description of this legislation.

3. Living Together, Living Apart: Interethnic Relations in New Immigrant Destinations

1. This is a pseudonym.

2. The Latino population of Cobb County increased from 2 percent of the total population in 1990 to more than 12 percent of the total population in 2008.

3. To gauge Cobb County residents' views on the impact of immigration, we conducted a series of focus group interviews. The focus groups were conducted specifically for our project by the A.L. Burruss Institute of Kennesaw State University during August 2008. Interviews were conducted with the following groups: African American females (N = 7), African American males (N = 8), Euro-American females (N = 11), Euro-American males (N = 10). All participants had lived in Cobb County for at least ten years. A moderator and note taker were present for each focus group. The interview guide included questions about the impact of immigration on

Cobb County (population growth, neighborhoods, local economy, schools, and English proficiency); immigration politics (state and local laws restricting immigration, the April–May 2006 immigration rights protests); and attitudes toward other ethnic groups.

4. See Humphrey Jeffrey, *The Multicultural Economy* (Waycross, GA: Selig Center for Economic Growth, University of Georgia, 2008).

5. Perryman Group, *An Analysis of the Economic Impact of Undocumented Workers on Business Activity in the US with Estimated Effects by State and by Industry* (Waco, TX: Perryman Group, 2008).

6. See Sarah Coffrey. *Undocumented Immigrants in Georgia: Tax Contribution and Fiscal Concern* (Atlanta: Georgia Budget and Policy Institute, 2006).

7. See California Immigrant Policy Center, *Looking Forward: Immigrant Contributions to the Golden State/A Compilation of Recent Research Findings in California* (Sacramento: CIPC, 2008).

8. See Emily Eisenhower, Alex Angee, Cynthia Hernandez, and Yue Zhang, *Immigrants in Florida: Characteristics and Contributions* (Miami: Research Institute for Social and Economic Policy of the Center for Labor Research and Studies at Florida International University, 2007).

9. See Sarita Mohanty, *Unequal Access: Immigrants and U.S. Health Care* (Washington, DC: Immigration Policy Center, 2006).

10. See Peter Cunningham, "What Accounts for Differences in the Use of Hospital Emergency Departments Across U.S. Communities?" *Health Affairs* 25, no. 5 (2006): 324–36.

11. See Leighton Ku, Shawn Fermstad, and Matthew Broadus, "Noncitizens' Use of Public Benefits Has Declined Since 1996," Center on Budget and Policy Priorities, April 21, 2003, http://www.cbpp.org/cms/index.cfm?fa=view&id=1810 (accessed December 1, 2010). See also Karen Cunnynham and Beth Brown, *Characteristics of Food Stamp Households: Fiscal Year 2003* (Washington, DC: USDA Nutrition Assistance Program Report Series, 2004).

12. The survey for this study was conducted specifically for our project by the A.L. Burruss Institute of Kennesaw State University utilizing random digit dialing (RDD) samples purchased from Survey Sampling Inc. (SSI) of Fairfield, Connecticut. A randomly generated sample of five thousand numbers drawn from Cobb, DeKalb, Fulton, Gwinnett, and Clayton counties made up our general sample. Calling for that sample took place between February 26 and March 19, 2009. The response rate for the general RDD survey was 23 percent with a margin of error of .05. A total of 403 completed interviews were conducted from the RDD sample (225 Euro-American respondents, 156 African American respondents, and 22 Latino respondents). In order to supplement the number of African American respondents in our samples we drew two further samples (of three thousand and four thousand numbers) targeting high-density African American census tracts in the same counties over the same time period. Those samples produced another

eighty-five completed interviews with African American and Latino respondents. The margin of error for those samples was .07. Finally, a sample of five thousand Latino surnames was utilized for surveys collected between April 7 and May 12, 2009, with a response rate of 14 percent. A total of 8,426 numbers were attempted during the survey, with 12,037 English call attempts and 3,394 Spanish call attempts. In all, interviews were completed with 227 Euro-Americans, 231 African Americans, 255 Latinos, and 1 respondent who reported another ethnic category.

13. See George J. Borjas, "The Labor Demand Curve Is Downward Sloping: Reexamining the Impact of Immigration on the Labor Market," *Quarterly Journal of Economics* 118, no. 4 (2003): 1335–74.

14. See Tim Bolin, *The Economic and Fiscal Impacts of Immigration* (Berkeley, CA: Institute for Research on Labor and Employment, 2006), 9.

15. Pew Hispanic Center, *The New Latino South: The Context and Consequences of Rapid Population Growth* (Washington, DC: Pew Hispanic Center, 2005), 27.

16. Ibid.

17. See Samuel Huntington, "The Hispanic Challenge," *Foreign Policy*, March–April 2004, 40.

18. See Georgia Department of Education, "School Year 1994–1995 Enrollment by Gender, Race/Ethnicity and Grade (PK-12)," Georgia Department of Education, http://app.doe.k12.ga.us/ows-bin/owa/fte_pack_ethnicsex.display_proc (accessed December 1, 2010). See also Georgia Department of Education, "School Year 2010–2011 Enrollment by Gender, Race/Ethnicity and Grade (PK-12)," Georgia Department of Education, http://app.doe.k12.ga.us/ows-bin/owa/fte_pack_ethnicsex.display_proc (accessed December 1, 2010).

19. According to the U.S. Census, the non-Hispanic white population grew by 8 percent from 1990 to 2000.

20. Georgia Department of Education, "School Year 1994–1995 Enrollment." See also Georgia Department of Education, "School Year 2010–2011 Enrollment."

21. See Mike Davis, *Magical Urbanism: Latinos Reinvent the US City* (London: Verso, 2000).

22. See Alejandro Portes and Rubén G. Rumbaut, *Legacies: The Story of the Immigrant Second Generation* (Berkeley: University of California Press, 2001), 239.

23. See Huntington, "The Hispanic Challenge."

24. Anti-Defamation League, "Immigrants Targeted: Extremist Rhetoric Moves into the Mainstream," http://www.adl.org/civil_rights/anti_immigrant/da_king.asp (accessed December 1, 2010).

25. Governor Brewer went so far as to mistakenly declare: "Oh, our law enforcement agencies have found bodies in the desert, either buried or just lying out there, that have been beheaded." See Aliyah Shahid, "Jan Brewer,

GOP Governor of Arizona and SB 1070 Supporter: I Was Wrong on Headless Bodies Claim," *Daily News* (New York), September 4, 2010.

25. See Randall Archibald, "On Border Violence, Truth Pales Compared to Ideas," *New York Times*, June 19, 2010.

26. "Statistics show that even as Arizona's population swelled, buoyed in part by illegal immigrants funneling across the border, violent crime rates declined, to 447 incidents per 100,000 residents in 2008, the most recent year for which comprehensive data is available from the F.B.I. In 2000, the rate was 532 incidents per 100,000. Nationally, the crime rate declined to 455 incidents per 100,000 people, from 507 in 2000." See Archibald, "On Border Violence."

27. See Suzanne Gamboa and Kathleen Miller, "Death of Nun, Sister Denise Mosier, Sparks Anti-Immigration Backlash In Virginia," *Huffington Post*, August 8, 2010.

28. See Rubén G. Rumbaut and Walter Ewing, *The Myth of Immigrant Criminality and the Paradox of Assimilation: Incarceration Rates Among Native and Foreign-Born Men* (Washington, DC: Immigration Policy Center, 2007).

29. See Robert Sampson, "Rethinking Crime and Immigration," *Contexts* 7, no. 1 (2008): 28–33.

30. Missy Diaz, "Teen Robber Faces Life in Prison," *South Florida Sun Sentinel*, September 6, 2007.

31. Bob Moser, "The Battle of 'Georgiafornia,' " *Intelligence Report*, Winter 2004, 33.

32. Southern Poverty Law Center, *Under Siege: Life for Low-Income Latinos in the South* (Montgomery, AL: 2009), 33.

33. See U.S. Department of Justice, *Uniform Crime Report: Hate Crime Statistics 2008* (Washington, DC: Federal Bureau of Investigation, 2009), 33.

34. See Southern Poverty Law Center, *Under Siege*.

35. Christian Dustman and Ian Preston, "Racial and Economic Factors in Attitudes to Immigration," *B.E. Journal of Economic Analysis Policy* 7, no. 1 (2007): 20.

36. See Shang Ha, "The Consequences of Multiracial Contexts on Public Attitudes Toward Immigration," *Political Research Quarterly* 63, no. 1 (2010): 39.

37. National Conference of State Legislatures, *State Laws Related to Immigrants and Immigration* (Washington, DC: Immigrant Policy Project, 2009).

38. Ordinances directly targeting undocumented immigrants have surfaced in places as diverse as Avon Park, Florida; Hazleton, Pennsylvania; Arcadia, Wisconsin; Farmingville, New York; and Riverside, New Jersey. See Philip J. Williams, Timothy J. Steigenga, and Manuel A. Vásquez, *A Place to Be Brazilian, Guatemalan, and Mexican Immigrants in Florida's New Destinations* (New Brunswick, NJ: Rutgers University Press, 2009), 224. See also David Fried, "Local Illegal Immigration Laws Draw a Diverse Group of

Cities," *North County Times-Californian,* September 3, 2006, http://www.nctimes.com/news/local/article_03dfcb93-677d-5b4f-blaf-ed123a8a49fc.html (accessed December 1, 2010).

39. See Cristina Rodriguez, Muzaffar Chishti, Randy Capps, and Laura St. John, *A Program in Flux: New Priorities and Implementation Challenges for 287(g)* (Washington, DC: Migration Policy Institute, 2010), 3.

40. See U.S. Immigration and Customs Enforcement, "Delegation of Immigration Authority Section 287(g) Immigration and Nationality Act Factsheet," 2010, http://www.ice.gov/pi/news/factsheets/section287_g.htm (accessed August 1, 2010).

41. According to a 2009 study 87 percent had a rate of Latino population growth higher than the national average. See Aarti Shahani and Judith Greene, *Local Democracy on Ice: Why State and Local Governments Have No Business in Federal Immigration Law Enforcement* (Brooklyn, NY: Justice Strategies Report, 2009).

42. See Azadeh Shahshahani, *Terror and Isolation in Cobb: How Unchecked Police Power Under 287(g) Has Torn Families Apart and Threatened Public Safety* (Atlanta: American Civil Liberties Union Foundation of Georgia, 2009).

43. Government Accountability Office, *Immigration Enforcement: Better Controls Needed over Program Authorizing State and Local Enforcement of Federal Immigration Laws* (Washington, DC: GAO, 2009).

44. Ibid., 5.

45. Ibid., 4.

46. See Shahshahani, *Terror and Isolation in Cobb.*

47. See Julia Preston and Robert Gebeloff, "Some Unlicensed Drivers Risk More than a Fine," *New York Times,* December 9, 2010. http://www.nytimes.com/2010/12/10/us/10license.html?_r=1&adxnnl=1&emc=eta1&adxnnlx=1292497203-6R5qz2WLg9Y/TzoHuwRkyw&pagewanted=all (accessed December 16, 2010).

48. Chelsea Cook, "Man Fishing Without a License Now Facing Deportation," *Atlanta Journal-Constitution,* June 10, 2010, http://www.ajc.com/news/man-fishing-without-a-546214.html (accessed 16 December 2010).

4. "Picking Up the Cross": Churches on the Front Lines

1. In this chapter, the names of religious organizations and their pastoral workers have not been changed. With the exception of P.J. and Amy Edwards, who requested that we use their names, the names of staff and members of these religious organizations have been changed to protect their anonymity.

2. Quoted from Emily Enders Odem, " 'A Little Picture of Heaven': Immigrants' Dreams and Visions Forge a New Multicultural Church," Presbyterian News Service, July 22, 2008, http://archive.pcusa.org/penews/2008/08527.htm (accessed December 20, 2010).

3. Ibid.

4. There is no doubt that throughout the United States, eleven o'clock on Sunday morning continues to be the most segregated hour in American life, and most churches continue to be ethnically homogeneous. However, congregations are increasingly developing different approaches to engaging with recent Latino immigrants, which range from separate and unequal existence under the same roof to full partnership. See Warner R. Stephen, "Religion and New (Post-1965) Immigrants: Some Principles Drawn from Field Research," in *A Church of Our Own: Disestablishment and Diversity in American Religion* (New Brunswick, NJ: Rutgers University Press, 2005), 232–52.

5. For an insightful analysis of the Santa Cena and further description of La Luz del Mundo Church, see Patricia Fortuny, "The Santa Cena of the Luz del Mundo Church: A Case of Contemporary Transnationalism," in Helen Rose Ebeaugh and Janet Saltzman Chafetz, eds., *Religion Across Borders: Transnational Immigrant Networks* (Walnut Creek, CA: Alta Mira Press, 2002), 15–50.

6. See Patricia Fortuny and Philip J. Williams, "Iglesias y espacios púbicos: lugares de identidad, de mexicanos en Metro Atlanta," in *Trayectorias. Revista de Ciencias Sociales* (Universidad Autónoma de Nuevo León) 10, no. 26 (2008).

7. For an excellent historical treatment of the role of black churches as alternative public spaces, see Evelyn Brooks Higginbotham, *Righteous Discontent: The Women's Movement in the Black Baptist Church, 1880–1920* (Cambridge, MA: Harvard University Press, 1994).

8. In Odem, "A Little Picture of Heaven."

9. For more information on renewalist Latino Christianity, see the Pew Research Center's 2007 study on Latino religion, "Changing Faiths: Latinos and the Transformation of American Religion," http://pewresearch.org/pubs/461/religion-hispanic-latino.

5. Migrants Mobilize: Finding a Voice in Local and National Debates

1. Story recounted from Anton Flores, *Engaging the Pharisees* (LaGrange, GA: Alterna Newsletter: After Pentecost, 2010).

2. U.S. Census Bureau decennial census and population estimates, as reported by Pew Hispanic Center, http://pewhispanic.org/states/?county id=13135.

3. For example, in Hazelton, Pennsylvania, the town administration passed a series of ordinances to curtail day labor. Among other restrictions, the ordinance required every business in town to sign an affidavit affirming that they had verified the status of all their employees, permanent or temporary, in order to obtain a license to do business within Hazelton. The ordinance also targeted day laborers by putting in place harsh penalties for landlords who were renting to undocumented people and requiring renters

in Hazelton to obtain an "occupancy permit" prior to renting. Farmingville, New York, Manassas, Virginia, and other towns across the United States have targeted day laborers similarly.

4. Libby Wells, "Day Labor Center Idea Discouraged," *Palm Beach Post*, November 13, 2004.

5. "January 2005 TC Minutes," Town of Jupiter, http://www.jupi ter.fl.us/Agendas/TownCouncil/2005-TC-Minutes.cfm (accessed November 30, 2010).

6. Lou Dobbs Tonight, aired November 18, 2004. Transcripts available at http://archives.cnn.com/TRANSCRIPTS/0411/18/ldt.01.html.

7. Jill Taylor and Pamela Perez, "Five Day Laborers Robbed, Dropped off in Martin," *Palm Beach Post*, September 24, 2005.

8. "5 April 2005 TC Minutes," Town of Jupiter, http://www.jupiter .fl.us/Agendas/TownCouncil/2005-TC-Minutes.cfm (accessed November 30, 2010).

9. "1 February 2005 TC Minutes," Town of Jupiter, http://www.jupiter .fl.us/Agendas/TownCouncil/2005-TC-Minutes.cfm (accessed November 30, 2010).

10. Dianna Cahn, "Center That Helps Immigrants in Jupiter Draws Protests: Protesters Say Center to Help Laborers Is Flouting Law; Jupiter Officials Call It Legal, Practical Solution," *South Florida Sun-Sentinel*, January 11, 2008.

11. See John C. Oliver, "Enforce Laws to Protect Americans," *Palm Beach Post*, December 23, 2007.

12. Dan Moffet, "See Real People by the Light of El Sol," *Palm Beach Post*, May 11, 2008.

13. *Brother Towns: Pueblos Hermanos*, DVD, directed by Charles Thompson (Durham, NC: Center for Documentary Studies at Duke University, 2010).

14. In Anton Flores, *Fearless Love* (LaGrange, GA: Alterna Newsletter: After Pentecost, 2010).

15. In Anton Flores, *In the Name of the Lord: Reflections on the 2010 Holy Week Pilgrimage for Immigrants* (LaGrange, GA: Alterna Newsletter: After Pentecost, 2010).

16. Flores, *Fearless Love*.

17. "Alterna: Love Crosses Borders/El Amor Cruza Fronteras," http:// www.alternacommunity (accessed November 30, 2010).

18. Sherri Brown, "Advocate from LaGrange Wins Top Honor from Atlanta Newspaper," *LaGrange Daily News*, February 9, 2010.

19. This and subsequent quotes come from interviews conducted in August and September 2010. Names have been changed to protect the anonymity of interviewees, with the exception of Anton and Charlotte Flores, who are public figures associated with Alterna.

20. 13 Matthew 31:32 (New Revised Standard Version).

21. "Alterna: Love Crosses Borders/El Amor Cruza Fronteras."

22. Ibid.

23. Ibid.

24. Ibid.

25. For an eye-opening account of the role of the Corrections Corporation of American in drafting and helping to pass Arizona's controversial SB 1070 as a means to fill their own prisons in Arizona, see the National Public Radio report "Prison Economics Help Drive Immigration Law," reported on *Morning Edition*, NPR, October 28, 2010, by Laura Sullivan, http://www.npr.org/templates/story/story.php?storyId=130833741.

26. "How Corporate Interests Got SB 1070 Passed," *Talk of the Nation*, NPR, November 9, 2010, http://www.npr.org/templates/story/story.php?storyId=131191523. The report focuses on the activities of the American Legislative Exchange Council (ALEC), whose board includes representatives from the Correction Corporation of America and other private prison companies as well as federal and state officials such as Russell Pearce, the Arizona state senator responsible for SB 1070. According to the NPR report, ALEC boasts about having passed two hundred pieces of legislation having to do with immigration enforcement and detention in statehouses across the country.

27. See http://Koinoniapartners.org (accessed December 17, 2010).

28. For an excellent treatment and ethical analysis of the work of utopian communities in the Americas and of the influence of the Anabaptist tradition on such communities, see Anna Lisa Peterson, *Seeds of the Kingdom: Utopian Communities in the Americas* (Oxford: Oxford University Press, 2005).

29. *The Purpose*, movie, in "The Trail of Dreams—Walkers for the Dream Act—AL DIA News," http://dreamact.pontealdia.com/purpose/the-trail-of-dreams (accessed November 30, 2010).

30. William Perez, *We Are Americans: Undocumented Students Pursuing the American Dream* (Sterling, VA: Stylus, 2009), xxv.

31. "Blog—Trail2010.org," http://www.trail2010.org/blog (accessed November 30, 2010).

32. Roberto Gonzalez, "Left Out but Not Shut Down: Political Activism and the Undocumented Student Movement," *Northwestern Journal of Law and Social Policy* 3 (2008): 219–39.

33. Roberto Gonzalez, "Young Lives on Hold: The College Dreams of Undocumented Students," *College Board Advocacy*, April 2009.

34. Perez, *We Are Americans*, xxv.

35. Gonzalez, *Young Lives on Hold*, 6.

36. Sharon White Senghor, "Undocumented Students and the Dream Act: Subsequent Developments and Trends," *NACUA Notes*, May 8, 2010.

37. Ibid.

38. Ibid.; Maura Dolan, "In-State Tuition for Illegal Immigrants Is Preserved with California Supreme Court Ruling," *Los Angeles Times*, http://www.latimes.com/news/la-immiganttuition15-m,0,512913.story (accessed December 1, 2010).

39. "DREAMActivist.org," http://www.dreamactivist.org (accessed November 30, 2010).

40. Ibid.

41. *Bob Edwards Weekend*, NPR, October 17, 2010.

42. *The Purpose.*

43. "Blog—Trail2010.org."

44. *The Purpose.*

45. "Trail of Dreams and Fast for Our Families," Facebook, http://www
.facebook.com/pages/Trail-of-Dreams-Fast-for-Our-Families/238380821
788#!/pages/Trail-of-Dreams-Fast-for-Our-Families/238380821788 (accessed November 30, 2010).

46. See http://trail2010.org/dreamactvideo (accessed December 17, 2010).

47. See http://colorlines.com/archives/2010/12/dreamers_storm_capi
tol_hill_before_senate_vote.html.

48. See http://americasvoiceonline.org/researchentry/the_ugly_face_
of_the_dream_act_debate (accessed December 17, 2010).

49. Julia Preston, "Immigration Vote Leaves Policy in Disarray," *New York Times*, December 19, 2010.

50. Ibid.

51. Ibid.

52. See http://trail2010.org/dreamactvideo (accessed December 17, 2010).

53. Felipe Matos, "No More Fear, Come Out!" trail2010.org, March 15, 2010.

Conclusion

1. Daniel Kanstroom, *Deportation Nation: Outsiders in American History* (Cambridge, MA: Harvard University Press, 2007), ix.

2. Tamara K. Nopper, "Why Black Immigrants Matter: Refocussing the Discussion on Racism and Immigration Enforcement," in *Keeping Out the Other: A Critical Introduction to Immigration Enforcement Today*, ed. David C. Brotherton and Philip Kretsedemas (New York: Columbia University Press, 2008), 205.

3. "Transcript & Video: President Obama's News Conference As Lame Duck Congress Concludes," Obama Foodorama, December 22, 2010, http://
obamafoodorama.blogspot.com/2010/12/transcript-video-president-obamas
-news.html (accessed January 1, 2011).

4. Ibid.

5. Ibid.

6. Leslie Berestein Rojas, "Q&A: UCSD Immigration Expert Wayne Cornelius on Why the Dream Act Went Down," Southern California Public Radio, December 21, 2010, http://multiamerican.scpr.org/2010/12/qa-uc
sd-immigration-expert-wayne-cornelius-on-why-the-dream-act-went-down/
(accessed January 1, 2011).

7. Marshall Fritz, Gebe Martínez, and Madura Wijewardena, *The Cost of Mass Deportation: Impractical, Costly, and Ineffective* (Washington, DC: Center for American Progress, 2010).

8. Mike M. Ahlers, "ICE: Tab to Remove Illegal Residents Would Approach \$100 billion," CNN.com, September 12, 2007, http://www.cnn .com/2007/US/09/12/deportation.cost/index.html (accessed December 26, 2010).

9. Jessica Vaughan, "Attrition Through Enforcement: A Cost-Effective Strategy to Shrink the Illegal Population," Center for Immigration Studies, April 2006, http://www.cis.org/Enforcement-IllegalPopulation (accessed December 26, 2010).

10. Jeffrey Passel and D'Vera Cohn, "U.S. Unauthorized Immigration Flows Are Down Sharply Since Mid-Decade," Pew Hispanic Center, September 1, 2010.

11. Ibid.

12. Miriam Jordan and Connor Dougherty, "Immigration Slows in Face of Economic Downturn: U.S. Crackdown on Illegal Workers Further Dims Opportunity," *Wall Street Journal*, September 23, 2008, http://online.wsj .com/article/SB122213015990965589.html (accessed January 1, 2011). The economic downturn also explains why in 2008 immigration as a whole "plateaued . . . following thirty years of unprecedented growth." See Audrey Singer and Jill Wilson, "The Impact of the Great Recession on Metropolitan Immigration Trends," Brookings, December 16, 2010, http://www.brookings .edu/papers/2010/1216_immigration_singer_wilson.aspx (accessed January 1, 2011).

13. "Transcript & Video: President Obama's News Conference As Lame Duck Congress Concludes."

14. "Statement on Law Enforcement Shooting in Pinal County by Governor Jan Brewer," April 30, 2010, http://azgovernor.gov/dms/upload/ PR_043010_StatementGovBrewer_Shooting.pdf (accessed February 17, 2011).

15. See "Table 4: Crime in the United States by Region, Geographic Division, and State, 2008–2009," Federal Bureau of Investigation, U.S. Department of Justice, http://www2.fbi.gov/ucr/cius2009/data/table_ 04.html (accessed January 5, 2011).

16. Ted Robbins, "Immigration Enforcement Working, Numbers Show," WBUR, January 4, 2011, http://www.wbur.org/npr/132657708/ immigration-enforcement-working-numbers-show (accessed January 5, 2011).

17. For a good summary of this debate, see Ruth Muñoz, *Labor and Legality: An Ethnography of a Mexican Immigrant Network* (New York: Oxford University Press, 2011), 124–36.

18. Eduardo Castillo, "APNewsBreak: Mexico Plans Immigration Shake-Up," Associated Press, available at http://abcnews.go.com/International/ wireStory?id=12523211 (accessed January 5, 2011).

19. Roger Daniels, *Coming to America: A History of Immigration and Ethnicity in American Life*, 2nd ed. (New York: HarperPerennial, 2002), 228.

20. Peggy Levitt, *God Needs No Passport: Immigrants and the Changing American Religious Landscape* (New York: The New Press, 2007), 196.

21. Douglas S. Massey and Magaly Sánchez R., *Brokered Boundaries: Creating Immigrant Identity in Anti-Immigrant Times* (New York: Russell Sage Foundation, 2010), 252.

22. Levitt, *God Needs No Passport*, 169.

23. Robert Putnam, "E Pluribus Unum: Diversity and Community in the Twenty-First Century: The 2006 Johan Skytte Prize Lecture," *Scandinavian Political Studies* 30, no. 2 (2007): 137–74.

24. Richard Alba, "Achieving a More Integrated America," *Dissent* 57, no. 3 (2010): 57.

25. Ibid.

26. Douglas S. Massey, Jorge Durand, and Nolan J. Malone, *Beyond Smoke and Mirrors: Mexican Immigration in an Era of Economic Integration* (New York: Russell Sage Foundation, 2002), 142–64.

27. Douglas S. Massey, "The Wall That Keeps Illegal Workers In," *New York Times*, April 4, 2006, http://www.nytimes.com/2006/04/04/opinion/04massey.html (accessed January 5, 2011).

28. Leslie Berestein Rokas, "Top Five Immigration Stories of 2010, #3: Secure Communities and 287(g)," Multi-American, Southern California Public Radio, December 29, 2010, http://multiamerican.scpr.org/2010/12/top-immigration-stories-of-2010-3-secure-communities-and-287g/ (accessed January 6, 2011).

29. This is already the case for EB-5 visas, which are given to investors who promise to create at least ten jobs in the United States.

30. James C. McKinley, "After Dream Act Setback, Weighing a Next Move," *New York Times*, December 20, 2010, http://www.nytimes.com/2010/12/21/us/politics/21immig.html (accessed January 6, 2011).

Epilogue

1. "Transcript of Benita Veliz Remarks as Prepared for Delivery, Democratic National Convention," *Daily Kos*, September 5, 2012, http://www.dailykos.com/story/2012/09/05/1128253/-Transcript-of-Benita-Veliz-remarks-as-prepared-for-delivery-Democratic-National-Convention (accessed October 29, 2012).

2. Jeffrey Passel and Mark Hugo Lopez, "Up to 1.7 Million Unauthorized Youth May Benefit from New Deportation Rules," Pew Research Center, August 14, 2012, http://www.pewhispanic.org/2012/08/14/up-to-1-7-million-unauthorized-immigrant-youth-may-benefit-from-new-deportation-rules/ (accessed October 30, 2012).

3. U.S. Customs and Immigration Service, "Deferred Action for Child-

hood Arrivals Process," http://www.uscis.gov/USCIS/Resources/Reports %20and%20Studies/Immigration%20Forms%20Data/All%20Form%20 Types/DACA/DACAOct2012.pdf (accessed October 30, 2012).

4. "ICE Agents v. Napolitano: Read the Complaint," NumbersUSA, October 12, 2012, https://www.numbersusa.com/content/news/august-23 -2012/ice-agents-v-napolitano-read-complaint.html (accessed October 28, 2012)

5. Marshall Fitz, Patrick Oakford, and Ann Garcia, "The Early Success of the Deferred Action for Childhood Arrivals Policy," Center for American Progress, October 26, 2012, http://www.americanprogress.org/issues/im migration/news/2012/10/26/43051/the-early-success-of-the-deferred -action-for-childhood-arrivals-policy/ (accessed October 30, 2012).

6. Janet Napolitano, "A Reality Check on Immigration," *Politico*, October 5, 2011, http://www.politico.com/news/stories/1011/65209.html (accessed October 8, 2012).

7. Suzy Khimm, "Obama Is Deporting Immigrants Faster than Bush. Republicans Don't Think That's Enough," *Washington Post*, August 27, 2012, http://www.washingtonpost.com/blogs/ezra-klein/wp/2012/08/27/ obama-is-deporting-more-immigrants-than-bush-republicans-dont-think -thats-enough/?print=1 (accessed September 18, 2012).

8. U.S. Customs and Immigration Service, "ICE Total Removals," http://www.ice.gov/doclib/about/offices/ero/pdf/ero-removals1.pdf (accessed September 21, 2012); U.S. Department of Homeland Security, "Immigration Enforcement Actions: 2010," June 2011, http://www.dhs.gov/ xlibrary/assets/statistics/publications/enforcement-ar-2010.pdf (accessed October 8, 2012).

9. U.S. Customs and Immigration Service, "Secure Communities. The Basics," http://www.ice.gov/secure_communities/ (accessed September 18, 2012); U.S. Customs and Immigration Service, "Activated Jurisdictions. Secure Communities," http://www.ice.gov/doclib/secure-communities/pdf/ sc-activated.pdf (accessed September 18, 2012).

10. Julia Preston, "Despite Opposition, Immigration Agency to Expand Fingerprint Program," *New York Times*, May 11, 2012, http://www.ny times.com/2012/05/12/us/ice-to-expand-secure-communities-program-in -mass-and-ny.html (accessed September 19, 2012).

11. Marie C. Baca, "Immigration Initiative May Put Domestic Violence Victims at Risk," California Watch, March 3, 2011, http://californiawatch .org/dailyreport/immigration-initiative-may-put-domestic-violence-victims -risk-8993 (accessed October 8, 2012).

12. See "State Laws Related to Immigration and Immigrants," National Conference of State Legislatures, http://www.ncsl.org/issues-research/ immig/state-laws-related-to-immigration-and-immigrants.aspx (accessed October 15, 2012).

13. See Pamela Constable, "A Tough New Alabama Law Targets Illegal Immigrants and Sends Families Fleeing," *Washington Post*, October 8, 2011,

http://www.washingtonpost.com/local/a-tough-new-alabama-law-targets -illegal-immigrants-and-sends-families-fleeing/2011/10/07/gIQAtZuPWL _story.html (accessed October 15, 2012).

14. Iulia Filip, "Bishops Say Alabama's Harsh Immigration Law Would Criminalize Religious Sacraments," *Courthouse News Service*, August 4, 2011, http://www.courthousenews.com/2011/08/04/38714.htm (accessed November 3, 2012).

15. Asian Law Caucus, "ICE's Shredding of 'S-Comm' Agreements: A Stunning Display of Bad Faith," August 5, 2011, http://arcof72.com/ 2011/08/05/ice's-shredding-of-"s-comm"-agreements-a-stunning-display -of-bad-faith/ (accessed September 24, 2012).

16. The Utah Compact: A Declaration of Five Principles to Guide Utah's Immigration Discussion, http://www.theutahcompact.com/read-the-utah -compact (accessed October 15, 2012).

17. Monica Varsanyi, *Taking Local Control: Immigration Policy Activism in U.S. Cities and States* (Stanford: Stanford University Press, 2010), 3.

18. Janice Fine, *Worker Centers: Organizing Communities at the Edge of the Dream* (Ithaca: EPI and Cornell University Press, 2006), 3.

19. Sandra Lazo de la Vega and Timothy J. Steigenga, *Against the Tide: Immigrants, Day Laborers and Community in Jupiter, Florida* (Madison: University of Wisconsin Press, 2013).

20. Julia Preston and Fernanda Santos, "A Record Latino Turnout, Solidly Backing Obama," *New York Times*, November 8, 2012, http://www .nytimes.com/2012/11/08/us/politics/with-record-turnout-latinos-solidly -back-obama-and-wield-influence.html (accessed November 8, 2012).

21. "Exit Polls 2012: How Votes Are Shifting," *Washington Post*, November 6, 2012, http://www.washingtonpost.com/wp-srv/special/politics/ 2012-exit-polls/#Florida (accessed November 8, 2012).

22. "ImpreMedia/Latino Decisions 2012 Latino Election Eve Poll," *La Opinión*, http://www.laopinion.com/section/voto_latinovote (accessed November 8, 2012).

23. Matt Barreto, "New Poll: Latino Voters in Battle ground States Enthusiastic About Obama DREAM Announcement, Oppose Romney 'Self-Deport' Alternative," Latino Decisions, June 17, 2012, http://www.latinode cisions.com/blog/2012/06/17/new-poll-latino-voters-enthusiastic-about -obama-dream-announcement-oppose-romney-policy-of-self-deport/ (accessed November 8, 2012).

24. Ezra Klein, "Wonkbook: For 2 Million Illegal Immigrants, Change Has Come," *Washington Post*, August 16, 2012, http://www.washington post.com/blogs/ezra-klein/wp/2012/08/16/wonkbook-for-2-million-illegal -immigrants-change-has-come/ (accessed November 8, 2012).

25. Peyton Craighill, "Why Republicans' Position on Immigration Is a Political Loser—in 1 Chart," *Washington Post*, November 9, 2012, http:// www.washingtonpost.com/blogs/the-fix/wp/2012/11/09/immigration -reform-has-clear-support-in-exit-poll/ (accessed November 10, 2012).

Appendix: Time Line of Important Immigration Policy

For another complete list of immigration legislation, see Lisa Magaña, *Straddling the Border: Immigration Policy and the INS* (Austin: University of Texas Press, 2003).

1. See Edward P. Hutchinson, *Legislative History of American Immigration Policy, 1798–1965* (Philadelphia: University of Pennsylvania Press, 1981), 11–16.

2. Ibid., 17.

3. Ibid., 22.

4. Ibid., 66.

5. Ibid., 80.

6. Ibid., 89.

7. Ibid., 539.

8. Ibid., 538.

9. Ibid., 176.

10. Ibid., 194.

11. Ibid., 258.

12. Ibid., 265.

13. Ibid., 280.

14. Ibid., 307.

15. See Reed Ueda, *Postwar Immigrant America: A Social History* (Boston: Bedford/St. Martin's, 1994), 44–45.

16. See Bernadette Maguire, *Immigration: Public Legislation and Private Bills* (Lanham, MD: University Press of America, 1997), 258.

17. See U.S. Citizenship and Immigration Services website, http://www.uscis.gov/portal/site/uscis (accessed February 16, 2011).

18. Ibid.

19. See U.S. Immigration and Customs Enforcement, "Fact Sheet: 287(g) and the Immigration and Nationality Act," Office of Public Affairs, Department of Homeland Security, August 16, 2006.

20. See Udi Ofer, Ari Rosmarin, and Michael Cummings, *No Freedom Without Privacy: The REAL ID Act's Assault on Americans' Everyday Life* (New York: New York Civil Liberties Union, 2009).

INDEX